Faith. Works. Wonders.®

Faith. Works. Wonders.®

An Insider's Guide to Catholic Charities

FRED KAMMER, SJ

PICKWICK *Publications* · Eugene, Oregon

FAITH. WORKS. WONDERS. ®
An Insider's Guide to Catholic Charities

The title—*Faith. Works. Wonders.*—is the registered trademark of Catholic Charities of the Archdiocese of Washington, D.C., and is used with their permission.

Pickwick Publications
An imprint of Wipf and Stock Publishers
199 W. 8th Ave., Suite 3
Eugene, OR 97401

ISBN 13: 978-1-60608-927-9

Cataloging-in-Publication data:

Kammer, Fred

Faith. works. wonders.® : an insider's guide to Catholic Charities / Fred Kammer, SJ.

ISBN 13: 978-1-60608-927-9

xii + 206 p. ; 23 cm. —Includes index.

1. Catholic Church—United States—Charities—History. 2. Church work with the poor—Catholic Church—History. 3. Christianity and justice—Catholic Church. I. Title.

BX2347.8 P66 K36 2009

Manufactured in the U.S.A.

To the women and men of Catholic Charities
across the nation,
in appreciation of the joy and hope
which you bring daily to God's little ones.

Contents

Introduction / ix

PART ONE: Faith.

1   Mission: What We Do and Why / 1

2   Catholic Identity: Who We Are and How / 31

PART TWO: Works.

3   Service: "Providing Help. Creating Hope. Transforming Lives." / 53

4   Advocacy: Changing Society with and for the Poor / 68

5   Convening: Building Communities That Care / 85

PART THREE: Wonders.

6   Volunteers: The Lifeblood of the Network / 105

7   Pluralism: From Jefferson to Obama / 120

8   Quality and Innovation: Doing Good as Well as Possible / 145

9   Spirituality: Seeing the Divine in Their Midst / 161

Appendix A—An Historical Outline: Important Dates in the History of Catholic Charities and Catholic Charities USA / 187

Appendix B—The Profitization of Social Services: Where Do We Set Limits on a Market-driven Social Service System? / 193

Index / 201

Introduction

My thirty-year association with Catholic Charities began by serving on the board of Catholic Social Services of Atlanta in the late 1970s. In the years that followed, I was the director of Catholic Community Services of Baton Rouge from 1984 to 1989, then president of the national organization Catholic Charities USA from 1992 to 2001, and most recently a board member again, this time for Catholic Charities of the Archdiocese of New Orleans. While at Catholic Charities USA I visited Catholic Charities in about forty states, the District of Columbia, and Guam. I also served on the executive committee and as North American vice-president for *Caritas Internationalis*, the Rome-based international federation of Catholic charitable organizations. While many people have heard of Catholic Charities and 300,000 people work as staff, board members, or volunteers with Catholic Charities agencies around the country in any given year, there is much about these organizations today, what they do, and what they stand for which is largely unknown.

Next year in 2010, Catholic Charities USA will celebrate its centennial. In preparation for and celebration of this centennial, it is my hope that this book will serve multiple purposes: encouraging the work of the three hundred thousand staff, board members, and volunteers in local Charities agencies; informing the Catholic and general public of the scope and wonderful impact of Catholic Charities agencies in communities across the nation; and explaining some of the positions which Catholic Charities have taken in our continuing national discussions on social welfare, faith-inspired organizations, and the appropriate roles of the private and public sectors in promoting the common good and caring for the least fortunate among us.

I have always been inspired by the slogan of Catholic Charities of the Archdiocese of Washington, D.C.—*Faith. Works. Wonders.*®[1] With their

---

1. Used with permission of Catholic Charities of the Archdiocese of Washington.

permission, that is both the title of this book and its internal structure. Under *faith*, the chapters explain the mission and religious identity of Catholic Charities in this country. Under *works*, the three core activities of agencies are described and explained (service, advocacy, and convening). And, under *wonders*, are discussed four marvelous characteristics of the people and agencies involved (volunteers, pluralism, innovation, and spirituality).

In their 1997 comprehensive study titled *The Poor Belong to Us*, Georgetown University Professors Dorothy M. Brown and Elizabeth McKeown focused on Catholic Charities and American welfare as they evolved through the period from the Civil War to World War II. In the introduction, they note the current state of Catholic Charities in these words, "By the 1990s the umbrella organization, Catholic Charities, U.S.A., represented the largest system of private social provision in the nation."[2] It is that network of locally based organizations, services, and advocates which I am describing and, yes, defending in this volume. I say "defending" because during its history, as Catholic Charities have fought to defend the poor, protect their rights, and assure their wellbeing, attackers have been abundant, most recently in the course of the welfare-reform debate of the 1990s.

The concluding paragraph of *The Poor Belong to Us* uses the word "complexity" twice. It reads as follows:

> From its beginnings, Catholic Charities in the United States has demonstrated both remarkable adaptability and consistency: adaptability in responding to the changing environment of American welfare and consistency in its advocacy for the poor. Part of the complexity in this historic development has been its resistance to the secularization of charity and its simultaneous and deliberate accommodation to the emergence of the modern welfare state. The complexity remains. The issues confronted in the 1870s persist: Children are still in peril and poverty still haunts the land. The challenge continues—to provide *Catholic charity* in the changing context of American welfare.

This book is about understanding and appreciating the complexity of Catholic Charities as it exists today and how agencies and individuals work to maintain and expand their service to people in need, while si-

---

2. Dorothy M. Brown and Elizabeth McKeown, *The Poor Belong to Us: Catholic Charities and American Welfare* (Cambridge, MA: Harvard University Press, 1997), 1.

multaneously challenging their cities, counties, and this nation to be communities of justice and compassion.

Each chapter opens with a person, an event, or a text which has been crucial to the history of Catholic Charities in this country or is illustrative of the chapter's content. Sometimes this initial person, event, or text is referred to explicitly later in the chapter, but often they are merely suggestive of the contents and approach to be taken.

I am grateful to the New Orleans Jesuit Province for allowing me to have these months free to write, to Catholic Charities USA for wonderful resources which I have been able to access long distance, to *Charities USA* magazine for keeping me informed after I left the national organization, to Sharon Daly for review of parts of this book, to Kathryn Mahon Peach for helping me with an earlier draft of this book, and to Catholic Charities of New Orleans, Baton Rouge, and so many other places for helping my hometown New Orleans and the State of Louisiana to continue to recover from Hurricanes Katrina and Rita. I also thank Pickwick Publications (a division of Wipf and Stock Publishers) and, in particular, Dr. K. C. Hanson for bringing this book into being. My deepest gratitude, however, goes to the men and women of Catholic Charities across this nation who have shown me over three decades what it means to love tenderly, act justly, and walk humbly with their God (Micah 6:8).

PART ONE

Faith.

1

Mission

What We Do and Why

IN THE NINE YEARS *that I travelled the country working with Catholic Charities staffs, board members, and volunteers, our days together often began with a prayer service arranged by the local agency. Invariably, the most common text used at these prayer services was the great judgment scene from Matthew's Gospel:*

> *When the Son of Man comes in his glory with all of his angels, he will sit on his royal throne. The people of all nations will be brought before him, and he will separate them, as shepherds separate their sheep from their goats.*
>
> *He will place the sheep on his right and the goats on his left. Then the king will say to those on his right, "My father has blessed you! Come and receive the kingdom that was prepared for you before the world was created. When I was hungry, you gave me something to eat, and when I was thirsty, you gave me something to drink. When I was a stranger, you welcomed me, and when I was naked, you gave me clothes to wear. When I was sick, you took care of me, and when I was in jail, you visited me."*
>
> *Then the ones who pleased the Lord will ask, "When did we give you something to eat or drink? When did we welcome you as a stranger or give you clothes to wear or visit you while you were sick or in jail?"*
>
> *The king will answer, "Whenever you did it for any of my people, no matter how unimportant they seemed, you did it for me."*
>
> *Then the king will say to those on his left, "Get away from me! You are under God's curse. Go into the everlasting fire prepared for the devil and his angels! I was hungry, but you did not give me anything to eat, and I was thirsty, but you did not give me anything to drink.*

I was a stranger, but you did not welcome me, and I was naked, but you did not give me any clothes to wear. I was sick and in jail, but you did not take care of me."

Then the people will ask, "Lord, when did we fail to help you when you were hungry or thirsty or a stranger or naked or sick or in jail?"

The king will say to them, "Whenever you failed to help any of my people, no matter now unimportant they seemed, you failed to do it for me." [1]

༄

In the mid-1980s, Catholic Community Services, the Catholic Charities agency where I worked in the diocese of Baton Rouge, approved its first strategic plan with the following mission statement at its head: "Catholic Community Services of Baton Rouge proclaims the gospel vision of Jesus Christ as its mission by serving the needs of individuals and families, especially the poorest, and working with Church and community for justice, peace, and compassion in society." Woven through this single sentence were three roles with long and complex histories in the world of Catholic Charities: "service, advocacy, and convening." Also included were strong and principled themes from the centuries of Catholic Social Teaching— justice, peace, compassion, the importance of family, evangelization, the preferential option for the poor, and, of course, the Good News of Jesus of Nazareth. All across the country, the boards, staff, and volunteers of hundreds of Catholic Charities agencies and institutions had developed or would develop similar mission and vision statements whose fabric was woven from the same three core roles and the same principles that underlie Catholic social morality.

THE NATIONAL CONFERENCE OF CATHOLIC CHARITIES (1910)

The formal "mission" story for Catholic Charities USA begins in 1910 on the campus of Catholic University of America (CUA). At the invitation of Bishop Thomas Shahan, CUA's President, the National Conference of Catholic Charities (NCCC) was founded to promote the foundation of diocesan Catholic Charities bureaus, to encourage professional social work

---

1. Matthew 25:31–45, *The Holy Bible: Contemporary English Version* (New York: American Bible Society, 1995).

practices, "to bring about a sense of solidarity" among those in charitable ministries, and "to be the attorney for the poor." The four hundred or so delegates from twenty-four states were predominantly laypeople, representative of the women and men who had founded the many charitable institutions in various ethnic communities, members of the Society of St. Vincent de Paul, and Catholic academics and public figures concerned about the poor in this society. President Taft hosted the closing ceremonies at the White House. The *Proceedings* recited the purposes as follows:

> The National Conference has been created to meet a definite situation. It aims to preserve the organic spiritual character of Catholic Charity. It aims to seek out and understand causes of dependency. It aims to take advantage of the ripest wisdom in relief and preventive work to which persons have anywhere attained, and to serve as a bond of union for the unnumbered organizations in the United States which are doing the work of Charity. It aims to become, finally, the attorney for the Poor in Modern Society, to present their point of view and defend them unto the days when social justice may secure to them their rights.[2]

In the early years of the NCCC, an intense effort—especially by Msgr. John O'Grady, NCCC Executive Secretary (1920–1960)—focused on the development of the diocesan Catholic Charities bureau or agency as a vehicle for organizing and professionalizing the works of charity within various dioceses. By 1922 there were thirty-five central bureaus of Catholic Charities formed in cities or dioceses. By 1937 the number of diocesan bureaus had increased to sixty-eight in thirty-five states.

In a way, this diocesan-level development was a focus on the service role of Catholic Charities; and it was complemented by efforts to improve the quality of services in keeping with the newly developing field of social work. For example, in 1923 NCCC published *A Program for Catholic Child-Caring Homes*, a work of its Conference on Religious, to stimulate improvement of standards in existing homes. In 1934, The National Catholic School of Social Service was founded at Catholic University of America at the urging of NCCC with Msgr. O'Grady as its first dean. The reach of NCCC extended internationally as the first meeting of the International

---

2. "Proceedings" of the first annual meeting of the National Conference of Catholic Charities, (September 25–28, 1910), 11; quoted in *Cadre Study: Toward a Renewed Catholic Charities Movement* (Alexandria, VA: Catholic Charities USA, 1972; 1992 revised and annotated), 63.

Conference of Catholic Charities (later Caritas Internationalis) is held in Rome in 1951. Msgr. O'Grady had been one of the planning committee for the founding of the international conference.

The second role of Catholic Charities—advocating for a more just society—was smelted in the social and economic caldron that was dominated by the depression, the New Deal, and World War II and its aftermath. NCCC and diocesan bureaus promoted social legislation based upon Catholic social principles, and Msgr. O'Grady became a major national voice on social reform. Two examples stand out. In 1935, the Social Security Act passed Congress for the first time, with strong support from NCCC for the concept of insurance benefits based upon rights as opposed to a needs test for benefits. The act provided the framework (and still does) for what are called social security benefits (for worker retirement, survivors, and dependents), workers' compensation, unemployment compensation, and social welfare (Aid to the Aged, Blind, and Disabled, now Supplemental Security Income, and Aid to Families with Dependent Children, now Temporary Assistance to Needy Families). This framework would later include Medicare and Medicaid as well. Then, in 1949 the National Housing Act was passed with strong support from NCCC and Msgr. O'Grady, culminating twenty years of O'Grady's leadership of the Catholic community and the nation on housing needs.

In its third role—convening—NCCC and local charities found common cause with a number of other social welfare organization, child caring institutions, and other advocates for improving the quality of social services and expanding the government's responsibilities for social welfare. Among Church organizations with whom NCCC collaborated were the Society of St. Vincent de Paul, the Christ Child Society, the Association of Ladies of Charity, the National Conference of Catholic Women, and the National Catholic Welfare Conference (now the United States Conference of Catholic Bishops).

THE CADRE REPORT (1969–1972)

In the wake of the political, social and cultural turmoil of the 1960s, its significant new civil rights and social legislation, and the momentous Catholic transformation promoted by the Second Vatican Council (1962–1965), NCCC members in 1969 undertook a three-year self-study aimed at clarifying the mission of Catholic Charities agencies and the

national conference. It was called the "Cadre" for the core group of charities and other Catholic leaders who spearheaded the process. At the 1972
annual meeting in Miami, NCCC membership approved the Cadre Report
Toward a Renewed Catholic Charities Movement with its triple roles for the
national organization and, by implication, local member organizations:

> *The Continuing Commitment to Service.* Catholic Charities
> must stand ready to serve those most in need, especially those
> most alienated, most oppressed, most distressed. Our credibility
> as Christians is established when we offer ourselves in service to
> individuals, to our communities, to our country, to our Church.
> Focus should be given to the increased services needed, to all those
> who remain unserved, and to the unfinished work before us.
>
> *Humanizing and Transforming the Social Order.* This is based
> on a belief in the necessity of pursuing social justice for all and
> particularly for those unable to do so for themselves, which, in
> turn, involves effecting changes in the existing social systems. One
> component is that of advocacy, courageously calling attention to
> the root causes of poverty and oppression. Other components are
> those of social planning, policy development, and contributing to
> the shaping of social welfare legislation.
>
> *The Convening of the Christian Community and Other Concern-
> ed People.* This is a process of reaching out to others to stimulate
> them to social awareness and to recruit them as active partners
> in the pursuit of the goals of the Catholic Charities movement.
> One method of this should be the convening of meetings and as-
> semblies in order to discern more clearly the roots of distress and
> poverty and to reach decisions which enable those convened to
> act. This role includes reaching out to and working with the parish
> community to assist it in its ministry of service. It involves recruit-
> ment, consciousness raising, discernment, and action.[3]

The shorthand statement of the Cadre mission—*service, advocacy, and
convening*—has carried the mission-understanding of the national organization and its members to the present moment.

POPE JOHN PAUL II AND CATHOLIC CHARITIES (1987)

In his address to the members of Catholic Charities USA at their 1987
annual meeting in San Antonio, Pope John Paul II emphasized the multiple roles of Catholic Charities and Catholic social teaching. Tracing

3. *Cadre Study*, 100.

the history of charitable service back to the Scriptures, the Holy Father emphasized that the Church has worked from its beginnings to carry out the teaching of Jesus about his close identification with the poor (Matthew 25:31–46) and the "dire consequences" of "gross disparities of wealth between nations, classes and persons . . ." (citing the parable of the rich man and the poor Lazarus). He emphasized the service role in these words: "Service to those in need must take the form of direct action to relieve their anxieties, and to remove their burdens, and at the same time lead them to the dignity of self-reliance."[4] Interestingly, his reference to self-reliance anticipates the emphasis on "empowering service" in the Catholic Charities USA Vision 2000 process that followed in the 1990s and is discussed below.

The Holy Father also underscored the advocacy or transformational role of the Catholic Charities mission as follows: "Service to the poor also involves speaking up for them and trying to reform structures which cause or perpetuate their oppression." In the context of the global dimensions of poverty and injustice, he went on urge the members of Catholic Charities to "see what can be done as soon as possible to purify the social structures of all society in this regard." Then, in his closing exhortation to his audience, the members heard the Pope emphasize all three parts of their mission in the words, "Gather, transform, and serve!"

VISION 2000 (1993–1996)

In the mid-1990s, now as Catholic Charities USA, the members of the national organization undertook another multi-year, in-depth study of their mission and organization in preparation for a new millennium. Vision 2000 engaged thousands of Charities staff, board members, clients, and volunteers in asking anew about the mission of their organizations, priorities arising from contemporary social and economic conditions, and how best to position themselves for the future.[5] The concluding

---

4. Pope John Paul II, address to the annual meeting of Catholic Charities USA, September 13, 1987 in *Charities USA* 14.9 (1987), 7–12.

5. Vision 2000 Task Force members who steered this three-year process were: Edward Orzechowski, Chairman; Kathleen McGowan, Vice-Chairwoman; Connie Andry; Raoul Aroz; Brian Corbin; Thomas DeStefano; Briston Fernandes; Msgr. John Gilmartin; Michael Haggerty; Patrick Johnson, Jr.; Eugene Matsusaka; James Mauck; Sister Barbara Moore, C.S.J.; Kristan Schlichte; Barbara Terrazas; John Young; Most Rev. Joseph Sullivan (ex-officio); and Rev. Timothy Hogan (ex-officio).

report, approved by the Board of Trustees in 1996, highlighted the following Vision Statement: "Believing in the presence of God in our midst, we proclaim the sanctity of human life and the dignity of the person by sharing in the mission of Jesus given to the Church. To this end, Catholic Charities works with individuals, families, and communities to help them meet their needs, address their issues, eliminate oppression, and build a just and compassionate society."[6] The report then developed four strategic directions flowing from the Vision Statement and the numerous regional and local convenings of Catholic Charities staff, board members, and volunteers, as well as listening sessions of the task force members with others within the Church and larger society:

Strategic Direction I: Relating to Those We Serve

Enhance our historical commitment to quality service by making the empowerment of those we serve, especially people who are poor and vulnerable, central to our work.

Strategic Direction II: Relating to Community

Build an inclusive Catholic Charities which engages diverse people, organizations, and communities in transforming the structures of society that perpetuate poverty, undermine family life, and destroy communities.

Strategic Direction III: Relating to Church

Strengthen our identity with, and relationship to, the broader Church and witness to its social mission.

Strategic Direction IV: Relating to One Another

Build the organizational and resource capacity for people to participate in effecting the vision of Catholic Charities.[7]

The Vision 2000 process and final report came at a time of significant challenges within a rapidly changing environment for Catholic Charities agencies across the country. These challenges affected not just Catholic Charities, but all non-profits, especially those deeply committed to the

---

6. *Vision 2000* (Alexandria, VA: Catholic Charities USA, 1997), 7.
7. Ibid., 9.

poorest and most vulnerable people. One of the best summaries of those challenges was in a 1995 book by economist Lester Salamon entitled *Partners in Public Service: Government-Nonprofit Relations in the Modern Welfare State.*[8] Salamon described five major trends impacting the voluntary sector: (1) resource constraints; (2) the move from categorical aid to universal entitlements, including the federal spending shift from lower income programs to middle class entitlements; (3) the shift from producer subsidies to consumer subsidies (e.g., vouchers); (4) four demographic changes—graying of the population, changing social and economic position of women, changes in family structure, and emergence of the urban underclass; and (5) the move from cultural to economic explanations of poverty.

From these trends, Salamon named four specific implications for the nonprofit sector: (1) overall sector growth due to increasing demand for such services as day care, nursing homes, family counseling, hospital services—among both the poor and the middle class; (2) commercialization of the sector whereby its growth occurred through greater integration of the voluntary sector into the market economy, including penetration of profit-oriented agencies into the welfare state and penetration of the mechanics of the market (e.g. growth of fee-for-service) into the operation of nonprofits; (3) reorganizing of assistance to the needy whereby, while many human service agencies assumed an increasingly commercial cast—subsidized and not—other institutions would assume increased responsibility for the traditional charitable mission of the nonprofit sector (we can hear *Vision 2000*'s "especially people who are poor and vulnerable"), that would require new skills and partnership arrangements, especially in preparation of skilled workers for the labor market; and (4) an intensification of the competition between for-profits and non-profits that would weaken the traditional rationale for the tax-exempt status of non-profits.

In view of all this, Salamon cited the following four implications for non-profit managers like the leaders of Catholic Charities agencies: (1) market savvy: they would need a more sophisticated awareness of market trends and increasing use of advertising, market surveys, "industry analyses," etc.; (2) they would face increasing personnel challenges for better pay and other working conditions at the same time that competi-

8. Lester Salamon, *Partners in Public Service: Government-Nonprofit Relations in the Modern Welfare State* (Baltimore: Johns Hopkins University Press, 1995), chap. 13.

tion was pressuring them to cut costs; and this could affect solidarity in the workplace and the willingness of volunteers to support the organization when it was increasingly fee-for-service; (3) they would be challenged to maintain and embody the agency's mission while adapting as necessary to the pressures of the external world that in turn would threaten the distinctiveness of organizational mission and identity; and (4) they would be pressed to downplay the traditional advocacy role of the sector—being "policy innovators and social critics"—in the interest of marketing their agency's services and improving the financial bottom-line.

In his chapter conclusion, Salamon wrote:

> Whether these implications will materialize as predicted here depends, of course, on the speed with which the developments outlined above proceed, and on the way nonprofit managers react to them. Properly fortified with a sense of the mission of the nonprofit sector and the values that are critical to its continuance, nonprofit managers may fend off some of the pressures that are looming. *But this will require a high level of self-consciousness within the sector and a concerted effort to revitalize the value base on which the sector rests.*[9]

It would not be a stretch to observe that Vision 2000 was for Catholic Charities a most timely "concerted effort to revitalize the value base" upon which their mission and work rested. The Vision Statement invited deep reflection on key relationships and the work of Catholic Charities in the light of the Scriptures and Catholic social teaching. Some elements of that value base from the vision statement follow, with my comments on each:

> *The presence of God in our midst.* This phrase reflected the Jewish sense of God within the Hebrew community and the Christian sense of the mystical God in Jesus Christ present in the Church and to be found specifically within the *anawim*—contemporary society's widows, orphans, and strangers.
>
> *The mission of Jesus given to the Church.* Jesus told Peter and, through him, all his disciples, "If you love me, feed my lambs . . . tend my sheep" (John 21). As we saw earlier, his portrayal of the last judgment focused on compassion shown to the least among us. This too was the mission of Catholic Charities USA, allowing staff and volunteers to share in the mission of Jesus given to the Church.

---

9. Ibid., 218 (emphasis supplied).

Catholic Charities works with *individuals, families, and communities.* Catholic Charities aimed to empower the people it served. By working "with" individual clients and local communities, agencies formed a partnership with the people they served.

Meet their needs, address their issues, eliminate oppression, and to build a just and compassionate society. This part of the Vision Statement called for a renewal of the message of the *Cadre Study* written twenty-five years earlier. "Meet their needs" reflected service; "address their issues" and "eliminate oppression" reflected advocacy; and "build a just and compassionate society" reflected convening. So, in some ways, the Vision Statement, and in turn *Vision 2000's* strategic directions, directly paralleled the threefold mission of the Cadre Study. The building of a just and compassionate society also reiterated the Old Testament themes of social justice and the responsibility of society to care for the *anawim.*

The four strategic directions reinforced and built upon the three roles (service, advocacy, convening) first enunciated in the *Cadre Study,* but then they called the members of Catholic Charities USA to further specifics demanded by the contemporary context within which Vision 2000 occurred.

Strategic Direction I

Strategic Direction 1 called for a deep and transforming commitment to those served and to their self-determination in these words: "*Enhance our historical commitment to quality service by making the empowerment of those we serve, especially people who are poor and vulnerable, central to our work.*" This direction reflected the twenty-five-year-old call of the Cadre to quality social service, self-help, and self-actualizing. But there was a new insistence on empowerment of clients—especially in the face of the demographics of need in which two-thirds of those served in the nineties came for emergency services, especially food and shelter.[10] Ironically, this demand for emergency services particularly aggravated the challenge of making empowerment integral to Catholic Charities' services, since empowerment seemed so far from the local soup kitchen, shelter,

10. The 1995 Annual Survey of Catholic Charities USA indicated that, of 10.8 million people served in the year prior to the completion of *Vision 2000,* 7.2 million had come to the agencies for emergency services, primarily food. Patrice Flynn, PhD, *Catholic Charities USA 1995 Annual Survey: National Findings* (Alexandria, VA: Catholic Charities USA, November, 1996), 1.

or food bank. And yet, many agencies were developing very creative ways to make even food and shelter services empowering (see chapter eight). Those innovative methods needed to be highlighted, shared, replicated, and celebrated.

But "empowerment" as used in Vision 2000 was broader than the individual client and client service. *Key Characteristics* were developed in the final report for each strategic direction. With regard to Direction One these characteristics reminded members of powerful community-building devices and dynamics such as community organizing and economic development, both of which had become more important and more common in the Catholic community in the decades after the *Cadre*. For example, the local offices for the Catholic Campaign for Human Development—the US bishops' anti-poverty program focusing on community and economic development—were situated within the structures of about 40% of Catholic Charities agencies. But Vision 2000 challenged the agencies to think about CCHD as more than an individual program. How could that empowerment approach be broadened to affect agencies' overall approach to the communities which they served and their assets, needs, and challenges? This Strategic Direction aimed to encourage members to amplify client services in a number of new community-based-and-focused ways and in an incredible variety of new alliances with community groups and others.

Strategic Direction II

Strategic Direction 2 challenged members to confront deep societal divisions, beginning with racism, and the sinful social structures that ravage families and communities and intensify poverty. The direction read as follows: "*Build an inclusive Catholic Charities which engages diverse people, organizations, and communities in transforming the structures of society that perpetuate poverty, undermine family life, and destroy communities.*" This Strategic Direction clearly reflected the Cadre's second goal of "humanizing and transforming the social structures." But, after 25 years of trying to understand and appropriate that goal, this Direction recognized two powerful barriers to effective action.

First was the reality and pervasiveness of *racism* in two contexts. The internal context was member agencies themselves, a sad fact emphasized to the task force members as they met with staff and volunteers in the state and regional listening sessions during the first year of the *Vision 2000* process. This was reinforced by the lack of racial and ethnic diversity apparent among diocesan directors of Catholic Charities and senior management and staff. The external context was the continuing reality of racism within our society at large. Prime examples were the 1992 Los Angeles riots, the 1996 church burnings,[11] running black homeowners out of white neighborhoods, and the perception that racism was only barely "masked" in political discussions about welfare reform and anti-immigrant legislation. Later, in 2005, America was shocked again at the racism unmasked in the horrible aftermath of Hurricane Katrina.

The second social reality emphasized by the Vision 2000 report was *"sinful social structures"* as an intrinsic part of the Church's social teaching since Vatican II, emphasized heavily in the teachings of Pope John Paul II and in the pastoral letters of the U.S. bishops. For charities workers, they experienced many of these structures—inadequate wages and benefits, punitive and degrading welfare programs, substandard and unaffordable housing—as harsh facts profoundly affecting family life and structure, the nature of poverty, and the quality of communities across the nation.

The racism part of this Strategic Direction seemed easier to define, and its challenge to members easier to frame in the *Activities* developed under this heading in the final Vision 2000 report. Catholic Charities USA had initiated its Racial Equality Project as an "early initiative" in this effort even before the final report was approved. There was great openness and willingness to participate as shown, for example, in the very positive interest on the part of the first eight local agency directors invited by the national organization to participate in the Racial Equality Project. Interest has continued to be strong since the mid-1990s and has given rise to the development by Catholic Charities USA of an agency cultural assessment to assist local agencies in moving beyond tolerance to promoting racial and cultural diversity, scholarships to promote increased participation of minorities in Catholic Charities USA meetings and its Leadership Institute, and a commitment to understand and confront the intrinsic connection between racial injustice and poverty in this society.

11. William Booth, "In Church Fires, a Pattern but No Conspiracy," *Washington Post*, June 19, 1996, A1. This article reported on thirty-seven suspicious fires at Black churches in the previous eighteen months, approval by the U.S. House of Representatives of legislation making it easier for federal officials to prosecute, and President Clinton's request for $12 million for investigations into the fires.

This connection has been highlighted most recently in the 2008 Catholic Charities policy paper titled, *Poverty and Racism: Overlapping Threats to the Common Good.*[12]

The social change part was acknowledged by Task Force members to be much more difficult. They believed that racism lay at the heart of the social question in this country, and that confronting racism was a privileged place for entering into social change as well. But they also understood that beyond racism much of what this strategic direction implied was still inchoate, needing development as the work of charities moved into the new century. The members would have to struggle to understand social reality more deeply and to develop appropriate local and national responses. There were real unknowns here; but, as Msgr. John Gilmartin of New York said repeatedly to the Task Force, if Catholic Charities did not do major new things in terms of social change in this country, they would be looking at twice as many clients across the country in the not too distant future. Facing that unknown future required that members trust themselves and one another to take up the challenge and to put flesh on these bones. That could take them far beyond the present ways in which they worked, a threatening challenge and one for which they may have felt unprepared. But the task force believed that together Catholic Charities could take up this challenge and make real progress in this direction.

Strategic Direction III

Strategic Direction 3 urged members to deepen their connection to, and animation of, the Catholic Church for the sake of the Gospel and the clarity and power of their own mission. In its words: "*Strengthen our identity with, and relationship to, the broader Church and witness to its social mission.*" In the course of the first year's listening sessions, task force members had heard this theme repeatedly, especially from directors of agencies. "How do I shape and lead religiously diverse staff, volunteers, and board members in a *Catholic* agency?" and "How does new lay leadership—not priests and religious—learn and pass on (teach) Catholic social teaching and Catholic Charities tradition?"

First, the *Vision 2000* report recognized that these were truly complex issues, and that the challenges came from the left, the right, and the

12. *Poverty and Racism: Overlapping Threats to the Common Good* (Alexandria, VA: Catholic Charities USA, 2008).

middle of the religious and political spectrum. Thus, at Catholic Charities USA the Catholic Identity Project had already begun as another "early initiative" of *Vision 2000*, with a goal to produce within a year or so additional focused resources to assist all its members in this matter. By 1997 Catholic Charities USA published, *Who Do You Say We Are?—Perspectives on Catholic Identity in Catholic Charities*.[13] The book contained reflections from charities veterans, canonical guidance, values and ethical principles, spirituality, and practical recommendations for implementation at the local level.

This Strategic Direction also focuses on the importance of Church parish. This was intended to call for more than "parish social ministry" as practiced at that time in many diocesan agencies. It meant reaching out to Catholics-beyond-parish: e.g., in small faith communities; in the public sector; in the business community; in government; and in the professions. It involved being present at what Father Bryan Hehir called the "fault-lines" of society, where the Catholic Church included both the wealthiest and most powerful as well as the poorest and least understood. This required re-appropriating the old concept of "pontifex" or bridge-builder into their ministry in Catholic Charities, bridging the divide between those with wealth and power and those without.

This Strategic Direction further called for promoting the Church's own social mission. Catholic Charities was to undertake a prophetic stance drawn from the Scriptures and Catholic social teaching. Some members had urged the Task Force during the Vision 2000 process to scale back the goal of promotion of Catholic social teaching to target only those involved in Catholic Charities, but Task Force members explicitly rejected that suggestion and maintained that this responsibility should be focused on the whole Church community.

During the 1990s, Catholic Charities USA had developed the closest working relationship with U.S. bishops' conference (then the National Conference of Catholic Bishops and the United States Catholic Conference) that anyone could remember. The two organizations worked closely on Washington advocacy, issued joint alerts and publications, sponsored common training for their local constituents, and had a number of committees on which respective staff served each other. While these were positive organizational developments beneficial to all those

13. *Who Do You Say We Are?—Perspectives on Catholic Identity in Catholic Charities* (Alexandria, VA: Catholic Charities USA, 1997).

involved, this strategic direction urged the promotion of Catholic social teaching as critical to the credibility of the Church's own mission, as well as that of Catholic Charities. As the Synod of Bishops of 1971 had put it, action for justice is a constitutive element of the preaching of the gospel.[14] The gospel would simply not be credible without the work of charity and justice. This was not an option, but lay at the heart of the Church's mission and ministry.

Strategic Direction IV

To do all that was implied in the first three strategic directions, Strategic Direction 4 made it clear that members needed to strengthen both their national organization and their local members. *"Build the organizational and resource capacity for people to participate in effecting the vision of Catholic Charities."* In the task force's thinking, there were four threshold issues here for the national organization: membership, governance, fundraising, and dues. Each of these was a difficult challenge. After extensive consultation over the first two years and a special meeting with diocesan directors of Catholic Charities in March 1996 in Kansas City, the Task Force developed specific proposals affecting membership, governance, and the financing of the national organization. These were mailed out to all the members in June of that year.

These related recommendations touched on the ways in which the organization conducted its annual meeting, how groups of specialists would belong to the national organization, and more effective engagement of the diocesan directors. They also included planning for the application of new communications technologies, including the internet, to membership needs.

Similar pressing concerns faced Catholic Charities at the state and local levels. The factors enumerated by Lester Salamon, above, and other external forces challenged members to develop stronger state alliances, both with one another in Catholic agencies and with other voluntary organizations. Among these forces were the expansion of managed care, the devolution of federal money and power to states in block grants, and

---

14. The actual text from the Synod of Bishops of 1971 reads: "Action for justice and participation in the transformation of the world fully appear to us as a constitutive dimension of the preaching of the Gospel, or, in other words, of the Church's mission for the redemption of the human race and its liberation from every oppressive situation." *Justice in the World* (Vatican City: Synod of Bishops, 1971), introduction.

recent decisions about "regionalization" of refugee resettlement which had been made by the United States Catholic Conference/Migration and Refugee Services. It was equally important to strengthen agency capacities and resources at the local and diocesan levels. This meant revisiting questions of funding, volunteers, relations to parishes and other diocesan agencies, alliances with other providers, collaboration between and among charities offices and programs, and the training and further professional development of staff, boards, and volunteers.

Ultimately, Vision 2000 called members to attend more proactively to a complex set of relationships that grew out of the special character of Catholic Charities within the Church and larger society. Edward J. Orzechowski, Chairman of the *Vision 2000* Task Force and Director of Catholic Charities of the Archdiocese of Washington, DC, spelled this out in his introductory remarks to the 1996 Kansas City meeting of diocesan directors. These four Strategic Directions, he said, were really about renewing and reforming our relationships:

- relationships with those whom Catholic Charities serve,

- relationships with the larger community,

- relationships with the Church, and

- relationships with one another.

Catholic charitable works had been changing ever since the first Catholic charitable foundation in New Orleans in 1727. That reality of change would continue into the future because of changing needs and the wonderful combination of talent, commitment, and resources which Catholic Charities workers brought to the Church's ministry of charity and justice. Despite political mean-spiritedness in the air on issues like welfare reform and the rights of refugees and immigrants, despite the assault of managed care on health and human services, and despite increasing needs and sometimes diminishing resources, Vision 2000 challenged Catholic Charities to trust their own gifts and resources and the presence of the God of justice and compassion in their midst. As people of the Gospel, they had to believe in the power of the seed to grow into the harvest and the transforming power of the few to reshape history. And they needed to reach out to one another to renew their partnerships and to shape new alliances for the future.

IN ALL THINGS CHARITY (U.S. BISHOPS, 1999)

On Thursday, November 18, 1999, the week before Thanksgiving, the U.S. bishops underscored the mission of Catholic Charities and the directions it had undertaken in a wide-ranging Pastoral Message entitled *In All Things Charity: A Pastoral Challenge for the New Millennium.*[15] The document, connected to Pope John Paul's preparation for the Jubilee Year 2000, first rooted the work of all the Church's charities in the Scriptures and the history of the Church. It went on to challenge U.S. society to new emphases on the inextricable link between charity and justice, global awareness, and increased generosity and involvement in the coming millennium.

The bishops recited the accomplishments of individuals and organizations in the history of the Church across the world and in the United States. They highlighted Catholic Charities (including the Cadre Report), the Society of St. Vincent de Paul, the Ladies of Charity, and others. They urged individuals, families, parishes, religious congregations, unions and business, to deepen their commitment to charity and justice. They also described the respective responsibilities of the voluntary sector, the private sector, and the public sector in working for charity and justice and in the delivery of needed social services in an era of increasing privatization.

Specifically, the bishops singled out those who made Catholic Charities a reality in this country, "We take this opportunity to extend our heartfelt gratitude and encouragement to those countless individuals who, over the years, have been engaged in Catholic Charities service at the parish, diocesan, and national levels."[16] With respect to Charities' work, the bishops recognized the need to develop professional and specialized competencies, increase leadership formation and staff and board development, respect the cultural and faith traditions of those served, and preserve and promote the Catholic roots, identity, and mission of Charities agencies. They urged agencies to provide fair salaries and comprehensive

15. Chaired by Bishop Joseph M. Sullivan of Brooklyn, the ad hoc writing committee for the pastoral message consisted of Bishops Edwin M. Conway of Chicago, Nicholas A. Di Marzio of Camden, Howard Hubbard of Albany, Ricardo Ramirez, CSB, of Las Cruces, and John H. Ricard, SSJ, of Pensacola-Tallahassee. Father Robert J. Vitillo of the Catholic Campaign for Human Development was the lead staff member for the pastoral message. Many Catholic Charities staff and volunteers had an opportunity to make suggestions in the process of the development of the pastoral message.

16. *In All Things Charity: A Pastoral Challenge for the New Millennium* (Washington, DC: United States Catholic Conference, 1999), 30.

benefits to employees and to maintain appropriate support systems for volunteers. In a spirit of ecumenism, the pastoral thanked "the many staff and volunteers of other faith traditions who generously bring their own commitment to the poor and needy and thereby enrich the work of Catholic social agencies across the country."[17]

In addition, the pastoral message quoted the Vision Statement of the Vision 2000 report of Catholic Charities USA and went on to "*strongly appeal to diocesan and parish communities to support the activities and form partnerships with Catholic Charities.*"[18]

POPE BENEDICT XVI AND *DEUS CARITAS EST* (2005)

In the first year of his pontificate, Pope Benedict XVI issued his first encyclical letter, entitled, "God Is Love" (*Deus Caritas Est*).[19] There are two parts of the letter that he addresses to bishops, priests, deacons, men and women religious, and all the lay faithful "on Christian Love." The first part, which he terms "more speculative," is a rich theological, scriptural, and spiritual essay on the mysterious love which God offers to us and its intrinsic link to human love. In the second part, Pope Benedict discusses "the ecclesial exercise of the commandment of love of neighbor" focusing on the work of charity and justice within the contemporary Church. It is this second part on which I will focus.

In the first part are some important themes that ground the "more concrete" work of the second part. These themes coalesce to make it clear that one cannot call oneself a Christian believer without living a life filled with active love for one's neighbor, especially those who are poor. This includes a portrayal of God's love for humanity as a passionate[20] and gratuitous[21] involvement in the human community, the Eucharist of Jesus as essentially social in character,[22] and a fascinating choice of "the great parables of Jesus."[23] The three parables that Pope Benedict selects are the

17. Ibid., 31.

18. Ibid., (emphasis original). Further, the bishops endorsed the work of the Campaign for Human Development, USCC Migration and Refugee Services, the USCC Department of Social Development and World Peace, and Catholic Relief Services.

19. Pope Benedict XVI, *Deus Caritas Est*, December 25, 2005.

20. Ibid., no. 9.

21. Ibid., no. 10.

22. Ibid., no. 14.

23. Ibid., no. 15.

rich man and Lazarus in Luke 16 (a favorite of Pope John Paul II in addressing audiences in prosperous nations), the Good Samaritan in Luke 10, and the Last Judgment in Matthew 25. All are strongly social in character and message.

In discussing the interconnection of the two great commandments in Part One, working from the First Epistle of John, the Pope emphasizes the "unbreakable bond between love of God and love of neighbor."[24] Through this unity, made possible in the revelation of God in Jesus, Benedict states that, in God and with God, we are able to love those persons whom we do not like or even know. To them we can offer what they need and, going beyond their outward necessities, can "give them the look of love which they crave." Without such love of neighbor, our relationship to God becomes arid, "proper," and loveless. The two commandments are "thus inseparable, they form a single commandment." And each reinforces and deepens the other so that, "Love grows through love."[25]

Part Two is entitled, "*Caritas:* The Practice of Love by the Church as a 'Community of Love.'" Its focus is on the Church's institutional practice of love, so we find here less of the broad social analysis and application of Catholic Social Teaching to social reality than we came to expect from the social encyclicals of Pope John Paul II. However, Benedict does discuss both charity and justice and the relative responsibilities of both the laity and the Church as institution; and he affirms the history of modern Catholic Social Teaching beginning with the encyclical *Rerum Novarum* in 1891 and extending to *Centesimus Annus* in 1991.[26]

Pope Benedict begins from a double foundation: love of neighbor is a responsibility of the entire ecclesial community, of individuals and Church at all levels; and love also "needs to be organized if it is to be an ordered service to the community."[27] He traces a two thousand-year-old tradition of *diaconia*—"the ministry of charity exercised in a communitarian, orderly way"—from its beginning in the appointment of the seven deacons in the Acts of the Apostles to its institutionalization within each of the Egyptian monasteries in the fourth century to its evolution into juridical corporations in the sixth century to which the civil authorities

24. Ibid., no. 16.
25. Ibid., no. 18.
26. Ibid., no. 27.
27. Ibid., no. 20.

entrusted part of the grain for public distribution.[28] (Thus began a partnership with government which has extended to the Catholic Charities agencies of the U.S. and the *Caritas* agencies of many other countries and which will be discussed further in chapters two and seven.)

Benedict notes that charitable activity on behalf of the poor and suffering was an essential part of the Church of Rome from its earliest days, continuing in the third century work of St. Lawrence and imitated by the emperor Julian the Apostate in the fourth century.[29] He concludes from his survey of the earliest Christian centuries that, "The Church's deepest nature is expressed in her three-fold responsibility: proclaiming the word of God (*kerygma-martyria*), celebrating the sacraments (*leitourgia*), and exercising the ministry of charity (*diakonia*).[30] He also notes approvingly that this ministry of charity extended beyond the membership of the Church to embrace—a lesson from the Good Samaritan—a "standard which imposes universal love towards the needy whom we encounter," whomever they may be. (Again, the pope affirms the contemporary practice of serving people of all faiths and none, as practiced by Catholic Charities and *Caritas* agencies.)

The encyclical also includes a substantive discussion of the relative duties of State and Church, laity and Church organizations, with regard to charity and justice. He begins by affirming that, "the pursuit of justice must be a fundamental norm of the State"[31] and the just ordering of society and the State is "a central responsibility of politics."[32] This reflects the proper autonomy of the State, but there are distinct relationships to that role on the part of laity and Church organizations. First, the laity have a *direct* duty to work towards a just ordering of society, with a specific responsibility to take part in public life.[33] "Building a just social and civil order . . . is an essential task which every generation must take up anew."[34]

The Church as institution, however, while respecting the autonomy of the state, has multiple responsibilities set out in different parts of the

28. Ibid., no. 23.
29. *Ibid.*, no. 24.
30. Ibid., no. 25.
31. Ibid., no. 26.
32. Ibid., no. 28.
33. Ibid., no. 29.
34. Ibid., no. 28.

letter. First, with regard to the just ordering of society, the Church, in a posture of dialogue with the larger society, has an *indirect* role with respect to its just ordering. The Church presents its social doctrine as "a set of fundamental guidelines offering approaches that are valid even beyond the confines of the Church . . ."[35] Within a framework that sees faith as a purifying and liberating force for the work of reason, Catholic social doctrine is not intended to give the Church power over the State, but "to contribute, here and now, to the acknowledgment and attainment of what is just."[36]

Pope Benedict writes that the Church should not take on the political battle to create a more just society, replacing the State. "Yet at the same time she cannot and must not remain on the sidelines of the fight for justice." Besides the rational public discourse indicated above, "she has to reawaken the spiritual energy without which justice, which always demands sacrifice, cannot prevail and prosper."[37] The pontiff also indicates that the Church as teacher has a role in forming and animating the consciences of the Catholic laity who have a more direct role vis-à-vis the State.[38]

The Church also has a more *direct* role through its charitable organizations to meet the immediate needs of people who are needy and suffering. That role is always needed, even in the most just civil society, because there are always people suffering, people who are lonely, and people with material needs that require a response that extends beyond the material to the care and refreshment of their souls.

That more direct role takes place within the context of an increasingly globalized world. This global society features the ability of mass media to broadcast the fact and faces of suffering to every continent and a worldwide network of humanitarian assistance made possible by governmental agencies and humanitarian organizations. And, for those who think that relief can be the work of individuals alone, Benedict notes, "The solidarity shown by civil society thus significantly surpasses that shown by individuals."[39] In this context, the pope emphasizes his gratitude for the many forms of cooperation that exist between governments and Church

35. Ibid., no. 27.
36. Ibid., no. 28.
37. Ibid.
38. Ibid., no. 29.
39. Ibid., no. 30.

agencies, the role of philanthropic and charitable organizations, and the generosity of volunteers, especially the young for whom such involvement offers "a formation in solidarity."[40]

Pope Benedict pledges the readiness of the Catholic Church to cooperate with a wide range of charitable agencies, noting their common goal of "a true humanism, which acknowledges that man is made in the image of God . . ."[41] In that context he stresses what must remain distinctive about the Church's own charitable activity. In this part of the letter, the characteristics highlighted by the Holy Father are consistent with the experience of Catholic Charities agencies within the United States. These include: 1) charity as an immediate response to human need; 2) professional competence and training; 3) a heartfelt concern for those in need, including "formation of the heart" to see where love is needed and to act accordingly; 4) the refusal to proselytize those who are hungry and poor, forcing faith as the price of care and concern; and 5) an openness to speak of God balanced with a sense of "when it is better to say nothing and to let love speak."[42]

Finally, Pope Benedict enumerates those who are responsible for the Church's duty of charity, including parishes and all levels of the Church. (Sadly, there was not the kind of developed specifics of "parish social ministry" which has marked the writings of the U.S. bishops or the work of Catholic Charities USA. This will be discussed below in chapters two and five.) He includes the responsibilities of each bishop for the organization and support of the ministry of charity within his diocese and the need for leadership personnel who are guided by faith and urged by the love of Christ to do the Church's work of charity and to embody in their own persons that same love. He notes the need for deep prayer that can sustain those workers in the midst of human suffering, failure, and discouragement, and emphasizes the importance of a robust faith, hope, and love.[43]

CATHOLIC CHARITIES USA CODE OF ETHICS (2007)

First published in 1983 and modified only slightly over the next twenty years, the *Catholic Charities USA Code of Ethics* recently underwent a

---

40. Ibid.
41. Ibid.
42. Ibid., no. 31.
43. Ibid., nos. 35–39.

thorough revision in light of member needs, the first encyclical of Pope Benedict, the new *Compendium of the Social Doctrine of the Church*,[44] and the new and complex issues that have emerged for members in recent years. The new code was approved by the Board of Trustees of Catholic Charities USA on September 12, 2007 and is important in understanding the current thinking among Charities leaders about their mission in the world. It contains significant parts dealing with the use and purpose of the code, its Scriptural and theological foundations, applicable principles of Catholic social teaching, fundamental values, and then ethical standards. In the *Prologue* to the code we find the familiar tripartite mission first enunciated by the Cadre Report of 1972: "Catholic Charities USA, in concert with Caritas Internationalis, is committed to providing quality social services, advocating for just structures in society and working to convene the Catholic community, along with all people of good will, to provide help and create hope."[45] Extensively detailed sections apply to the responsibility to the clients, competence of staff, and the work of volunteers, all of which would apply to the *service* goal of the Catholic Charities mission. Further specific sections of the code, such as Section 5.01 on "Mission Engagement" and 5.02 on "Staff Participation" and 5.03 on "Coalition Building," spell out the responsibilities of agencies, boards, management, and staff for *advocacy* for social change and social justice and engaging with others in the wider community (*convening*).

THE SCRIPTURAL AND THEOLOGICAL FOUNDATIONS FOR MISSION

As did the 2007 *Code of Ethics*, it is important to briefly explain how the mission of Catholic Charities fits within the larger context of Catholic social teaching, including its deep roots in the Scriptures. That revelation begins with the nature of the human person. The new *Compendium of the Social Doctrine of the Church* puts it this way: "*The fundamental message of Sacred Scripture proclaims that the human person is a creature of God (cf. Ps 139:14–18), and sees in his being in the image of God the element that characterizes and distinguishes him:* "God created man in

---

44. Pontifical Council for Justice and Peace, *Compendium of the Social Doctrine of the Church* (Vatican City: Vatican Library Press, 2004).

45. *Catholic Charities USA Code of Ethics*, rev. ed. (Alexandria, VA: Catholic Charities USA, 2007), 2.

his own image, in the image of God he created him; male and female he created them" (Gen 1:27). God places the human creature at the centre and summit of the created order."[46] The human person is not just sacred, however, but he or she is social as well. The social nature of the person is not revealed solely in the incompleteness of Adam without Eve in the narrative of *Genesis*, but it is revealed all through the Jewish Scriptures in the compelling story of God's love for a people—Israel—and the intimate bond which this God has with them and which they in turn have with God and with one another. The Covenants of God with Israel are expressive of this intimate bondedness and call the people to duties of justice and charity towards one another, with a special care for the poor among them, those whom God especially loves.

The U.S. Catholic bishops, writing in their pastoral message *In All Things Charity*, reminded their readers of the Jewish tradition in these words:

> The Old Testament writers describe the great covenant of Sinai, which concretized the relationship of the community of Israel with God. This divine revelation illumines our understanding of the breadth and depth of charity. In the covenant, God promises steadfast love and faithfulness to the people of Israel. They, in turn, pledge to worship him alone and to direct their lives in accordance with God's will, made explicit in Israel's great legal codes. Integral to those codes is the special concern charged to the community for the widows, orphans, and strangers who comprised God's beloved poor. While the poor remain faithful to God, they are oppressed by a combination of poverty, powerlessness, and exploitation by others. "What these groups of people have in common is their vulnerability and lack of power. They are often alone and have no protector or advocate." The poor are oppressed politically and denied a decent share in the blessings of God's creation, which are intended to be shared by all of humanity.[47]

The bishops then describe the role of the jubilee in light of this tradition of community and its responsibility for God's beloved poor.

> The jubilee year (cf. Lv 25), which fell every fifty years, was meant to restore equality among all the children of Israel, "offering new

46. *Compendium of the Social Doctrine of the Church* (Vatican City: Pontifical Council for Justice and Peace, 2005), 108.

47. *In All Things Charity*, 12, quoting the 1986 U.S. Bishops' Pastoral Letter *Economic Justice for All*, 38.

possibilities to families which had lost their property and even their personal freedom." The jubilee year was proclaimed to assist those in need, to free those enslaved (often for debt), to restore property to its original owners, and to allow the poor to share fully in God's abundant blessings.

... Proclaiming jubilee was a requirement of just government, and the jubilee year was meant to restore social justice among the people. In doing so, it followed the tradition that those who possessed goods such as personal property were really only stewards charged with working for the good of all in the name of God, the sole owner of creation. God willed that these goods should serve everyone in a just way.[48]

Jesus in turn came to usher in this new millennium, to restore right relationships among people and with their God. Justice lies at the heart of those right relationships, of the jubilee year, and of what we call Catholic social teaching. Quoting Jesus in the fourth chapter of Luke's Gospel, the bishops declared that, "Jesus himself is the proclamation of the Great Jubilee." They went on to explain: "In the fullness of time, it is Jesus who proclaims the good news to the poor. It is Jesus who gives sight to the blind and frees the oppressed. By His words and above all by His actions, Jesus ushered in a "year of the Lord's favor," becoming in his passion and death the ransom for many."[49] In addition, as noted by Pope Benedict XVI, "the great parables of Jesus"—the rich man and the poor Lazarus, the Good Samaritan, and the Judgment scene in Matthew 25—all deepen our understanding of the centrality of love and justice at the heart of the revelation of the love of God embodied in Jesus of Nazareth. Further, as Benedict emphasized, the exercise of the ministry of charity (*diakonia*) is part of the threefold responsibility of the Church. Catholic social teaching is also a part of the proclamation of the Gospel (*kerygma-martyria*) which too is part of that threefold responsibility.

At this point it might be good to formally introduce what we call "Catholic social teaching," which the *Catechism of the Catholic Church* describes in these general terms:

The Church's social teaching comprises a body of doctrine, which is articulated as the Church interprets events in the course of his-

48. Ibid., 13, quoting Pope John Paul II in *Tertio Millennio Adveniente*, 13.
49. Ibid., 14.

tory, with the assistance of the Holy Spirit in light of the whole of what has been revealed by Jesus Christ.[50]

The Church's social teaching proposes principles for reflection; it provides criteria for judgment; it gives guidelines for action . . .[51]

As the Catechism further explains, the Church makes moral judgments about economic and social matters "when the fundamental rights of the person or the salvation of souls requires it."[52] These kinds of judgments date back two millennia to the earliest days of the community of followers of "the Way" of Jesus. The appointments of deacons to insure the feeding of the Greek-speaking widows and orphans, the collection promoted by St. Paul for the Christians suffering in Jerusalem, and the powerful and graphic warnings about the dangers of wealth in the Epistle of James are all early applications of the gospel to social realities.

In the post-apostolic centuries, Cyprian, St. John Chrysostom, Origen, St. Augustine, St. Clement of Alexandria, and St. Basil all strongly warn about the dangers of wealth and the punishment earned by those who failed to give alms. The community of believers was to be as generous and compassionate as they knew that their God was towards them, and they knew well the close identification that Christ had made between himself and the poor.

In the Middle Ages, while the monasteries and religious congregations were notable for their organized care for orphans, widows, the elderly, the sick, and the poor, the philosophers and theologians were developing a comprehensive body of thought that married Christian values with the philosophical traditions of the Greek, Latin, Arab, and Jewish worlds. From these were developed the underlying concepts of both personal and social justice and the nature of the virtuous life that provided the foundations for what we now call "modern Catholic social teaching."

The key building blocks in modern Catholic social teaching are the encyclical or teaching letters of the popes and the conciliar documents of the Second Vatican Council and synods of bishops. Among these are what I call "the classics, moderns, and contemporaries."[53] The

---

50. *Catechism of the Catholic Church* (Vatican City: Libreria Editrice Vaticana, 1994), 2422.

51. Ibid., 2423.

52. Ibid., 2420 quoting Vatican II's *Gaudium et Spes* (1965), 76, sec. 5.

53. See, for example, my treatment of these encyclicals in chapter three of *Doing*

two great classics among the encyclicals were written by Pope Leo XIII (*Rerum Novarum,* 1891) and Pope Pius XI (*Quadragesimo Anno,* 1931), forged in the heat of the industrial revolution and laying the foundations for much of the Church's discussion until the present. Pope John XXIII wrote *Mater et Magistra* in 1961 and *Pacem in Terris* in 1963 and these two encyclicals heavily influenced the work of the Second Vatican Council. The council's landmark document on *The Church in the Modern World (Gaudium et Spes,* 1965) is the most authoritative document of the last century and it began a more intense forty years of Church teaching which has brought us to Pope Benedict's *Deus Caritas Est* in 2005 and *Caritas in Veritate* in 2009.

What does all this mean now? How does the scriptural tradition of justice and charity and the two thousand year old tradition of Catholic social teaching come to bear on our contemporary realities and the mission of Catholic Charities? Most commentators have enunciated a series of principles of Catholic social teaching which can be drawn from the long and complex history of the Church's interface with political, social, economic, and cultural realities of the modern world.[54]

Faithjustice: An Introduction to Catholic Social Thought, rev. ed. (Mahwah, NJ: Paulist, 2004).

54. For example:

(1) Economist William J. Byron, SJ, writing in *America* on October 31, 1998 [vol. 179, no. 13] offered "ten building blocks of Catholic social teaching."

(2) In a recent book, theologian Thomas Massaro, SJ, offers nine themes around which to organize the key texts within the tradition. Cf. *Living Justice: Catholic Social Teaching in Action* (Franklin, WI: Sheed & Ward, 2000).

(3) The bishops of the United States also have worked to develop summaries of major themes from Catholic social teaching. Their efforts also demonstrate how summaries can evolve over time, as Catholic social teaching itself evolves. In 1991, on the hundredth anniversary of *Rerum Novarum,* the bishops wrote a short pastoral message in which they highlighted the following six themes from the tradition: the life and dignity of the human person; the rights and responsibilities of the human person; the call to family, community, and participation; the dignity of work and the rights of workers; the option for the poor and vulnerable; solidarity (*A Century of Social Teaching: A Common Heritage, A Continuing Challenge,* 1991). Seven years later, in a new document on the teaching of Catholic social teaching, the bishops reiterated the above six themes, but added a seventh: care for God's creation.

(4) In *Doing Faithjustice,* I identified twenty-six "key ideas" that occur in the first one hundred years of modern Catholic social teaching—from *Rerum Novarum* to *Centesimus Annus.* The fact of so many is an indication of the richness of the tradition and the inadequacy of any short list of principles or values to be drawn from over a century of this line of Catholic thought.

The *Compendium*, in an effort to be synthetic, perhaps overly so, identifies four core principles of Catholic social teaching, including extensive commentary on each. A short description of each is taken from the *Compendium*:

The Principle of Human Dignity

A just society can become a reality only when it is based on respect of the transcendent dignity of the human person. The person represents the ultimate end of society, by which it is ordered to the person: "Hence, the social order and its development must invariably work to the benefit of the human person, since the order of things is to be subordinate to the order of persons, not the other way around."[55]

The Principle of the Common Good

The principle of the common good, to which every aspect of social life must be related if it is to attain its fullest meaning, stems from the dignity, unity and equality of all people. According to its primary and broadly accepted sense, *the common good* indicates "the sum total of social conditions which allow people, either as groups or as individuals, to reach their fulfillment more fully and more easily."

... *The common good does not consist in the simple sum of the particular goods of each subject of a social entity. Belonging to everyone and to each person, it is and remains "common," because it is indivisible and because only together is it possible to attain it, increase it and safeguard its effectiveness, with regard also to the future.*[56]

The Principle of Subsidiarity

It is impossible to promote the dignity of the person without showing concern for the family, groups, associations, local territorial realities; in short, for that aggregate of economic, social, cultural, sports-oriented, recreational, professional and political expressions to which people spontaneously give life and which make it possible for them to achieve effective social growth ...

On the basis of this principle, all societies of a superior order must adopt attitudes of help ("subsidium")—therefore of support, promotion, development—with respect to lower-order societies ...

---

55. *Compendium*, no. 132, quoting Vatican Council II, *Gaudium et Spes*, 26 (emphasis in original).

56. Ibid., 164, quoting *Gaudium et Spes*, 26 (emphasis in original).

The principle of subsidiarity protects people from abuses by higher-level social authority and calls on these same authorities to help individuals and intermediate groups to fulfill their duties. This principle is imperative because every person, family and intermediate group has something original to offer to the community.[57]

The Principle of Solidarity

Solidarity highlights in a particular way the intrinsic social nature of the human person, the equality of all in dignity and rights and the common path of individuals and peoples towards an ever more committed unity . . .

In the presence of the phenomenon of interdependence and its constant expansion, however, there persist in every part of the world stark inequalities between developed and developing countries, inequalities stoked also by various forms of exploitation, oppression and corruption that have a negative influence on the internal and international life of many States. *The acceleration of interdependence between persons and peoples needs to be accompanied by equally intense efforts on the ethical-social plane,* in order to avoid the dangerous consequences of perpetrating injustice on a global scale.[58]

As the *Catholic Charities USA Code of Ethics* explains, the values and work of Catholic Charities are in keeping with the principles of Catholic social teaching and promote them in society. In terms of *human dignity*, Catholic Charities work to affirm and respect the dignity of each person and to promote their rights and duties. Catholic Charities promote the *common good* in their efforts to help all people to access what they need in society to reach their fulfillment, to encourage all persons to work for the rights of all, and in their advocacy for justice within society. Catholic Charities, in keeping with the principle of *subsidiarity*, encourage decision-making by all those capable of doing so, participation by those affected by decisions, and empowerment of those most in need. Further expressions of *subsidiarity* are the participation of Catholic Charities in the public discourse of this nation about charity and justice, especially for those with little or no voice of their own, and their own work as an "intermediate group" in providing services in society, including their partnership with government at all levels. Insofar as *solidarity* is concerned, Catholic

57. Ibid., 185–87 (emphasis in original).
58. Ibid., 192 (emphasis in original).

Charities embody the special concern for the poor in their priorities for the most needy, the emphasis on participation by those served in agency decision-making, and their advocacy for and with those most in need in public discourse.[59]

CONCLUSION

By articulating its mission in terms of service, advocacy, and convening, Catholic Charities in the United States stands squarely in the lines of a two-thousand-year-old theological tradition which is rooted in the Judeo-Christian Scriptures, expressed in the teachings of the popes and the U.S. bishops, and consistent in its embrace of both charity and justice as Gospel values. What was more inchoate in the founding documents of 1910, hammered out in the experiences of the next sixty years, clarified in the *Cadre Report* of 1972, and refined in the *Vision 2000* directions of 1996 has been repeatedly endorsed by the Church. The mission of Catholic Charities is to serve compassionately, empower enthusiastically, advocate prophetically, and genuinely engage others in this mission.

59. See discussion of how Catholic Charities implements these principles in *Code of Ethics*, part II.

2

Catholic Identity

Who We Are and How

A T CATHOLIC COMMUNITY SERVICES *in Baton Rouge in the 1980s, we arranged for staff to be educated on the Catholic identity of the agency and to have the opportunity to discuss its meaning and implications for their daily work. At the end of one such session, an elderly woman who I knew was Baptist came up to me and said, "Father Kammer, I just love working at Catholic Community Services. I just wish my church had a Catholic Community Services!" Her enthusiasm for working at a Catholic agency was shared by many of our staff of many faiths.*

I thought of her a decade later when the Catholic Identity Task Force of Catholic Charities USA was meeting for the first time in our offices in Alexandria, Virginia. One veteran director initially summarized the internal challenges the Task Force faced in terms of three sets of employees within the typical Catholic Charities agency. First, he said, there are the devout Catholics who are active in their local parishes and in the diocese in many ways and for whom working at Catholic Charities is icing on the cake of their overall active commitment to the Church. Second, there are those who were raised Catholic, but who have drifted away from active participation in the Church, often angry with the Church about one or another matter. For them, working at Catholic Charities is the last vestige of their Catholic upbringing and identity. The third group is those of many other faiths, who have a deep sense of sharing the underlying values upon which our agencies are based. He concluded by saying that it is not the third group that has trouble with our focus on Catholic identity, but it is the second!

To this analysis, another veteran responded, "To those three groups you have to add a fourth—those for whom working at Catholic Charities is just a J-O-B!"

What these veteran directors were highlighting was the incredible variety of people within Catholic Charities agencies, and how their efforts to mold the Catholic identity of their agencies was a complex and challenging endeavor requiring a great deal of effort and inventiveness. They also underlined the importance of this task for the Charities leader.

⌒

THE CATHOLIC IDENTITY OF CATHOLIC CHARITIES

Across this nation there are literally hundreds of independent organizations, involving thousands of programs, which make up the Catholic Charities network. In 2007, over 64,875 staff, 6,342 board members, and 230,357 volunteers served 7.7 million people.[1] They were the face and hands and heart of Catholic Charities. And despite the incredible variety of people of many faiths and none who make Catholic Charities a reality, certain essentials make the agencies *Catholic* Charities. Ten of them stand out.[2] They are drawn from the history of the mission of Catholic Charities sketched out in chapter 1, from authoritative documents of the Catholic Church, and from the experiences of Catholic Charities agencies across the country.

First, this ministry is rooted in the Scriptures. The work done by Catholic Charities has its roots deep in the Scriptures. In the Jewish Scriptures, at the heart of the biblical concept of *justice* was the care of the widow, orphan, and the stranger. Responding to their needs was a special responsibility of the Jewish people, and this justice was the gauge of whether they understood their relationship to God and to one another. Ironically, the contemporary work of Catholic Charities worldwide continues to be primarily to these same groups who comprised the biblical *anawim*: poor women; poor children; and those marginalized because, literally, they are foreign workers, immigrants, and refugees, or because

1 Mary L. Gautier, PhD, and Anna Campbell Buck, PhD, *Catholic Charities USA 2007 Annual Survey, Final Report* (Washington, DC: Center for Applied Research in the Apostolate, 2008) 3, 103.

2. This first part of chapter two is adapted and updated from my article, "10 Ways Catholic Charities are Catholic," *Charities USA* 25.1 (1998) 1–4.

they are racially different, or because they have a disability, HIV/AIDS, or some other condition that sets them apart. How these people are treated tests every society's justice and whether people understand that we are all children of one God who is passionately concerned about the least among us.

This was the teaching of Jesus as well. In the famous judgment scene in Matthew 25, one of Pope Benedict's "great parables," Jesus tells his followers that the nations will be judged by how they treat him—found among the hungry, homeless, sick, imprisoned, and poor. This teaching is reinforced in the great scene in the thirteenth chapter of the Gospel of John when Jesus washes the feet of his disciples and charges them to do so for others. It is an expression of the servant model of Church underscored in the teaching of the Second Vatican Council (see, *The Church in the Modern World*).

Second, this ministry has been an integral part of the Catholic Church for two thousand years. As the apostolic Church formed, the apostles faced a challenge that threatened to tear apart the new Christian community. The charge brought by the Greek-speaking Christians was that their widows were not receiving a share of the community's goods. The apostles then appointed the seven deacons; and their first ministry was to make sure that justice was reflected in the life of the community—that poor widows and children were cared for. As Pope Benedict pointed out, this ministry was institutionalized in the Egyptian monasteries of the fourth century, then in Church corporate structures of the sixth century, which were entrusted by government with the means to assist the poor.

This ministry of caring for the needy also was institutionalized in the great monasteries of the first millennium spread across the Church. The monastic communities of men and women took care of orphans, the sick, the elderly, travelers, and the poor. Centuries later, from the monasteries it was carried by women and men religious back into the cities where orphanages, homes for the sick and elderly, hospices, and many other centers for health and social services were established. Still later, lay and religious associations such as those begun by St. Vincent de Paul in France in the seventeenth century expanded and deepened this work. Many other great Saints were known for their ministries to the poor and vulnerable: St. Francis of Assisi, St. Clare, St. Peter Claver, St. Catherine of Siena, St. Martin de Porres, St. Ignatius of Loyola, and, in the United States, Sts. Elizabeth Ann Seton, Frances Cabrini, and Katherine Drexel.

Carried to the New World, this tradition of caring for the needy became part of the institutional and parish life of the Catholic Church here. The first such foundation was the orphanage, home for "women of ill repute," school, and health care facility begun by the Ursuline Sisters in New Orleans in 1727. By 1900, over eight hundred Catholic charitable institutions existed in the United States. Now, staff and volunteers, serving almost eight million persons a year, care for fetal alcohol syndrome infants, sponsor group homes for persons with mental disabilities, provide high-rise apartments for the elderly, resettle refugees and immigrants, counsel troubled families, offer hospice to persons with HIV/AIDS, feed hungry families, and shelter people who are homeless.

Third, Catholic Charities promote the sanctity of human life and the dignity of the human person. The ultimate rationale for these services is the belief in the sanctity of the human person and the dignity of human life, the underlying foundation for all of Catholic social teaching. This is reflected, for example, in adoption services that are among the most traditional in Charities and the care for the sick and the elderly which is a hallmark of the work of Catholic Charities. While society may exclude some people because they are sick, disabled, poor, or racially different, Catholic Charities reach out to them with respect for their human dignity. While society may reject some people because they are in prison or undocumented, Catholic Charities work to enhance their dignity, improve their lives, and meet their needs. Jesus Christ rejected no one from his healing touch and was known for his fellowship meals with tax collectors and sinners. So, too, Catholic Charities welcome persons with HIV, undocumented migrants, or others whom political majorities would ignore or punish.

Because of the theological and philosophical traditions of this faith community, at the heart of which are human sanctity and dignity, Catholic Charities have certain values and ethical standards to shape their work; these are set out in the *Catholic Charities USA Code of Ethics*, discussed in chapter 1. Among these values is the preferential concern for the poor articulated by Pope John Paul II and so many others. This preference is fleshed out in the nature of their services, the locations of their offices, the use of sliding fee scales, and advocacy for social justice.

Fourth, Catholic Charities are authorized to exercise their ministry by the diocesan bishop. Whether founded by a diocese, parish, religious congregation, or lay activists, Catholic charitable works and institutions root their formal Catholic identity in relationship to the Church and the diocesan bishop. As emphasized by Pope Benedict in *Deus Caritas Est,* the bishop is charged in Church teaching and canon law with responsibility for the apostolate within diocesan boundaries and with a special charge to care for the poor. However organized in terms of canon and civil law, Catholic Charities have responsibilities to operate consistently with the teachings and values of the Church. While there is great organizational variety, the civil law structure of even a separately incorporated charities agency generally allows the diocesan bishop to exercise his canonical responsibilities for the apostolate.

Fifth, Catholic Charities respect the religious beliefs of those they serve. Many people are surprised to learn that Catholic Charities serve people of all faiths. They may be even more surprised to learn that most agencies do not keep statistics on the religious affiliation of those coming to them. This is not an accident of history or a result of receiving funding from the United Way or government entities. Instead, it reflects a determined position to serve the entire community, a custom going back as far as the fourth century and, in this country, to the Ursuline Sisters in New Orleans in 1727. Again, in the pattern of Christ Jesus, the agencies' response is to families and persons in need—those who are hungry, homeless, depressed, troubled, and frail—regardless of their religious beliefs. We see this in Jesus' own ministry, where he cured the daughter of the Canaanite woman in Matthew 15 and the centurion's servant in Luke 7. Pope Benedict emphasized this inclusiveness in his encyclical's treatment of the Parable of the Good Samaritan and its lesson of universal love.

This decidedly ecumenical approach is simultaneously very Catholic. It reflects our respect for human dignity, religious liberty, and the ecumenical sensitivity promoted at Vatican II. Many people come to Catholic Charities for particular needs: a hot meal, a safe place to stay, a voucher for prescription medicine, resettlement in a new nation, and resources to rebuild after a natural disaster. They do not seek or need religious proselytizing, nor would staff members and volunteers offer it. It would be more than strange to preach Catholic beliefs to a devout Muslim family being resettled from Bosnia, a Buddhist Vietnamese grandmother coming to a Catholic Charities senior center, a Baptist elder to whom volunteers deliver a meal at home, or an Evangelical father entering a job-training program. Agencies are Catholic precisely in their respect for others' religious beliefs. As Pope John Paul II told the members meeting in San Antonio in

1986, "For your long and persevering service—creative and courageous, and blind to the distinctions of race *or religion*—you will hear Jesus' words of gratitude, 'You did it for me.'"[3]

Ten years later, Pope John Paul addressed the Pontifical Council "Cor Unum" on the role of charitable activity worldwide. Charitable activity is an eloquent means of Catholic evangelization because it witnesses to a spirit of giving and of communion inspired by God who created all men and women, the pope said. But, he continued, the primary motivation for Catholic giving is to serve Christ in the poor and suffering and to promote the justice, peace, and development worthy of the children of God. "Actions of aid, relief, and assistance should be conducted in a spirit of service and free giving for the benefit of all persons without the ulterior motive of eventual tutelage or proselytism."[4] Pope Benedict was equally explicit in his encyclical on love: "Charity, furthermore, cannot be used as a means of engaging in what is nowadays considered proselytism. Love is free; it is not practiced as a way of achieving other ends."[5] The love of God is to be shown in the work of Catholic Charities, not imposed as a condition for housing, food, or counseling services.

For a variety of reasons, however, Catholic Charities also may sponsor particular programs for the Catholic community, including marriage preparation and counseling, parish outreach and training, Catholic school counseling, or other more specific services. These are usually funded by the Catholic Church, used primarily by Catholics, and have a more explicitly Catholic content where appropriate.

Sixth, Catholic Charities recognize that some services require attention to the physical, mental, and spiritual needs of those they serve. In some services, it is appropriate and necessary to recognize and respond to the physical, mental, and spiritual needs of those Charities serve. Addiction treatment programs, marriage and family counseling, grief ministries, and other services call for attention to all the integrated facets of human beings. Catholic Charities do this in many ways consistent with their respect for the individual's religious beliefs. For example, twelve-step programs have a distinctive spiritual component essential to their success. Homeless shelters often provide opportunities for sharing faith and hope, prayer of

3. Pope John Paul II, address to the 1987 annual meeting, 12 (see chap. 1 n. 4).

4. Source: Catholic News Service, reporting on Pope John Paul II's address to the Pontifical Council "Cor Unum," April 18, 1997.

5. *Deus Caritas Est*, 31(c).

all kinds, and expressions of belief in a higher power. Senior centers and residences may provide opportunities for chaplaincy services of various denominations, depending on the desires of those served. And marriage and family counseling often must attend to the spiritual beliefs and values of those involved and how those beliefs help or hinder movement towards healing within the family. Counselors recognize and affirm the importance of this spiritual dimension of those they serve, again without imposing religious beliefs upon those involved.

Pope Benedict underscores this openness to the spiritual in all of Charities' services when he emphasizes the concern of charity for the whole person. Often, he says, no matter what the need in question, people crave "the look of love" because of their interior desire for a sign of love, of concern.[6] Pope John Paul had made a similar point in his 1987 San Antonio address to Catholic Charities USA when he declared, "[N]o institution can by itself replace the human heart, human compassion, human love or human initiative, when it is a question of dealing with the sufferings of others."[7]

The deepest cause of their suffering may well be "the very absence of God," wrote Pope Benedict. The Church's charitable activity, then, does not impose religion, but remains open to communicate God's love in deeds:

> Those who practice charity in the Church's name will never seek to impose the Church's faith upon others. They realize that a pure and generous love is the best witness to the God in whom we believe and by whom we are driven to love. A Christian knows when it is time to speak of God and when it is better to say nothing and let love alone speak. He knows that God is love (cf. 1 Jn 4:8) and that God's presence is felt at the very time when the only thing we do is to love.[8]

St. Francis of Assisi is reputed to have made the same point to his followers, saying, "Preach the Gospel, if necessary use words."

Seventh, Catholic Charities have a special relationship to the Catholic diocese and to Catholic parishes. In over half of U.S. dioceses, Catholic Charities agencies have formal programs through which the agency seeks to support and encourage the parish in its ministry to the community and

---

6. Ibid., 18.

7. Pope John Paul II, address to the 1987 annual meeting, 11.

8. *Deus Caritas Est,* 31(c).

its needs.[9] In many others this parish relationship also exists, although more informally. In this capacity, agencies assist parishioners in the exercise of their baptismal commitment to the poor and needy.[10] Agencies provide professional resources, training, support, and encouragement to parish-based ministries such as food pantries, outreach to the frail elderly, community organizing, legislative networks working for social justice, and action for global solidarity and peace. By so doing, agencies help pastors and parishes to carry out their responsibilities to form caring faith communities. They also expand agencies' own ministry through the hands and hearts of many thousands of parishioners, and even enlist parishes and parishioners in joint ventures such as community-wide soup kitchens, sponsorship of refugee families, and prison visitations. The U.S. bishops, writing in *In All Things Charity*, urged parish leaders and members to develop links with diocesan Catholic Charities agencies and encouraged Charities agencies to reach out to parishes to support their social concern activities.[11]

Catholic Charities also cooperate with diocesan leadership by operating or collaborating with diocesan offices and programs, funded largely by the Church. These would include the Catholic Campaign for Human Development anti-poverty program, family life and respect life programs, youth organizations, offices for African-American or Hispanic-American Catholics, Catholic Relief Services, the St. Vincent de Paul Society, and justice and peace offices. In so doing, Catholic Charities assist the Catholic Church in carrying out other related aspects of the Church's ministry within and to the wider community and help fulfill their own mission to serve people in need, advocate for a just society, and bring people together to solve community problems. (More of this collaboration and parish social ministry is discussed below in chapter 5.)

Eighth, Catholic Charities work in active partnership with other religiously sponsored charities and with the civic community. Reflecting the teaching of the Second Vatican Council and an even longer experience

---

9. The 2007 Annual Survey reports that 97 of 171 responding agencies reported that 445 agency staff are involved in Parish Social Ministry, averaging 4.6 staff (in FTEs) involved in Parish Social Ministry. *Survey*, 110.

10. See *Communities of Salt and Light*, National Conference of Catholic Bishops, 1993, and *Called to Global Solidarity*, 1998, in which the bishops call upon parishes to exercise their baptismal social responsibility.

11. *In All Things Charity*, 23.

with practical ecumenism, Catholic Charities express the willingness and even responsibility of the Catholic Church to work hand in hand with other religions and other people of good will to serve community needs. They often support community-wide fundraising for the benefit of Catholic Charities, the charities sponsored by other churches, and other non-profit organizations, such as those conducted by the United Way. They build coalitions to address emerging community needs by developing new collaborative responses, community education, and combined advocacy before public and private forums. The U.S. bishops have encouraged such activities and partnerships: "Voluntary organizations play an important part in our collective efforts to promote the common good, protect human life, reach out to people in need, and work for a more just and compassionate society . . . Parishes, diocesan organizations, and Catholic charity and justice organizations should take every reasonable opportunity to work with such associations as well as with those organizations sponsored by other faith communities."[12] The bishops also urged collaboration with the private sector where businesses, corporations, and unions could play a strong role in promoting jobs with decent wages, providing volunteers and financial support, and supporting charities with technical assistance, business skills, and capital.[13] Pope Benedict urged charity workers to "work in harmony with other organizations in serving various forms of need, but in a way that respects what is distinctive about the service that Christ requested of his disciples."[14] (Further discussion of this collaboration follows in chapters 5 and 7.)

Ninth, Catholic Charities support an active public-private partnership with government at all levels. The Catholic Church has a long and strong tradition of teaching about the responsibilities of governments for promoting the common good and protecting the least among us and the responsibilities of Catholics as citizens and taxpayers for support of those roles and active participation in civic life. In his encyclical, Pope Benedict taught that, "The just ordering of society and the State is a central responsibility of politics." In carrying out this responsibility, "justice is both the aim and the intrinsic criterion of all politics."[15] The Church's role

12. Ibid., 36–37.
13. Ibid., 37.
14. *Deus Caritas Est*, 34.
15. Ibid., 28(a).

here is the formation of consciences and education as to the "authentic requirements of justice" in the civic realm in which everyone has a duty. "Building a just social and civil order, wherein each person receives what is his or her due, is an essential task which every generation must take up anew."[16] The Church does not replace the State, but has a duty to promote justice in the public dialogue.

An additional relationship exists between Church and State, Benedict teaches, whereby there has been "the growth of many forms of cooperation between State and Church agencies."[17] In keeping with the principle of subsidiarity, the government encourages various forms of subsidiary organizations such as Catholic Charities, who bring their own strong mission, resources, and volunteers to serve the needs of the public. In many cases as well, government provides the kinds of financial resources which are far beyond the wherewithal of private charities who in turn bring to bear the human and spiritual resources which are unavailable to government.

Two instances come to mind. One is the provision of income support, often to the elderly, disabled, and needy families, a role for which only government has the resources. The *Compendium* speaks of such redistribution of income under the heading of social justice and the pursuit of authentic well-being within a country.[18] Charities cannot replace this function of government—basic income support—but they often provide additional financial and in-kind support (food, clothing, a rent payment) in times of crisis, when government income programs are clearly inadequate to meet family needs (which is the case all too often), and for short-term needs of families otherwise able to support themselves.

The second area of complementarity between government and voluntary agencies such as Catholic Charities is in the provision of needed social services. In the light of these teachings, Catholic Charities have sought and accepted partnerships with cities, counties, states, and the Federal Government in which they receive government funding for services to the wider community that they judge to be consistent with their own missions. These payments may take the form of contracts to deliver particular services such as foster care of vulnerable youth, reimbursement

16. Ibid.

17. Ibid., 38(b).

18. *Compendium*, 303.

for care of individuals paid by government such as Medicaid, and government funding of construction such as housing. Government provides funding; and agencies bring additional funding, volunteers, efficiency, values, community credibility, and dedication to the service of local communities and their needy families. As the U.S. bishops explain approvingly: "The U.S. government has also provided funding for needed social services by purchasing service contracts and providing other funding for nonprofit agencies. These agencies, in turn, have provided hands-on care by trained staff, enrichment of volunteers, private fund raising, and dedicated commitment to deliver the services to children, families, elders, and people with disabilities."[19] What the bishops describe at the level of the federal government is also true of state and local governments as well, either with federal funding delivered through block grants and other devices to the states and localities or with separate state or local funds.

The bishops have an important caveat as well. In describing positively this partnership between State and Church, they provided this caution: "In establishing partnerships with voluntary agencies, public sector authorities must not make requirements that weaken agency identities and integrity or undermine agency commitments to serve people in need."[20]

This was a timely warning in view of the increasing tendency of those in government to disregard the strongly held values of charitable agencies—especially religious organizations—by imposing inconsistent requirements. This occurred in California at the turn of this century when the legislature defined "religious employer" to include only those whose purpose was to inculcate religious tenets and who employed and served primarily those who share its tenets—thus removing Catholic health care and charities from the religious employer category and their ability to invoke traditional conscience clauses in refusing to include recently mandated contraceptive coverage from their prescription plans. The legislature's action was upheld by the California Supreme Court (6–1) in 2004,[21] and later that year the U.S. Supreme Court declined to review that decision on appeal by Catholic Charities of Sacramento.

Most recently, Catholic Charities of Boston experienced similar intrusion in the insistence of the State of Massachusetts that adoptions

19. *In All Things Charity,* 39.

20. Ibid.

21. Rick Mockler, "When States Define 'Religious Employer': California's Ruling against Catholic Charities in Sacramento," *Charities USA* 31.2 (2004) 17.

by gay couples be mandatory for all Massachusetts adoption agencies. Ultimately, in 2006, Catholic Charities of Boston—unable to accept the state's mandate—was forced to discontinue adoptions after almost a century of service to the community rather than to retreat from its religious values, even though there were other agencies in Boston that would provide adoptions to gay couples.

Tenth, Catholic Charities blend advocacy for those in need and public education about social justice with service to individuals, families, and communities. Throughout the last century, the Catholic Church has been increasingly outspoken about the need for economic and political change. This change is consistent with the obligations of social justice in order to meet the needs of the entire community, with a special concern for the poorest and most vulnerable (e.g., *Economic Justice for All*, National Conference of Catholic Bishops, 1986). Such change is in addition to the obligations of individuals to reach out to those nearest to them in charity and justice.

Catholic Charities, following the lead of the Vatican and the bishops of the United States, have made working for a more just society an integral part of its understanding of its mission. It is not enough to feed more and more hungry families; Charities also must raise the public question about why so much hunger persists in this wealthy nation and how that condition might be changed by individual, community, business, and government action. Thus, local Catholic Charities understand that advocacy, empowerment, and work for justice are intrinsic parts of their mission of caring for individuals, families, and communities in need. In taking this position, Catholic agencies understand the intimate connection between justice and charity arising from the Gospel. The U.S. bishops have consistently taught this connection:

> In his apostolic exhortation *The Church in America (Ecclesia in America)*, Pope John Paul II clearly presents the Christian responsibility to ensure that charity and justice result in individual actions and work for systemic change. We Christians must "reflect the attitude of Jesus, who came to 'proclaim Good News to the poor' (Lk 4:18) . . . This constant dedication to the poor and disadvantaged emerges in the Church's social teaching, which ceaselessly invites the Christian community to a commitment to overcome every form of exploitation and oppression. It is a question not only of alleviating the most serious and urgent needs through individual

actions here and there, but of uncovering the roots of evil and pro-
posing initiatives to make social, political and economic structures
more just and fraternal."[22]

This connection has been a central theme for Catholic Charities USA from
its founding in 1910, promoted consistently in the recommendations of
the Cadre and Vision 2000, and contained in the mission and requirements of the various editions of the Code of Ethics of the organization.

THE POWER OF CATHOLIC IDENTITY IN *CATHOLIC CHARITIES*[23]

These ten ways that Catholic Charities is *Catholic*, when taken together,
mean resistance to those on the extreme left and extreme right of politics
and religion who would have Catholic Charities be "Catholic" in some
half-a-loaf, half-baked, or half-true fashion to satisfy their political or po-
lemical agenda. From two thousand years of history, it is clear that being
truly Catholic is multiform, complex, shaded with meanings, filled with
creative tensions, developing over time, responsive to many cultures and
peoples, a religious mystery, and yet dynamically alive in so many ways.
This can be better understood when Church itself is known to be simultaneously institution, community, word, sacrament, servant, and, as Vatican
II emphasized, a pilgrim people still searching for its way.[24]

These agencies should make no apologies for being *Catholic* or being
Catholic Charities! This can be appreciated better by moving from merely
being Catholic to an understanding of the *power* of being Catholic. It is
a fact that many of the 64,875 staff, 6,342 board members, and 230,357
volunteers who serve millions of needy people each year in the name of
Catholic Charities are themselves other-than-Catholic. But the power
of being Catholic Charities is a power in which every one of these staff,
volunteers, board members, and supporters can all share—for the sake of
the individuals, families, and communities that Catholic Charities serve.
Part of that power is the recognition by many people of many faiths that
they want to be part of this enterprise that is so rooted in the scriptures, in

---

22. Ibid. 17, citing Pope John Paul II, *Ecclesia in America* (1999), 18.

23. This part of chapter two draws upon points first made in my address in the 1st
Annual John M. Lally Lecture; Catholic Charities, St. Louis; April 8, 1999.

24. Avery Dulles, SJ, *Models of the Church* (Garden City, NY: Doubleday, 1974).

the ministry of Jesus, and in the inestimable value of each human person they encounter.

What do I mean by power? Let me start with two sentences from the 1998 report of the Catholic Charities USA Task Force on Empowerment: "For our purposes, power is simply the ability of an individual, community, or organization to act, to get things done and/or to change things. In its best and purest form, power is shared."[25]

The power of being Catholic Charities is about their ability to support families, fight poverty, and build communities—the threefold mission framed in 1972 by the Cadre. And power is about doing that mission *effectively*! The power is also about the credibility that comes from effective ministry, wide collaboration in the community, deeply held values, and a mission which is understood and admired by many in the communities in which Charities work. In Texas in the late 1990s, I asked board members of a local Catholic Charities why they had agreed to serve in that capacity. A woman forthrightly responded, "It was because of the widespread credibility of Catholic Charities in the community." That is the power of Catholic Charities, and it can be shared by all of those so involved.

The reason for attacks upon Catholic Charities when it does advocacy for the poor is precisely because the people involved in making Catholic Charities a reality are powerful—in the sense the task force suggests. Their power is rooted not just in the ten ways Catholic Charities is Catholic, but even more in their everyday experience with needy families, commitment to the well-being and empowerment of those they serve, advocacy for and with them for a just society, and their "mission-driven-ness." Many of those in politics, the media, universities, or think-tanks simply do not have this experience or rootedness. The shared experience of the lives of those in need is what has made the voices of Catholic Charities heard in the halls of Congress and in various Administrations. It is also precisely what has made these same voices resented by some whose only qualification for speaking about the poor is that their opinions play well in the media or in the lifestyle enclaves of the privileged and powerful.

The power of Catholic Charities is rooted simply in daily contact with Christ among the homeless, hungry, poor, illiterate, imprisoned, refugee, lonely, and despised. That is a gift that is given only by the poor

25. Task Force on Empowerment, *A Catholic Charities Framework for Empowerment* (Alexandria, VA: Catholic Charities USA, 1998), 2.

and which must be carried with reverent respect for its effects and for its demands. What are these effects and demands?

The *effects* of this power of being Catholic Charities are at least several. First, it makes it possible for the staff and volunteers to continue their work year-after-year, day-after-day, even while those coming to the agencies for help increase dramatically in number and needs and the financial resources always lag far behind the agencies' desires to serve and the aspirations of the needy for new lives. Despite years and years of serving millions and millions of people in need, volunteers and staff have continued to serve creatively and courageously in the power of Catholic Charities. That is precisely because of the combination of factors that make these charities *Catholic* and that keep staff and volunteers actively engaged: their deep roots in the Scriptures and in the mission of Jesus; their connection to the larger Church; their values; their respect for those they serve; their collaborative approach; their partnerships with government at all levels; and the ways they blend service to the needy with community building and advocacy for justice.

Second, this power creates relationships for Charities with those who carry the name *Catholic* on their persons or institutions. This *relationship-creating power* allows them to partner across ministries within the Church, from the thirty-five-year-old commitment to nurture parish social ministry to reaching out to the Catholic institutions which span pre-school to post-doctoral education to the increasingly logical collaboration with Catholic health ministry which has been urged so strongly in the past ten to fifteen years (see chapter 5). These are no small opportunities when Charities' boards and staff consider that the Catholic community in the United States now comprises a quarter of the population, half of the Fortune 500 CEO's, almost 20,000 "local offices" called parishes, and the largest voluntary school system, health care system, and social services system in the nation. Catholics are as well, as Catholic Charities USA's President Father Bryan Hehir has noted frequently, a Church whose membership spans those who have arrived at the center of American political and economic life and those new arrivals and others who wait at the periphery to be allowed to enter our national community.

This *relationship power* also allows agencies and individuals, through their national organization and network, Catholic Charities USA, to have personal, professional, and faith-based friendships which cross the nation, span lifetimes in this ministry, generate new ideas, encourage members to take bold steps, and bind them to one another in prayer and solidarity in times of sickness, disability, retirement, grief, and death. And, within states, this power invites Catholic Charities workers to reach out to form alliances with one another in order to be more effective advocates as states shape welfare programs or to be more effective partners with states or other organizations in the service of needy families.

The third effect of this power of being Catholic Charities is that it urges Charities workers to take the long view. The success of their ministries is not dependent on the events of today, this week, or even this year. This work has been an integral part of this Church for almost 2,000 years and their national organization since 1910. While the daily commitment to and with the poor and needy may not be too trendy at times or popular with today's media or tomorrow's, Catholic Charities will be around when today's critics, policy makers, and even some competitors are long forgotten. That awareness undergirds the sense that agencies do and should not trade off long-term, faith-based values for short-term economic or political gain.

These are just three effects of the power of being Catholic: it renews those who work in Charities for the daily struggle, creates effective relationships for the future, and urges staff and volunteers to take the long-term view of the people served and the problems agencies face.

Being entrusted with the power of Catholic Charities also makes certain *demands* on those involved in agencies today. I also would like to underscore three of those demands. First, what is done as Catholic Charities must be more than just service-as-provided-by-others. This commits members to the service-that-empowers that was the hallmark of the first Strategic Direction of the 1996 *Vision 2000* plan: "*making the empowerment of those we serve, especially people who are poor and vulnerable, central to our work.*" This implies not only the helping-people-to-help-themselves that the Cadre recommended in 1972. It also demands that agencies make central to their work the full arsenal of community organizing and consensus building, economic and community development, personal and political advocacy, and as wide a range of responses to family, neighborhood, and community problems as can be imagined consistent with the dignity and empowerment of those served and the values Catholic Charities espouses. These responses challenge members to learn new skills, form new alliances with business, universities, government, churches, and non-profits, and take the risks of new ventures with and for those they care about. That can be scary when agencies already have so much to do and seemingly too little to do it with. But the power of being Catholic Charities is to continually innovate and to create new hope where there is none and new possibilities where others have despaired or have resigned themselves to service-as-usual. (see chapter 8 on innovation and quality.)

The second demand of this power is that, even taking the long view, Catholic Charities must confront the structural and technological issues that affect their ability to continue to provide services tomorrow to many people served today. This implies a duty to preserve their heritage and to position themselves for the immediate future. The very viability of this Church to provide services to the poor and vulnerable is threatened by changes in the environment for Catholic Charities agencies. Public and private funders are targeting their support to the most efficient operators, regardless of mission and values, to integrated delivery networks, and to those providers whose program effectiveness can be documented through outcome measures. These environmental changes demand that, to preserve Catholic identity and their value-driven services, agencies must be prepared to compete effectively, to enter into networks of service, and to document program effectiveness through such measures as agency accreditation—all the while preserving and enhancing their power-laden Catholic identity. This will take not just the wisdom of Solomon, but the patience of Job, the courage of David, the wiles of Judith, and the faithfulness of Mary.

The third demand of the power of being Catholic Charities addresses itself to Catholic Charities USA, as a national organization with local members, and to the leadership of those local members. Members embodied that demand in the third Strategic Direction of the 1996 *Vision 2000* plan when they pledged to: "*Strengthen our identity with, and relationship to, the larger Church and witness to its social mission.*" Those directions targeted local Catholic Charities and their national organization. They demanded significant steps to enhance leadership development and mission effectiveness, integration of theology and spirituality into leadership and staff formation, clarity about Catholic identity, and clear guidelines for governance, operations, and management under civil and canon law as they affect a Catholic sponsored agency entering into partnership with Catholic and non-Catholic providers in various networks.

One such initiative was the work of the Task Force on Catholic Identity and their 1997 publication of the book *Who Do You Say We Are: Perspectives on Catholic Identity in Catholic Charities.*[26] In 2001, national staff engaged in a year-long process to develop a Catholic Identity and Mission Self-Assessment tool that any local agency would be able to use. Together with a consultant, after a year of consultation on the draft with diocesan directors, piloting at five agencies, and the development of survey instruments to be used with board members and staff, the national organization made available to member agencies a complete set of materials for the Catholic Identity and Mission Assessment.[27] Another more recent effort was the thorough revision of the *Catholic Charities USA Code of Ethics* in 2007, discussed above.

In terms of leadership development, the national organization for two decades has conducted an intense week-long leadership institute for agency directors and senior managers that blends together leadership skills, organizational development, and Catholic Charities history and values.[28] More recently, Catholic Charities USA has initiated a new Executive Leadership Program in conjunction with Notre Dame University for agency leadership teams of staff and boards to assist them in integrating Catholic identity, spirituality, and mission with sound management in a values-based context.[29] Most recently, it also has launched a new on-site Vocation of the Trustee program to educate local board members on mission and responsibilities[30] and, in 2008, a New Diocesan Directors Institute, offered at the national organization's offices, to introduce directors to Catholic Charities and their responsibilities and challenges in the context of Catholic identity and mission.[31] Many local agencies have also developed their own programs for board members and staff, including,

26. *Who Do You Say We Are? Perspectives on Catholic Identity in Catholic Charities* (Alexandria, VA: Catholic Charities USA, 1997).

27. Dr. Terry McGuire, EdD, "Developing a Catholic Identity and Mission Self-Assessment: Results of a Year-long Process," *Charities USA* 29.1 (2002) 14–15.

28. See, "Leadership Institute: Building the Capacity of Individual Leaders," *Charities USA* 35.1 (2008) 14–16.

29. See, "From Mission to Service: The Notre Dame Executive Leadership Program," in ibid., 17–19.

30. See, "Vocation of the Trustee: Leadership Development for Catholic Charities Board Members," in ibid., 20.

31. See, "New Diocesan Directors Institute: A 'Charities 101' Course for New Directors," in ibid., 21.

for example, the innovative "Catholic Charities University" of Charities of Spokane, a monthly leadership development seminar for fifteen program directors.[32]

These efforts at the national and local level are designed to preserve Catholic identity and its power as agencies position themselves for future ministry in the environment just described. Local staff and volunteer leadership, however, must insure that their agencies take the time and concern and make the human and financial investments to update mission statements, adopt a code of ethics, orient new staff to agency mission and values, educate board and staff and volunteers in agency values, design and select programs and services consistent with mission and values, and, ultimately, serve and empower individuals, families, and communities in ways demanded by that same mission (see chapter 7 on pluralism).

So far, I have described three demands on agencies due to the power of Catholic Charities entrusted to them: that they provide far more than just service as usual; that they preserve and position their agencies for future service in terms of structural and technological issues; and that their national and local organizations provide improved resources to enhance Catholic identity and power and that local leaders make that identity effective in communities across the nation.

Despite a variety of factors in their environment that threaten or will threaten agencies and their mission, being Catholic carries strength, power, and resiliency that give Charities both the tenacity and the flexibility to face internal and external challenges of the present and the future. These are the lessons of a Resurrection Church—that God's love embodied in the risen Jesus is stronger than anything we humans and our endeavors suffer from. All we need do is to remember the stories of the risen Jesus and how his love for each of those he encounters is stronger than whatever apparent calamity they saw:

- for Mary Magdalene: stronger than the loss of the one she loved (John 20:11–18);

- for the disciples locked in the upper room after the crucifixion: stronger than their fear of being known as his followers (John 20:19–23);

32. Joannie Eppinga, "Catholic Charities University: An Innovative Program Grows Leaders at Catholic Charities Spokane," in ibid., 9–11.

- for Thomas: stronger than his skepticism and pragmatism (John 20:24–29);
- for the two on the road to Emmaus: stronger than their disappointment and hopelessness (Luke 24:13–35); and
- for Peter: stronger than his own failures (John 21:15–19).

God's love—enfleshed in our own time in ministries to the poor and vulnerable—will survive any challenges from contemporary hopelessness, cynicism, loss, disappointment, failure, skepticism, or fear. The ultimate power of being Catholic Charities is that there is no challenge that they face today that can overcome their faith and hope in the power of the risen Lord and his love which is their message to the world.

PART TWO

Works.

3

Service

"Providing Help. Creating Hope. Transforming Lives."[1]

"THE URSULINES CAME TO *New Orleans in response to a call from Governor Bienville, who recognized that education was of vital importance if the fledgling colony were to grow and prosper, and who knew the esteem the Ursulines enjoyed in Europe for their work, dedication, and determination. This occurred only nine years after Bienville and his men had cleared the site for fortifications on the muddy banks of the Mississippi River.*

"Under the auspices of King Louis XV, 12 courageous women, in the spirit of St. Angela,[2] *answered Governor Bienville. On a cold, foggy morning in February 1727, in Rouen, France, they boarded the ship La Gironde, which was bound for the New World and New Orleans. They had no idea what might be awaiting them, but simply and humbly stepped into that vast void with faith and a sense of mission. On a hot and steamy day in August of 1727, with not even so much as a wooden sidewalk in the New Orleans colony to welcome them, the sisters landed and went immediately to work.*

"The strenuous voyage of the Ursulines from France lasted five months, during which they were plagued by terrible storms, threats by pirates, and seasickness. What food was not lost was meagerly rationed. The Ursulines

---

1. "Providing help. Creating hope. Transforming lives." This is the 2008 slogan of Catholic Charities of North Dakota, their version of a slogan promoted by Catholic Charities USA. The local agency has added the third phrase to more fully capture their understanding of their work for people in need.

2. St. Angela Merici (1474–1540) founded the "Company of St. Ursula," known as the Ursuline Sisters, in Brescia in Lombardy in 1535 to teach girls and young women, especially the poor.

53

met the challenge that few would have braved, and scarcely any have accomplished.

"When the Ursuline nuns arrived in New Orleans in 1727, Governor Bienville was no longer in charge and had returned to France. There were extraordinary squabbles among residents of the colony that were both political and ecclesiastical in nature. Through all of this, with characteristic Ursuline calm and faith, the nuns, under the direction of their prioress Mother St. Augustin, continued their own spiritual development and their educational efforts with boarders, day students, orphans that they had taken in from both the city and as a result of the Natchez massacre, and with the African and Native American girls of the colony.

"The Ursulines thereby not only established the first school for girls, but also ran the first free school and the first orphanage, held the first classes for African slave and Native American girls, and organized the first retreat for ladies within the present limits of the United States. They also performed outstanding work in the military hospital in the new colony, where one of the Ursulines, Sister Francis Xavier, became the first woman pharmacist in the New World. Most important of all, by their Christian living, they so influenced the wives and mothers in the colony that this Christian spirit endures today."[3]

This Ursuline foundation in the city of New Orleans has a unique triple significance: it marks the beginning of the extensive Catholic ministries of education, health care, and social services in what is now the United States. From this heroic but humble beginning have grown the largest non-governmental education, health care, and social services networks in the United States and, actually, in the world. Catholic schools and universities, hospitals and nursing facilities, and charities and social services, begun in most places by religious sisters, brothers, and priests, now serve tens of millions of people a year. While education and health care are each part of this achievement, the focus of this chapter is on the works of Catholic Charities.

The "works" of Catholic Charities begin with the services that most people readily associate with such organizations—helping people in need. What do Catholic Charities do? It seems a simple question, but the an-

3. From the history of the Ursulines, quoted in *Charities USA* 29.2 (2002) 18.

swers are very complex because of the amazing scope of services offered across the country and the diversity of the organizations that are called "Catholic Charities."

It may be helpful at first to understand that the Catholic Charities USA network is not a single national organization with local branches such as the Boy Scouts of America, the Salvation Army, or the Red Cross. Because of the structure of the Catholic Church into individual dioceses and the grassroots histories of these ministries, the Catholic Charities agencies are largely "home grown." Many are organized as a single not-for-profit corporation within a single diocese, for example, Catholic Community Services of Baton Rouge, where I worked. They also may have different names such as "Catholic Charities," "Catholic Social Services," or "Catholic Family Services."

In many dioceses, however, there are multiple affiliated organizations under the heading of Catholic Charities. In some there exist separate institutions, for example, an individual home for the elderly ("St. Christopher's Residence") or housing complex ("Hope Homes") created as separate legal corporations for legal, financial, and funding purposes. In other dioceses with large geographical areas to serve, there may be individual county organizations that are separately incorporated to serve local populations, e.g., Catholic Social Services of Monroe County, one of several branch agencies of Catholic Charities in the Archdiocese of Detroit. In still other dioceses, the separate agencies may be specialty organizations serving particular people in need, e.g., a housing corporation, a counseling agency, or an organization providing legal services for immigration and naturalization. To make it even more confusing some dioceses like Youngstown combine geographical agencies and specialty organizations under one organizational umbrella.[4] And, in a few rare situations, a single Catholic Charities agency may operate in more than one diocese, usually because of a specialty service—for example, a food-buying cooperative— or a statewide or regional contract to deliver services.

Such organizational diversity often reflects a sense of subsidiarity within the diocese. However, as discussed in chapter two, all of the diverse agencies are in some way subject to coordination or supervision by the diocesan Catholic Charities agency and/or the diocesan bishop, as is the

---

4. See, for example, the organizational structure of the Diocese of Youngstown. Brian R. Corbin, "Catholic Identity and Institutional Practice: A Case Study of Catholic Charities of Youngstown, OH," *Charities USA* 31.2 (2004) 11–14.

case in a diocese with a single agency. "While separately incorporated, Catholic Charities retains a public identity with the Church for religious reasons not only rooted in its origin, but also integral to its continuing identity and mission. Its religious integrity requires a formal connectedness to the diocese through corporate structures that meet the requirements of the law of the Church (canon law) and the state law governing the corporation, as well as federal and state laws that may regulate some funding programs."[5] Separately incorporated organizations can also be a challenge to the diocese in terms of keeping a strong sense of identification with the diocese and coordination among the agencies.[6]

WHO DO CATHOLIC CHARITIES SERVE?

But what do these organizations do and who do they serve? For an overview, we turn to the 111-page *Catholic Charities USA 2007 Annual Survey Final Report*, prepared by the Center for Applied Research in the Apostolate (CARA) at Georgetown University.[7] The survey reports that in 2007, "1668 local Catholic Charities agencies and affiliates provided services to 7,736,855 unduplicated clients."[8] An "unduplicated client" is a single person, although he or she may receive multiple services from local Catholic Charities. For example, a person with mental health problems may be counseled, as well as receive assistance with a medical bill and even housing in a shelter for the homeless. (Statistics on services provided in the pages that follow will report on the services provided by Catholic Charities agencies, although in some cases two or more services may be received by a single person.) The annual survey is itself a challenge for the statisticians since statistics have to be collected from a number of organizations and their staffs across the country, often working in multiple affiliated agencies within a single reporting diocese.[9]

5. Melanie DiPietro, SC, JD, JCL, "Organizational Overview," in *Who Do You Say We Are?* 25–41, at 28.

6. See Corbin, "Catholic Identity."

7. Gautier and Buck, *2007 Survey*. CARA began this annual survey work for Catholic Charities USA in December, 2002.

8. Ibid., 3.

9. CARA mailed the twenty-page 2007 Annual Survey in January 2008 to 171 executive directors for completion on-line. Between January and July, 2008, a total of 139 agencies and affiliates participated in the 2007 survey, a response rate of 81 percent. To make data from year to year more comparable, CARA substituted 2006 data (where available)

Who were these seven million people served by Catholic Charities in 2007? As the survey emphasizes, *"Children under age 18 and seniors age 65 and over comprise close to half of unduplicated clients served by Catholic Charities member agencies and affiliates."*[10] Of all those served, 2,219,644 or thirty-three percent were children under 18 years of age; 4,014,798 or fifty-two percent were adults 18 to 64 years of age; and 1,141,708 or fifteen percent were 65 years and older. (An additional 60,705, less than one percent, were not classified by age.) In terms of socio-economic characteristics, CARA reports that forty-four percent of the unduplicated clients were receiving means-tested public assistance including Temporary Assistance to Needy Families (TANF), Supplemental Security Income (SSI), Medicaid, and food stamps. A total of fifty-six percent of the persons served by Catholic Charities had family incomes below the federal poverty line ($20,650 for a family of four). This economic concentration reflects most people's perception that Catholic Charities serve the poor and needy, but the data also indicates that Catholic Charities serve many others in the community as well.

WHAT SERVICES DO CATHOLIC CHARITIES PROVIDE?

What services do these seven million people receive from Catholic Charities? First and foremost, it is food ("When did we see you hungry, Lord?"). Here, using the figures for *services* provided in a year (totaling 13,919,070 client services provided, where one client may be "duplicated" in the sense of receiving more than one service) and the categories provided by CARA, Catholic Charities in 2007 provided the following client services:

---

for 32 member agencies or affiliates that did not respond with 2007 data. Because of this and other variations in agency data collection methods, CARA advises that trend analysis should be made with care. Ibid., 1–2.

10. Ibid. (emphasis in original).

TABLE 1: Services Provided by Catholic Charities Agencies, 2007

Service Types	Number	Percent
Services that provide food	6,533,080	47%
Services that build strong communities	3,482,216	25%
Other basic needs services	1,568,964	11%
Services that strengthen families	1,156,240	8%
Housing related services	532,869	4%
Disaster services	420,422	3%
Programs for special populations	225,279	2%
Total client services provided	13,919,070	100%[11]

Since *food services* are those most received by people from Catholic Charities, it may be good to look more closely at those numbers. Approximately half of those services are in "prepared food services" meaning congregate dining facilities (1,667,236), soup kitchens (1,268,750), and home delivered meals (278,015). The other half is in what are called "food distribution services," which includes food banks and pantries (2,768,252) and other food services (550,827) which would include food co-ops and food vouchers. Despite the fact that over six million food services were provided, agencies reported that, in distributed food, "they were unable to provide services to 114,214 clients" and, in prepared meals, they had to turn away "11,289 clients requesting prepared food."[12] The CARA report also indicates, that, "Between 2003 and 2007 the total number of clients increased in each type of food service,"[13] with the greatest increase—*54 percent*—being in those persons served in soup kitchens. One can only imagine what the economic meltdown of 2008 will do in terms of people needing food in this country!

While the meaning of food services might be clear to most Americans, the need for the vast array of *services that build strong communities* reflect the many community problems that are often invisible to the ordinary person unaffected by them. Forty-nine percent of these services (1,704,258) addressed the need for social support by frail and vulnerable people. Key among these are the elderly and children. For seniors, ninety-seven re-

11. Ibid., 19.
12. Ibid., 21.
13. Ibid.

porting agencies provided such services as: counseling, case management, transportation, services for the homebound, caregiver support, respite care, chore services, employment services, homemaker services, Senior Companion Programs, home repairs, Retired Senior Volunteer Programs, Foster Grandparent Programs, adult day care, legal services, guardianships for seniors, assisted living, bereavement support, and senior centers.[14] For children, 109 agencies indicated this array of programs and services for toddlers, pre-schoolers (ages 2 to 5), and school-age children: support services for non-parent relatives raising children, childcare in centers and family settings, before-and-after-school care, enrolling children in health insurance coverage, respite care, transportation, and evening and week-end care.[15] Additional services to children and the elderly will be reported below in the part on services to families.

Besides care for children and the elderly, these community services include education and enrichment (612,092 people served), socialization and neighborhood services (555,730 served), services to at-risk folks (344,440), health-related services (265,696),[16] and employment services (50,080).[17] What might these categories mean? Education and enrich-ment programs include Head Start programs, financial literacy training, marriage promotion and strengthening, GED services, and responsible fatherhood programs.[18] Under socialization and neighborhood services agencies report operating neighborhood and community centers, camps, gyms, youth programs, family support groups, seafarer centers, summer programs, and mothers' support groups in 603 sites.[19] Persons at risk of abuse or neglect (children, spouses, elders, and others) are served by 157 agencies reporting programs in case management, prevention services, intensive home-based family support, family preservation services, men-toring, family mediation, supervised home visits, adoptions, counseling, emergency shelter, financial assistance, legal assistance, life skills training, respite care, visitation programs, and transitional housing.[20]

14. Ibid., 24.
15. Ibid., 25.
16. Ibid., 19.
17. Ibid., 26.
18. Ibid., 27.
19. Ibid., 28.
20. Ibid., 30–31.

Health-related services include prescription drug provision, medical and dental clinics, support groups, parish nursing programs, hospice, addiction treatment, HIV/AIDS services, home health, and intermediate care and skilled nursing facilities.[21] Employment services are job search and interview skills training, resume development, employment training, mentoring, and job bank services.[22] Just this listing, without data as to specific numbers or a variety of other programs under the above headings, reflects the breadth of Charities services at the community level and the disparate needs of communities across the country. No single agency provides all of these services, but larger and more diverse agencies will provide many of them.

Under the heading of *other basic needs services* CARA reports on assistance with clothing (576,000 persons), utilities (296,981), finances (157,871), prescriptions (49,930), and other basic needs (487,664).[23] The total of persons served is 1,568,964, fully eleven percent of the services of Catholic Charities in 2007. At the neighborhood, local office, and agency level, these needs—together with food—are often considered to be the focus of "emergency assistance" workers. When destitute families come to many offices or programs, they need "all of the above." Often near the end of the month, after the payment of the rent or mortgage and the exhaustion of the last paycheck or welfare check, families are basically without income for *anything*—food, clothing, utilities, medicine, diapers, bus fare, etc. Emergency assistance workers usually have small funds for assistance, food or transportation vouchers, and a telephone rolodex of numbers of other churches and social agencies who can be called to cobble together $25, $50, $100, or $400 for a utility bill, a rent deposit, a uniform for work, or shoes for school, just enough to help this or that individual or family to make it to another day. Watching these staff or volunteers work is a lesson in inspiration and frustration at the same time. It should be a requirement for all elected officials, news commentators, editorial writers, and clergy, if not all of the baptized.

Catholic social teaching views the family as the most basic and important of social units in society. If families in great numbers are unhealthy, then an entire society is unhealthy. Recognizing this reality,

21. Ibid., 31–32.
22. Ibid., 26.
23. Ibid., 33–34.

Catholic Charities focus a number of programs and services on the family, in addition to many of those already described as community-focused. In 2007, staff and volunteers provided *services that strengthen families* to 1,156, 240 persons. These services fell in the following categories:

TABLE 2: Services to families by Catholic Charities agencies, 2007

Service Types	Persons	Percent
Counseling and mental health services	442,286	38%
Immigration services	375,982	33%
Addiction services	122,289	11%
Pregnancy services	85,742	7%
Refugee services	82,576	7%
Adoption services	47,364	4%
Total services to strengthen families[24]	1,156,240	100%

In CARA's report each of these services is broken down into subparts and, in many cases, compared to the previous year's statistics. For our purposes, it is important to note that many of these programs require the intensive services of professionals such as psychologists, social workers, attorneys, addiction specialists, translators, and a wide variety of counselors with differing specialties (adoption, addiction, childbirth, housing, finance, employment, group therapy, skills training, case management, aging, violence prevention, child development, family systems, and emergency assistance). No one agency offers all of these services, but the focus on families is central to the mission of Catholic Charities agencies in communities across the nation.

In the larger category of *housing related services*, Charities agencies in 2007 served 532,869 clients, up twelve percent from the 474,999 clients reported in 2006. The mortgage and lending crisis of 2008 likely will drive those numbers even higher. Services reported under the heading of housing include: temporary shelter for 197,871 clients (37%), housing services for 193,834 persons (36%), supervised living services for 79,784 persons (15%), permanent housing for 43,334 (8%), and transitional housing for 18,046 (3%). The people served by this array of programs included intact

24. Ibid., 34. Details are set out at 35–39.

families, elderly and disabled persons, parents and children fleeing abuse, homeless individuals and families, persons with mental health and addiction problems, persons with developmental disabilities, ex-offenders, runaway youth, and young adults transitioning from foster care to more independent living.[25]

Disaster services, like disasters themselves, are often seasonal and localized. In 2007, Catholic Charities agencies reported serving 420,422 clients. This was a decrease from the 567,334 persons served in 2006, but twice as many as the 206,747 people served in 2005. Thousands of persons continued to need assistance to recover from the late 2005 hurricanes along the Gulf Coast, but other storms and disasters followed each year. Of those served, 53,125 were children or adolescents, 51,621 adults, and 9,149 were senior citizens (306,527 persons were not age-specified in reports). The nature of the services often depended on the kind of disaster involved, its duration, the services provided by other local and regional and national agencies, and the resources of the Church and local community. As a representative of the Salvation Army said at a meeting that we both attended in the early 1990s, "No disaster is like any other disaster." I took him to mean that the responses must be flexible and targeted for the people, places, and kinds of damage inflicted.

The CARA report also specifies that 225,279 other people in *special populations* received services from Catholic Charities in 2007. Among these groups were victims of crimes, women who have had abortions, prisoners and ex-offenders, families of prisoners, persons with disabilities, migrant workers, victims of international and domestic trafficking, veterans, gang members, undocumented persons, and military personnel. The details of the services are not specified, but we can conclude that they would span the gamut from counseling to emergency assistance to protection to work with families to legal advice to food and shelter.

WHO DOES THE WORK OF CATHOLIC CHARITIES?

As already indicated, the CARA survey for 2007 indicates that agencies report the involvement of 301,574 people in their programs and services. 64,875 people were paid staff; 6,342 were board members; and 230,357 were volunteers. The overall number was down three percent from 2006,

25. Ibid., 40–44.

largely due to a decrease of five percent in volunteers.[26] This last number can fluctuate easily depending on the number and kinds of programs using volunteers, the economy, disaster work, and other factors. The role of volunteers will be discussed further in chapter 6, below.

In terms of paid staff, seventy percent work full-time and thirty percent hold part-time positions on staff, a proportion that was the same in 2006. Fifty percent of all staff work at the program level, while four in ten work as administrative support staff, clerical workers, and other support staff. Those working at the program level include professionals, paraprofessionals, consultants, contractors, and program supervisors. Only seven percent of staff work at the executive or director level. The gender breakdown of staff is 65% female and 35% male, although the executive level is half female and half male. Staff are 53% white; 30% black or African American; 14% Hispanic or Latino; 3.4% Asian, Native Hawaiian, or Pacific Islanders; and 0.4% Native American or Alaskan Native.[27] As discussed above, their areas of specialization and expertise would be as varied as the wide range of services delivered by Catholic Charities and the different kinds of persons served (children, elders, migrants, families, the homeless, persons with addictions, etc.).

Board members tend to be male (59%) and predominantly white (85%), while females (41%) and persons of color (7% black, 6% Hispanic, 2% Asian, and 1% Native American) are underrepresented in terms of the people served by Catholic Charities or the composition of the Catholic and general population of this country. Their roles also may vary depending on the kind of board on which they are members, whether corporate members, advisory board members, or members of specialty corporations such as those focused on housing or immigration services.

WHO PAYS FOR THE WORK OF CATHOLIC CHARITIES

The total income reported in the CARA survey for 2007 was $3,855,340,823. This $3.8 billion dollars included cash revenue for Catholic Charities reflecting the diversity of the programs offered and the communities within which the agencies work: approximately 40% of total income from state and local governments; 12% from community support, including corporate, individual, and foundation funding; 11% from the federal govern-

26. Ibid., 103.
27. Ibid., 104–6.

ment; 11% from program fees charged to those who can afford to pay for services, often on a sliding scale; 5% from investments, business, and other income such as bequests, capital campaigns, gains on sale of property, membership dues, rental income, sales of assets, and thrift shop revenues; 3% from Diocesan and Church support; 2% from United Way and the Combined Federal Campaign (CFC); and 13% from unspecified other government revenue. Add to this the $115 million dollars (3%) of in-kind contributions including in-kind salaries, contributed supplies, equipment, and space, and other goods and services for total income in 2007.[28]

Catholic Charities 2007 Income

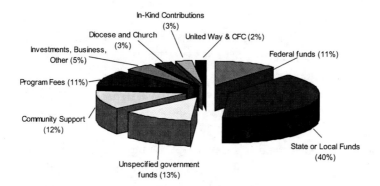

Of the funds received by Catholic Charities agencies from the federal, state, or local governments, CARA asked the agencies to report these funds in six important areas of governmental and human service activity: health and human services (87%); agriculture (6%); housing and urban development (5%); labor (1%); Federal Emergency Management Agency (FEMA) (0.6%); and justice (0.4%). Since the amount for health and human services ($1,527,726,446) is by far the bulk of any government funding, it might be good to look more closely at this funding. Of the total, thirty percent (over $440 million) went to programs to help children and families. These included foster care and residential care for children, independent living programs, child welfare programs, runaway youth services, head start, child day care, family support and reunification, social and community services, developmental disabilities programs, and services for those receiving Temporary Assistance for Needy Families (TANF).

28. Ibid., 8–9.

This focus on the family would reflect the priority given in Catholic Social Teaching to the family as the primary unit of society.

In addition to these programs, Catholic Charities received: (1) over $536 million dollars under Medicaid, Medicare, and programs for older Americans and for the resettlement of refugees; (2) more than $146 million dollars for public health programs, including those involving mental health services, alcoholism and substance abuse, HIV/AIDS, maternal, infant, and child health, adolescent family life, and abstinence; and (3) over $12 million dollars in Katrina Relief funds.[29] In most of these programs, individual agencies would engage in contracts with the respective branch of the government to provide services to a specific population or populations in a certain geographical area. Catholic Charities and a number of other voluntary organizations engage in these "purchase of service" contracts as a way to bring the resources of the local organizations—skills, commitment, organizational capacity, community base and credibility, volunteers, matching funds, and supervision—to the service of the wider community in ways requested and funded by elected officials to meet community, family, and individual needs. Often there are competitive preliminaries in government contracting processes and the large and varied scope of services provided by Catholic Charities in partnership with various governments reflects the credibility and proven services of so many local agencies and their leadership in the fields of human and social services, counseling, housing, and disaster relief. Just as the government turns to businesses to build airplanes and ships for the military and to universities and medical schools for health research, so it turns to the voluntary sector to meet human needs. This tradition, as Pope Benedict noted, began with the government in Egypt in the sixth century turning to the early Church to distribute grain to the public.

Expenses for the year 2007 for Catholic Charities agencies and affiliates totaled $3,690,683,436, of which approximately sixty percent ($2,238,219,696) was expended for salaries, wages, benefits, and payroll taxes. This seems normal for non-profit social service organizations where the greatest investment is in the people who make the services happen. Seven percent of expenditures went to direct cash assistance provided to or for clients ($268,698,524), often in the form of vouchers for food or bus tokens, payments to landlords or utility companies, direct payments

29. Ibid., 14–17.

to health care providers or for medicine, or other third-party payments. In my experience, it is rare for Catholic Charities agencies to actually disburse money directly to clients. Almost ninety percent of total expenditures were on the programs that provide services to the clients of Catholic Charities. As CARA notes, "Less than 10 percent of expenditures were on management and general expenses, and about 2 percent of total expenses went to fundraising."[30]

CONCLUSION

The vast scope of services by Catholic Charities agencies and their affiliates is itself amazing and, sadly, it reflects the tremendous needs of America's poor and vulnerable families. What is equally impressive is the incredible variety of programs and services within each local diocese, a variety that would be hard to achieve by a single national organization of even the same size. The local base of the Catholic Charities organization allows it to focus on local communities, to identify and try to respond to their needs, and to tap the human and financial resources available from local Church and civil society. They are doing, as the Ursuline Sisters did at the outset, "whatever needed to be done." By being part of a larger national network such as Catholic Charities USA and various professional associations, staff and volunteers are then able to apply the ideas tested in other communities, utilize research available in respective fields, and access state and national public and private resources as well. Their service to people in need and their reputation for mission-driven commitment to those people lays the foundation for their great credibility in the larger society.

The Catholic Charities agencies thus benefit from both the large size and scope of their network and the particular grounding of each agency in a local Church and community. In 2008, this combination resulted in two distinct recognitions:

> Catholic Charities USA—with its network of diocesan agencies—was named the country's top provider of social services in Charity Navigator's "Holiday Giving Guide 2008," and finished second overall in *The NonProfit Times* Top 100 list of the country's largest charities.

---

30. Ibid., 12–13.

Charity Navigator, America's most utilized evaluator of charities, uses an objective, numbers-based rating system to assess the financial health of more than 5,000 of America's best-known charities. The goal of "Holiday Giving Guide 2008" is to help people navigate the crowded charitable marketplace and make intelligent giving decisions.

The NonProfit Times is the leading business publication for non-profit management and compiles an annual list of the top 100 non-profits ranked by total revenue.[31]

These recognitions were not earned by a single organization or leadership team, but rather they reflect the efforts of hundreds or organizations, tens of thousands of staff and leaders, and hundreds of thousands of volunteers to serve millions of "the least among us."

The array of services provided by Catholic Charities also accomplish a number of other purposes that will be discussed in later chapters. They provide many opportunities for engaging the imagination and commitment of volunteers—230,357 of them! They connect staff and volunteers to the lives and communities of Americans in need, which in turn educates agencies on the nature of those needs, how to respond more effectively, and, spiritually, how to find Christ among the poor and needy. They also provide the information and credibility that makes Catholic Charities a powerful advocate for a more just and compassionate society.

---

31. "Catholic Charities Named Top Provider of Social Services by Charity Navigator and Ranked Second Overall in *The NonProfit Times* Top 100," *Charities USA* 35.4 (2008) 40.

4

Advocacy

Changing Society with and for the Poor

*I*N THE MID-EIGHTIES, *I attended the February social action gathering in Washington for the first time. This was then sponsored annually by the Department of Social Development and World Peace at the U.S. bishops' conference as a means to educate diocesan justice and peace advocates, Catholic Charities leaders, and others on the public policy issues facing the nation.*[1] *There were then two offices within the department, one on domestic policy and the other on international policy. The director of the domestic policy office was Sharon M. Daly, perhaps the most effective advocate for people who are poor whom I had ever met. At the end of my stint with Catholic Community Services in Baton Rouge, Sharon offered me a position at the "health and welfare desk" of the domestic policy office where I began in early 1990. A year or two later she moved over to the Children's Defense Fund to work with Marian Wright Edelman, another awesome advocate for poor children. Shortly after I moved over to Catholic Charities USA in 2002, I asked Sharon if she would be interested in being our Vice-President for Social Policy, one of the most important things that I did while I was there. She was a great gift to Catholic Charities across the nation and those whom they served.*

A few years ago, after having served for twelve years as the social policy leader for Catholic Charities USA, Sharon was asked why Catholic Charities does advocacy:

---

1. It is now co-sponsored by Catholic Charities USA, Catholic Relief Services, the Catholic Campaign for Human Development, and a number of other national Catholic organizations.

This has always been our tradition, from the very beginning of Catholic Charities agencies in this country. In 1910, when the National Conference of Catholic Charities was founded, the Charities directors came together to make recommendations to government. Agency directors have always been advocates for the poor, and not just for funding for the kinds of services that Catholic Charities provide, but for programs in which government helps poor people directly, like Social Security or food stamps.

We have a long tradition of seeking justice for the poor, and it is based in our theology going back to the Hebrew Scriptures. The prophets called on the kings of Israel to make justice for the poor, for the immigrants, for the widows and children their priority. The prophets said that the test of the faith of Israel was the quality of justice to the poor.

Of course, the practical reason why we advocate comes from our experience working with individuals, families, and communities. It's always been clear to Charities agencies that the direct services they provide are only part of the necessary equation for reducing poverty and deprivation . . .

If you talk to people who have made it their life's work to serve the poor directly, they will all say that what is needed is far beyond the capacity of religious groups or social services organizations and that some things need to be done systemically. Catholic Charities agencies are rightly known for a high standard of hands-on direct service that is motivated by the Scriptural call in Matthew 25 to see Jesus in the poor. I am proud that Catholic Charities agencies are also known for demanding that government pay attention to the need for more affordable housing, health care for the uninsured, higher wages, and more subsidized daycare. Those are things for which we have to turn to government."[2]

Daly's remarks focus on advocacy with government, which may take the form of legislative or administrative advocacy—supporting or opposing proposed laws or urging administrative or regulatory steps or providing consultation to government commissions or officials. Advocacy may also take a number of other forms including legal action on behalf of an individual, a group of persons, or an agency; community organizing, usually

2. "Why We Advocate: A Conversation with Sharon Daly," *Charities USA* 32.2 (2005) 3–4.

focused on state or local issues; institutional advocacy, for example, with lending institutions; economic development; or public education about matters of justice and peace.

A CHURCH THAT ADVOCATES

To understand the commitment to advocacy of Catholic Charities USA and its parameters, we need to situate the discussion in the context of a Church that believes that advocacy is a part of the responsibility of every Christian and of the Church itself. Every four years since 1976, in the context of presidential and congressional elections, the U.S. bishops have issued a statement on the responsibility of Catholics to the larger society, specifically their political responsibilities. In 2007, this document was entitled *Forming Consciences for Faithful Citizenship: A Call to Political Responsibility from the Catholic Bishops of the United States*. In the statement, the bishops discuss their right to speak out in this pluralistic society and the appropriateness of what they have to say:

> Some question whether it is appropriate for the Church to play a role in political life. However, the obligation to teach about moral values that should shape our lives, including our public lives, is central to the mission given to the Church by Jesus Christ. Moreover, the United States Constitution protects the right of individual believers and religious bodies to participate and speak out without government interference, favoritism, or discrimination. Civil law should fully recognize and protect the Church's right, obligation, and opportunities to participate in society without being forced to abandon or ignore its central moral convictions. Our nation's tradition of pluralism is enhanced, not threatened, when religious groups and people of faith bring their convictions and concerns into public life. Indeed, our Church's teaching is in accord with the foundational values that have shaped our nation's history: "life, liberty, and the pursuit of happiness."[3]

In the public debate, the bishops continue, the Catholic community brings two major contributions:

> The Catholic community brings important assets to the political dialogue about our nation's future. We bring a consistent moral

3. United States Conference of Catholic Bishops, *Forming Consciences for Faithful Citizenship: A Call to Political Responsibility from the Catholic Bishops of the United States*, November, 2007, 11.

framework—drawn from basic human reason that is illuminated by Scripture and the teaching of the Church for assessing issues, political platforms, and campaigns. We also bring broad experience in serving those in need—educating the young, caring for the sick, sheltering the homeless, helping women who face difficult pregnancies, feeding the hungry, welcoming immigrants and refugees, reaching out in global solidarity, and pursuing peace.[4]

When the bishops speak of the second contribution—"broad experience"— they are explicitly referencing the work of Catholic education, health care, and charities.

In addition to the bishops' two primary contributions of the Church to our nation's policy debates—our consistent moral framework and our broad experience is serving those in need—I would add two other contributions: (1) a passion for justice and God's own poor; and (2) a realistic assessment of the realities of power and evil. In some ways these two additions of mine may seem contradictory, but I would argue rather that they stand in healthy tension with one another. Our faith-filled passion keeps us committed to the task of working for justice and the poor, when others have given up on political or social advocacy, chosen the ever popular course of voting with the pollsters, or been silent in the face of popular or political opinion. In addition, our realism in the face of power and evil make us ever watchful about what is possible, probable, and/or foolish or prophetic. We recognize the limits of what can be accomplished on particular issues at particular times; and we steward our energies, time, and money to fight the battles where we can be most effective. Yet, all the while we recognize that certain issues may call for the prophetic action that is foolish in the world's eyes but which plants the seed for future harvests.

At this point it is important to make two distinctions that are key to Church statements about legislative and issue advocacy, and helpful in understanding community organizing efforts by the Church and its members, including Catholic Charities. The first distinction, made more than twenty years ago by the U.S. bishops in their comprehensive pastoral letter on economic justice, is in the approach to the audiences whom they address:

> We write, then, first of all to provide guidance for members our own Church as they seek to form their consciences about economic

4. Ibid., 12.

matters. No one may claim the name Christian and be comfortable in the face of the hunger, homelessness, insecurity, and injustice found in this country and the world. At the same time we want to add our voice to the public debate about the directions in which the U.S. economy should be moving. We seek the cooperation and support of those who do not share our faith or tradition. The common bond of humanity that links all persons is the source of our belief that the country can attain a renewed public moral vision.[5]

This distinction affects the policy advocacy conducted by Catholic Charities as it too seeks to persuade both fellow Catholics and others in this pluralistic society. It also colors the use of moral reasoning, logic, data, agency experience, and even the Scriptures.

The second distinction is between principle and policy application. For example, there is a principle in Catholic social teaching about the right of workers to receive a decent family wage. That principle is distinct from the question of whether to support a particular minimum wage bill at the federal, state, or local level, which would be a policy application. The bishops indicate that there are an important set of bridges, however, from principle to policy applications:

> In focusing on some of the central economic issues and choices in American life in the light of moral principles, we are aware that the movement from principle to policy is complex and difficult and that although moral values are essential in determining public policies, they do not dictate specific solutions. They must interact with empirical data, with historical, social, and political realities, and with competing demands on limited resources. The soundness of our prudential judgments depends not only on the moral force of our principles, but also on the accuracy of our information and the validity of our assumptions.[6]

Then, they conclude that because of the bridges from principle to policy applications, their "moral authority" is different:

> Our judgments and recommendations on specific economic issues, therefore, do not carry the same moral authority as our statements of universal moral principles and formal church teaching; the former are related to circumstances that can change or that

---

5. U.S. Catholic Bishops, *Economic Justice for All: Catholic Social Teaching and the U.S. Economy*, November 13, 1986 in *Origins* 16, p. 24 (November 27, 1986), 409–55 n. 27.

6. Ibid., 134.

can be interpreted differently by people of good will. We expect and welcome debate on our specific policy recommendations. Nevertheless, we want our statements on these matters to be given serious consideration by Catholics as they determine whether their own moral judgments are consistent with the Gospel and with Catholic social reaching.[7]

With Catholics, the bishops made an appeal to conscience, with a distinction between principle and policy application, but an urge to consider carefully the policy applications. With other-than-Catholics, the bishops often appeal to reason and human dignity and a hope that the bridges to policy application are convincing in themselves. In this light, under the umbrella of their national conference, the U.S. bishops employ a number of persons as policy analysts and others as government relations specialists at their headquarters in Northwest Washington, D.C. Their task is to look at the issues pending before Congress, their moral implications, and to advise the bishops on appropriate responses to such matters, including letters to government officials, testimony on pending legislation or regulations, and public statements. (The bishops' conference does not take a position on either candidates for public office or those considered for government appointment to the Executive or Judicial branches.)

THE ADVOCACY OF CATHOLIC CHARITIES

When it speaks publicly, Catholic Charities, of course, do not have the formal moral teaching authority of the bishops within the Catholic community; but they draw upon the various documents of the Popes, the Vatican, and the bishops for their moral principles. They then bring their own experience to questions of how to apply those principles to policy applications in the public debate at the federal, state, or local levels and especially how they will affect those whom Catholic Charities serve. This is often done in concert with the national or state conferences of Catholic bishops. (Charities too do not endorse or oppose particular candidates for elective or appointed office.)

Of approximately 140 separate agencies responding to the CARA study, only forty report having paid staff responsible for legislative advocacy.[8] Some staff may work on advocacy issues after-hours or on an often

7. Ibid., 135.
8. *2007 Survey*, 107.

very-part-time basis, and sometimes advocacy is done by volunteer board members on behalf of the agencies. In addition, many agencies belong to community coalitions on specific issues such as health care or housing, where the coalition may include advocacy in its agenda. Parish social ministry, discussed in chapter five, also may involve staff and volunteers assisting parishioners in doing advocacy on issues of justice and peace. Catholic Charities USA has only a handful of paid social policy staff working at the national level, although at times they have been assisted in their Washington advocacy by law students from Georgetown University or from Catholic University of America. With tens of thousands of staff and hundreds of thousands of volunteers, the number doing advocacy seems relatively small, but their impact can be very important for those Catholic Charities serve. The small number of paid staff doing legislative advocacy also keeps Catholic Charities well within the lobbying limits imposed on tax-exempt, non-profit organizations in the United States. Those limits also do not apply generally to issue education—for example, education of the public on the rights of migrants or the impact of hunger on the poor—that is not targeted to specific pending legislation.

If we look back twenty years to the Catholic Charities USA survey for 1987 activities, that survey reports that the top five legislative issues of members were: family issues; refugee and immigration issues; the economy; housing and homelessness; and hunger and nutrition issues. Over half of the diocesan agencies reported that they had participated on governmental commissions on the local (60%) or state (50%) levels, and two-thirds had offered consultation to public officials at these levels. In regulatory matters, 42% of agencies reported they had participated in the development or revision of regulations at the local level, 57% at the state level, and only 15% at the federal level. Approximately 80% of agencies indicated that their efforts to influence public policy were done in collaboration with other social service agencies.[9]

Ten years later in the 1997 survey, 89% of the respondents reported involvement in some kind of legislative action. The top five issues overall were: income security and welfare reform; international justice and refugees; economy, employment, and minimum wage; hunger and nutrition; and abortion. Again, the level of social action was much higher at the state

9. Rosemary Winder Strange, ACSW, Joseph J. Shields, PhD, Mary Jeanne Verdieck, PhD, *Annual Survey 1987 Catholic Charities USA* (Washington, DC: Catholic Charities USA, 1998), 25–28.

level than either the national or local levels. Common among the "top five" were three issues worked on at all three levels: income security and welfare reform; economy, employment, and minimum wage; and hunger and nutrition. Unique among the "top five" issues at different levels were international justice, refugees, and abortion at the national level; adoption and health care at the state level; and housing at the local level.

The CARA-administered Catholic Charities USA survey no longer tallies the issues of social policy worked on by member agencies in the year preceding. A review of the quarterly issues of *Charities USA* magazine for 2008, however, indicates the following key issues as those about which members—individuals and agencies—contacted Congress in conjunction with the work of the national organization: housing, poverty, the Farm Bill, Medicaid, immigration, the economic stimulus bill, and the federal budget.[10] On January 10, 2008, the national organization launched an ambitious Campaign to Reduce Poverty in America, aiming to cut the domestic poverty rate in half by the year 2020. The dire economic news of 2008 will make that education and advocacy campaign all the harder and all the more necessary.

As with the wide array of services discussed above in Chapter Three, the advocacy work of the many agencies within the Catholic Charities network really defies a simple description of the issues involved or the methods used by members. A sampling drawn from a 2005 special issue of *Charities USA* devoted to advocacy gives some flavor of these efforts:

- In New Mexico, the New Mexico Human Needs Coordinating Council, chaired by Gregory Kepferle, executive director of Catholic Charities of the Archdiocese of Santa Fe, involved Catholic Charities staff, volunteers, and residents of their transitional housing program, some of whom formerly had been homeless. Together with 152 other organizations and inspired by the testimony of residents, they helped persuade the legislature and Governor Bill Richardson to create a state affordable housing fund and allocate the first $10 million to the fund.[11]

---

10. "CCUSA Quarterly Update," *Charities USA* 35.1 (2008) 4; "CCUSA Quarterly Update," *Charities USA* 35.2 (2008) 4; "CCUSA Quarterly Update," *Charities USA* 35.3 (2008) 4; and "CCUSA Quarterly Update," *Charities USA* 35.4 (2008) 4.

11. Gregory R. Kepferle, "Grass Roots Advocacy in New Mexico Results in $10 Million Housing Trust Fund," *Charities USA* 32.2 (2005) 10.

- Catholic Charities Trenton included a public awareness campaign as part of its advocacy efforts. On issues like housing and minimum wage, it developed letters to the editor, op-eds, and editorial board meetings at key newspapers throughout New Jersey. The result was that op-eds authored by Francis Dolan, agency director, appeared in every major daily newspaper in New Jersey.[12]

- Undocumented clients of Santa Rosa Catholic Charities had paid thousands of dollars to a Sonoma County "notario" who falsely promised to file their applications for legalization of their immigration status. Staff members working after-hours compiled evidence and interviews, transported clients, tracked proceedings, and, with the help of a board member and the media, got the District Attorney to file charges of theft.[13]

- In Chicago, a growing number of board members met with legislators to educate them about agency services in their districts and agency priorities. In the spring of 2005, one priority was the Rental Housing Support Program to create rental assistance for 5,500 families in Illinois, which passed both House and Senate.[14]

- Advocacy efforts of Catholic Charities of the Archdiocese of Galveston-Houston involved creating a series of relationships with legislators, their aides, and other advocates. During the state legislative session, the Charities agency publishes a weekly on-line newsletter, *Peritus,* for advocates with health and human services news for advocates, advocacy developments, and Catholic social teaching.[15]

As you can see from these five examples, advocacy may involve public education through the media, individual meetings by board members with elected officials, testimony by clients before public bodies, promoting law enforcement, and participation in coalitions. Earlier examples from the

12. Lisa Thibault, "Catholic Charities of Trenton Scores Legislative Victories Through Multi-faceted Efforts," ibid., 10–11.

13. Betsy Timm, "Santa Rosa Advocates for Illegal Immigrants," in ibid., 12–13.

14. Laurie Barretto, "Catholic Charities in Chicago Utilizes Board Members in Advocacy," ibid., 11–12.

15. Jennifer Carr, "Galveston-Houston Defends Health and Human Services through Collaboration," in ibid., 13.

surveys included participation in public commissions, consultation with state and local officials, and comments on proposed local, state, or federal regulations. To all of these Catholic Charities brings its broad experience from serving seven million people a year, its professional expertise, its focus on the empowerment of those it serves, the Catholic moral framework, and its passion for justice and compassion in society.

Catholic Charities agencies and their staff and volunteers must be careful, however, to keep a close connection between what they do for people in need on the services side and what they set out to accomplish on the advocacy front. These are some questions they should ask and answer as they develop their advocacy agenda in any year:

1. What advocacy issues are rooted in the experience of our agencies and the people whom we serve?

2. What issues have been addressed in our Catholic social justice tradition, which provides principles upon which to build specific policy applications?

3. On what issues can we make a significant difference? Examples might be where the issue is a close call; or where the moral voice of Catholic Charities can be persuasive; or where Catholic Charities have a pertinent viewpoint on the issue from their experience and telling points to make; or where there is not already a well developed constituency of advocates.

4. What issues especially impact the poor and vulnerable people whom Charities serve?

5. On what issues can Catholic Charities develop effective coalitions—with other Catholic organizations, with other faith communities, and with others in the general community?

6. What can really be achieved on an issue? And, in tension with this, where do Catholic Charities need to be outspoken and prophetic even if the issue is judged to be "a loser"—at least in the short term?

7. What issues will affect the mission and work of the agencies, for example, legislation that would require staff or volunteers to report undocumented persons to the civil authorities?

It is important in their planning that organizations keep a manageable list of issues about which they commit their staff and volunteers to work. The above questions can help in this winnowing process so that energies are focused and agencies are not seen as "social gadflies" who issue statement after statement often disconnected from the service work upon which the credibility of Catholic Charities is founded. Agencies must be concerned not to be used by the political left or the right, by Republicans or Democrats for their partisan purposes. Their focus must remain centered on the needs of the poor and vulnerable whom they serve and the means to be *effective* advocates on their behalf in the light of the Scriptures and Catholic social teaching.

COMMUNITY ORGANIZING AND ECONOMIC DEVELOPMENT

Since the campaign of Barack H. Obama for the presidency, community organizing has become a more familiar term in the American political lexicon. After college, President Obama had worked initially as a community organizer in his native Chicago; and he seems to have taken the core organizing strategy of involvement of the grassroots into his campaign. Interestingly, Chicago boasts being the home of the "father" of community organizing—Saul Alinsky. Alinsky (1909–1972) is described by one source as follows: "He is generally considered to be the founder of modern community organizing in America, the political practice of organizing communities to act in common self-interest."[16] In the 1930s, he began his organizing in Chicago's "Back of the Yards" stockyards neighborhood, aligned with unions and the Catholic Church. In the 1940s, he founded the Industrial Areas Foundation (IAF) for the training of community and union organizers and wrote his first book *Reveille for Radicals* in 1946. He later promoted stockholder activism for corporate change. IAF has continued the training of organizers to this date. Interestingly, Alinsky was the subject of the senior college thesis of Wellesley graduate Hillary Rodham (Clinton), former first lady and senator, now Secretary of State.

In the 1960s and 1970s, a small but influential body of Catholic activists became involved in grassroots organizing of low-income communities, usually in urban centers. Some received their training at IAF. Their experience of empowerment among poor and middle-class neigh-

16. "Saul Alinsky," in *Wikipedia*.

borhoods and Vatican II's emphasis on the concerns of the poor helped to prime the founding by the U.S. Catholic bishops of the Catholic Campaign for Human Development in 1970.[17] The Campaign's website describes itself as follows:

> We invest in the dignity of people living below the poverty line. Our programs support self-sufficiency and self-determination for people who are working to bring permanent change to their communities.
>
> Our philosophy emphasizes empowerment and participation for those in poverty. By helping the poor to participate in the decisions and actions that affect their lives and communities, CCHD empowers them to move beyond poverty.[18]

The campaign tries to create new structures of empowerment for the poor or to challenge unjust structures. Often the organizing approaches of grantees involve coalitions of local church congregations, both Catholic parishes and churches of other dominations. By 2007, CCHD had allocated $280 million in self-help grants and loans to more than 4,000 local and national organizations for community organizing and economic development. In the single year 2006-2007, CCHD awarded almost $9 million to 236 projects in forty-seven states, the District of Columbia, and Puerto Rico.[19] Many of these projects are connected with local Catholic Charities agencies, often involving the assignment of Charities staff to work with the members of these organizations.

In the 2007 survey, 101 Catholic Charities agencies reported involvement in community organizing, forty-two of which indicated that they had paid staff doing this work.[20] Agencies reported thirty-one different target issues of community organizing. The top five were: access to health care; neighborhood improvement; tenants rights/housing; crime and public safety; and racism and diversity. The focus of many of these activities are local, since it is local issues that often bring together people in the same neighborhood or community.

---

17. See *Empowerment and Hope: Twenty-Five Years of Turning Lives Around* (Washington, D.C.: Campaign for Human Development, 1996).

18. CCHD website at www.usccb.org/cchd/povertyusa/about.shtml.

19. *Catholic Campaign for Human Development 2006-2007 Annual Report* (Washington, D.C.: Catholic Campaign for Human Development, 2007) 4.

20. *2007 Survey*, 28–29.

In the wake of *Vision 2000* and its emphasis on "empowering services," a special task force of Catholic Charities USA members and specialists in community organizing worked to develop, *A Catholic Charities Framework for Empowerment*. In that 1998 document, referred to in chapter 2, empowerment was defined as follows: "Empowerment is a process of engagement that increases the ability of individuals, families, organizations, and communities to build mutually respectful relationships and bring about fundamental, positive change in the conditions affecting their daily lives."[21] The task force described the process of empowerment as beginning with the individual and collective experiences of the people involved, building then on their strengths and hopes, and culminating in the transformation of life situations and/or social structures. Empowerment was about the root causes of problems, restoration of human dignity, and integral human development. Three principles were central to the task force concept of empowerment:

- People are the primary agents of change.

- Empowerment changes happen through participative relationships.

- The human person is both social and spiritual; what affects one aspect of the person, affects the other.[22]

From these three principles, the task force developed the above definition of empowerment in the context of the work of Catholic Charities. This emphasis on empowerment meant that Catholic Charities were obligated to move beyond the individual self-improvement of good social casework to emphasize deep, permanent, fundamental change within individuals, families, communities, and organizations, including the Charities agencies themselves.

This emphasis on empowerment was not necessarily new in the history of Catholic Charities. As theologian Kenneth Himes noted in a 1998 address to the annual Catholic Charities USA conference:

> Interest in empowerment, however, has long been part of the broader vision of Catholic Charities. William Kerby and John O'Grady in the formative years of Catholic Charities saw the pur-

---

21. *A Catholic Charities Framework for Empowerment*, 2 (see ch. 2 n. 25).
22. Ibid.

pose of such a national organization as providing resources and encouragement for local agencies to keep their vision wider than direct service to human need. The Cadre Study, the code of ethics and Vision 2000, using one or another formulation, have all seen empowering others as an important dimension of serving them.[23]

But these earlier documents contemplated neither the model of community organizing—often congregation-based—nor the extent of its use by Catholic groups and Catholic Charities in the past thirty or more years, nor its effectiveness in bringing people together in the awareness of their own power[24] and helping them to affect public policy and public services from city hall to the statehouse to Congress.

The approach of community organizing also reflects a distinct shift in Catholic social teaching and practice in recent decades that is shared by other people of good will. Instead of the focus on the negatives of the people they serve—their economic and social needs, lack of power over their own lives or in society, or failure to participate in political and civic processes—Catholic Charities and others have looked more deeply to see the resources that the same people have. Social assessments focus not just on "community needs," but on "community assets" as well. Individual client assessments look for personal strengths and capacities as well as weaknesses. This is in keeping with the emphasis in Catholic social teaching and practice to help people to be "artisans of their own destiny" reflected in the emphasis on cooperatives, participation in labor unions, worker ownership, shared decision-making, micro-enterprise loans, and the development of base Christian communities.

In recent decades, economic development programs have become a part of the portfolio of an increasing number of Catholic Charities agencies. Economic development models within Catholic Charities have included a variety of programs designed to introduce new economic resources into client communities or to develop the economic skills and assets of the persons whom they serve. (The 2007 survey reports that twelve

---

23. Kenneth Himes, OFM, "What 'Empowerment' Means: Toward Servant Friendship," *Origins* 28 (1998) 299 [297–300].

24. See Edward J. Ryle, "The Cadre Study: Twenty Years Later," in *Cadre Study*, 4–15, where he observes: "The *Cadre Study's* presentation on social action is not meant to be a complete treatise on the subject. Nevertheless, I believe it is seriously deficient in its failure to deal explicitly with the *importance of power* in humanizing and transforming the social order" (9).

agencies have staff dedicated specifically to economic development works. These would be in addition to hundreds of staff working in the area of housing.) Among these programs, Charities include the following:

1. Micro-enterprise loan programs provide the financial and business counseling and financing so that enterprising people can borrow small loans to begin businesses such as home-cleaning services, catering, and lawn services. The model for these programs is the lending first begun by Nobel Peace Prize winner Muhammed Yunus and his Grameen Bank that made very small loans to the poorest of the poor in Bangladesh, loans which made small businesses possible, transformed lives, and were paid back in astonishing numbers![25] Catholic Charities of Omaha, for example, offers training in business skills, micro-loans, and ongoing technical assistance in Spanish through its Microbusiness Training and Development Project at its Microbusiness and Latina Resource Center in South Omaha.[26]

2. Homeownership programs help buyers acquire the primary asset of many U.S. families. For example, in Chemung County, New York, 352 families have purchased their first home through the First Time Homebuyer Program at Catholic Charities. One report indicated that, in addition to their homes, participants cited other new assets: ". . . self-esteem, self-confidence, leadership skills, expanded horizons and expectations for themselves and their children, budgeting and priority-setting skills, interest in civic life and neighborliness, and peer support."[27]

3. Food cooperatives such as the SHARE Colorado Food Program of Catholic Charities of the Archdiocese of Denver make it possible for low-and-middle-income families to stretch the family food dollar by combining purchasing power of thousands of families with volunteer hours that they also contribute to food storage, packaging, and transportation.

25. Alan M. Webber, "Giving the Poor the Business," in *USA Today* (May 21, 2008) 11A.

26. See website for Catholic Charities of Omaha at www.ccomaha.org.

27. Jane Galvin, "A House, a Home, an Asset," *Charities USA* 35.4 (2008) 8–9.

4. The Gateway to Financial Fitness program was introduced by Catholic Charities of St. Louis and replicated by other agencies such as that in Fort Worth. This program "helps working families learn how to make their hard earned money work for their families by mastering important financial skills . . ."[28] Skills include financial planning, developing habits of saving, controlling credit, using tax savings, wise investing, and choosing good insurance.

5. The creation of housing facilities is a common economic development program of many Catholic Charities agencies. Housing may be apartments or individual homes, for rent or ownership. For example, Providence Housing Development Corporation, affiliated with Catholic Charities of the Diocese of Rochester, NY, "develops, finances, and manages affordable housing for seniors, individuals with special needs, and families."[29]

Through these means and others Catholic Charities actually change the society in which we live by changing the skills and resources available to low-income individuals and families who formerly have been thought to be without the means to improve their lives economically and socially.

CONCLUSION

In the face of the temptation to divide social service and social action, Catholic Charities agencies understand that the Gospel promotes their essential partnership. Service to those in need by thousands of staff and volunteers, as described in the previous chapter, is the immediate response of Gospel compassion to human suffering. These services also contain the seeds of Gospel justice, the advocacy that has been described in this chapter. When staff and volunteers encounter widespread poverty and suffering on a daily basis, they soon find themselves asking why such suffering continues to exist. Their daily service also proclaims to an uncaring society and its leaders that these people—no matter how poor or apparently powerless—are worthy of a humane response consistent with the dignity and sacredness of the human person. Service thus *is* advocacy

---

28. Lauren King, "Getting Smart about Money," in ibid., 10–11.

29. See website for Providence Housing Development Corporation at www.providencehousing.org.

in the sense that it declares loudly and clearly that persons matter and that injustice cannot be allowed to continue without challenge.

Advocacy for Gospel justice by Catholic Charities, as has been described in this chapter, thus is rooted in the compassionate services provided by staff and volunteers. It also is most on target when connected to the persons served by agencies and the injustices that staff and volunteers see daily, structured into the institutions and systems of our society. "Love is the soul of justice,"[30] declared the Latin American bishops; and advocacy for a more just and compassionate society is best energized by passionate concern for the least among us. Thus service and advocacy are wedded together in the work of Catholic Charities.

---

30 · Medellin conference of Latin American Catholic Bishops, 1968, final documents, section 2.14.

5

Convening

Building Communities That Care

WHEN I FIRST HEARD *Bishop Joseph Sullivan speak at a Catholic Charities USA annual conference in the mid-1980s, I knew that he was the real thing. Bishop Sullivan had been a member of the original Cadre, the director of Catholic Charities in the Diocese of Brooklyn and Queens, and is now the liaison between Catholic Charities USA and the bishops of the United States. During years of working with him, I came to know him as an inspiring speaker, a national Charities leader, the effective chair of the committee of bishops that drafted In All Things Charity in 1999, board chair of the Catholic Health Association, chair of the Domestic Policy Committee of the bishops' conference, a good friend, and a determined servant of the poor and advocate on their behalf. In recognition of all of this and much more, Catholic Charities USA awarded him their Vision Award in 2008.*

In a 1994 interview, Bishop Sullivan was asked to reflect on the goal of the Cadre in their focus on parish social ministry. He responded in part as follows:

> *Much of what we were trying to do through the cadre process was to get the rootedness of Charities centered in the life of the Church; not so much, I think, as part of the social welfare establishment. We were seeking to deepen the Church ties, principally at the local level. The Charities leadership felt that was critical to our participation in the whole arena of social services and advocacy. We needed to be not only designated by the Church, but to have representation and participation from the Church, and to be connected to the local Church.*
>
> *Born out of that was the effort to go back to the parishes and not just to the central diocese. That took off in very different ways. It*

was locally generated by the initiative of the executive director or the delegate. It took many different forms, usually dictated by the history of the local diocese and an understanding of the experience o the Church locally. It usually was the result of an awareness that the parish had a prime responsibility to respond to the needs of the people, and Charities was intended to be an enabler, basically a broker for support and backup systems.

The primary responsibility for the ministry of caring for one's brother or sister is rooted in one's Catholic identity from baptism. We were trying to get it clear and conscious in the minds of active lay Catholics, and the pastors and religious for that matter, that this was not something you could give away to some downtown professional agency. It had to be rooted in the life of a Catholic community.[1]

When the *Cadre Study* called for "The convening of the Christian community and other concerned people" in 1972, it was a wake-up call to Catholic Charities agencies and leaders about their connection to the local Church, especially the parish, and to other Church and civic organizations and people of good will in their communities. The purposes were several. With the Church, it was to renew the full sense of the meaning of their baptism among the Catholic faithful and partnership among Catholic organizations. With others in society, it was to enhance the commitment to the common good of all people within this democracy, especially the poor. With the poor and vulnerable, it was to enhance their roles in society and to enlarge the efforts of Church and society in their service. For Charities themselves, it was to strengthen their mission by making common cause with others and to root themselves more deeply in Church and community.

PARISH SOCIAL MINISTRY

The *2007 Survey* of Catholic Charities agencies indicates that the 171 responding agencies report active relationships with 8,235 (44%) of the 18,869 parishes in their dioceses. They also reported that 5,176 parishes are doing some form of what is called parish social ministry (PSM). Of the agencies, 97 report that 445 agency staff (in full-time equivalents) are

1. Interview by Catholic Charities USA Parish Social Ministry Director Polly Duncan Collum with Bishop Joseph M. Sullivan in *Charities USA* 21.3 (1994) 1–2 [1–8].

involved in PSM activities, averaging 4.6 staff doing this work.[2] Of the components of their PSM programs, the five most commonly reported by agencies were (in rank order): building partnerships with parishes; promoting formation on the Catholic social mission; raising awareness of parish social ministry (e.g., educating pastors and parish leadership); coordinating Catholic Campaign for Human Development efforts or promoting community organizing and economic development; and building capacity for parish social ministry (e.g., training or consultation on structuring social ministry in the parish and engaging the parish community).

As we saw in chapter one, in his first encyclical, Pope Benedict XVI had emphasized that organized *caritas* or social ministry was one of the three core responsibilities at the heart of the Church, along with proclaiming the word of God and celebrating the sacraments. While Pope Benedict did not expound on the details of parish social ministry, the U.S. Catholic bishops had done so in 1994 in a pastoral letter entitled *Communities of Salt and Light: Reflections on the Social Mission of the Parish*. In that letter, the bishops highlighted seven elements that might be included within a framework that would keep social ministry integrated within the parish and not, as often is the case, isolated within a single committee or a few active individuals:

1. Prayer and worship—bringing themes of justice and peace into the prayer life of the parish, especially the celebration of the Eucharist.

2. Preaching and education—reflecting the social dimensions of the Gospel in homilies and the curriculum and life of schools, religious education programs, sacramental preparation, and Christian initiation activities.

3. Family, work, and citizenship—helping the parishioners in their everyday choices as parents, workers, students, owners, investors, and advocates to bring a living faith into the world.

4. Outreach and charity—reaching out to the hurting, poor, and vulnerable through programs, partnerships with Catholic Charities, collaborative efforts with other churches, and changing the structures of society that deny people their dignity and rights.

2. *2007 Survey*, 110–11.

5. Legislative action—reviving a sense of political responsibility, informed citizenship, and outspoken advocacy through legislative networks and other advocacy groups.

6. Organizing for justice—participating as a parish in church-based and community organizations to rebuild a sense of community in their own neighborhoods and towns and to empower the poor to seek greater justice.

7. International solidarity—being part of a universal Church through parish twinning, support for Catholic Relief Services, mission efforts, migration and refugee activities, and other actions for global justice and peace.[3]

Four years later in 1998, the bishops expanded on the seventh element in *Called to Global Solidarity* where they "urged parishes to reach beyond their own boundaries to extend the Gospel, to serve those in need, and to work for global justice and peace in all parts of the world."[4] The bishops acknowledged in 1999 that, while much had been done "to enrich and carry out the social mission of our parishes, much more remains to be done."[5]

Catholic Charities agencies with PSM programs were well aware of the need for far more participation in the social mission of the Church at the parish level. This is why the third strategic direction of the 1996 Vision 2000 report had urged members to, "Strengthen our identity with, and relationship to, the broader Church and witness to its social mission."[6] Since 1996, PSM has continued to be a priority of members and their national organization. The *2007 Survey*, in addition to reporting common components of PSM programs, indicated above, also reported the priorities espoused by those programs. Again, the top five (in rank order) were: building relationships with parishes; raising awareness of parish social ministry; coordinating volunteer recruitment between Catholic Charities and parishes; promoting formation on the Catholic social mission; and

---

3. National Conference of Catholic Bishops, *Communities of Salt and Light: Reflections on the Social Mission of the Parish*, 1993.

4. *In All Things Charity*, 23, referencing the U.S. bishops' *Called to Global Solidarity* (1998).

5. Ibid.

6. *Vision 2000 Report*, 9.

coordinating a referrals line for social services specifically for people in need who come to parishes. These are well-known ways to try to flesh out the responsibility of parishes for the social mission and to assist them in making that mission a parish reality.

The national organization has included a PSM Advisory Committee since the eighties,[7] when that committee produced the first PSM Manual, *Parish Social Ministry: A Vision and Resource*[8] and began planning formal PSM training programs for members,[9] including two certificate programs at Loyola University New Orleans and Catholic University of America beginning in the summer of 1987.[10] Since the early 1990s, Catholic Charities USA has provided continued staffing for a national PSM office and a number of materials have been developed during the past twenty years to promote its development both within the Catholic Charities network and by others active in the Church's social ministries.[11] The recent activities of the national Charities organization have included: the legislative manual, *Parish Strategy for Legislative Advocacy*; a PSM membership section to bring members together to share ideas and strategies for promoting this ministry; regional training opportunities and PSM consultations (in the past year, these occurred in Memphis, Phoenix, Oklahoma City, St. Cloud, Indianapolis, and West Virginia[12]); and, new in 2008, the publication of *Catalysts and Collaborators in Social Ministry: Strategies for Parish Partnerships and Parish Social Ministry in Catholic Charities*,[13] a new manual for PSM development and partnerships.

7. Rosemary Winder Strange, "Service, Advocacy, Empowerment" column, *Charities USA* 12.6 (1985) 6.

8. NCCC, *Parish Social Ministry: A Vision and Resource* (Washington, DC: National Conference of Catholic Charities, 1985).

9. Rosemary Winder Strange, "Service, Advocacy, Empowerment" column, *Charities USA* 13.2 (1986) 4.

10. Same column, *Charities USA* 13.10 (1986) 30.

11. See, for example: Mary L. Heidkamp and James R. Lund, *Moving Faith into Action: A Facilitator's Guide for Creating Parish Social Ministry Organizations* (Mahwah, NJ: Paulist, 1990); Tom Ulrich, *Parish Social Ministry: Strategies for Success* (Notre Dame, IN: Ave Maria, 2001); Peggy Prevoznik Heins, *Becoming a Community of Salt and Light: Formation for Parish Social Ministry* (Notre Dame, IN: Ave Maria, 2003); and *Taking Action: A Parish Strategy for Legislative Action* (Alexandria, VA: Catholic Charities USA, 2003 and later revisions).

12. Trainings are indicated in the four 2008 issues of *Charities USA* 35, nos. 1–4.

13. Catalysts and Collaborators in Social Ministry: Strategies for Parish Partnerships and Parish Social Ministry in Catholic Charities (Alexandria, VA: Catholic Charities USA, 2008).

In 2001, Catholic Charities USA teamed up with Jack Jezreel of Louisville, creator of the program *JustFaith*, to promote and develop his program for a national audience—truly the most extensive program for justice formation that exists. In 2005, this partnership expanded to include the Catholic Campaign for Human Development and Catholic Relief Services, both of whom had financially supported the *JustFaith* program for some years.[14] By 2005, 7,000 people had already completed the basic program. Jezreel's thirty-week program, including weekly meetings, two retreats, and four Saturdays of hands-on ministry with the poor and needy, is a conversion-focused process that includes books, videos, speakers, discussion in small groups, and prayer in order to "empower people of faith to develop a passion and thirst for justice."[15]

In addition, local agencies, sometimes in association with the national organization, have provided a number of resources to help develop PSM in parishes across the country. Some methodologies, each with a single local example, are: training for PSM at the parish level, indicated above, PSM certificate programs (Catholic Charities of the Archdiocese of Galveston-Houston), intentional formation programs (The Leadership Institute co-sponsored by Catholic Charities of the Archdiocese of Washington, DC and the Washington Theological Union), and PSM newsletters ("JustMatters," newsletter of the Office of Parish Social Ministry of Catholic Charities of the Archdiocese of Baltimore).

If we look back to the surveys of 1997 and 1987, in light of the *2007 Survey*—while comparisons cannot be perfect due to the changes in the number and format of PSM data collected—we can see real growth in the commitment of Charities agencies to PSM and its effectiveness. In 1987, the survey reported that Charities had 137 full-time and 208 part-time staff engaged in PSM, working with 2,523 parishes.[16] In 1997, Charities reported having 168 full-time and 219 part-time staff working with 4,372 parishes.[17] Finally, in 2007, Charities had 445 FTE (full-time equivalent)

---

14. "New Partnership with JustFaith Announced," *Charities USA* 32.1 (2005) 9.

15. See JustFaith website at www.justfaith.org for more details, including new programs for youth (Justice Walking) and advanced training (JustSkills) in PSM for those who have completed the basic program. A new ecumenical program for protestant groups has also begun.

16. *1987 Survey*, 30–33.

17. *1997 Survey*, 37–40.

staff working with 5,176 parishes that had a PSM program.[18] Not all PSM is conducted in parishes having working relationships with Catholic Charities, so the scope of PSM within the Catholic Church is broader than these statistics indicate. Training for PSM, as indicated above, is also supported by other national Catholic organizations. What is clear, however, as the bishops noted in *Communities of Salt and Light*, is that much more needs to be done to arrive at Pope Benedict's 2005 declaration that organized *caritas* is one of the three essentials of the Church and its parishes.

Before leaving this topic, it might be good to look briefly at three examples of what the work of a local Catholic Charities agency actually looks like in promoting PSM in the parishes of its diocese. The first represents a thirty-year commitment to PSM, while the others represent major PSM rethinking that began in 2000 and 2004:

- In the diocese of Rockville Centre, NY, the eighth largest U.S. diocese with nearly 1.5 million Catholics and a national model of PSM, more than 110 of 134 parishes have a PSM coordinator hired, supervised, and paid by the parish. The PSM Department of Catholic Charities "provides support services such as training, opportunities for prayer and convening, case management consultation, additional direct services, and an organizing network for advocacy, public policy analysis, and action on local, national, and global issues."[19] The PSM effort in the diocese has been in place for thirty years as a partnership between Catholic Charities and the parishes of the diocese. At the parish level, key roles are played by the pastor, the PSM coordinator, and, often, an advisory committee to help assess the needs of the community and to guide the work of the PSM program. At Charities, PSM is considered to be a core ministry of the agency, utilizing significant staff and resources, including a director, three social ministry developers, a coordinator for education and mission, two social workers, and staff members to coordinate emergency assistance,

18. *2007 Survey,* 109–11.

19. Anthony P. Mullen, "Reaping What Others Have Sown," *Charities USA* 32.1 (2005) 16–18.

the Catholic Campaign for Human Development, and the Public Policy Education Network.[20]

- In the Diocese of Spokane, Catholic Charities initiated a comprehensive campaign in 2000 to reconnect with parishes across the diocese. During a seven month period, a series of ten diocesan-wide listening sessions were conducted by Bishop William Skylstad and Dr. Corrine McGuigan, a volunteer consultant from Gonzaga University. The findings allowed the agency to ground significant philosophical shifts and strategic plans, so much so that parish partnerships "have become the focal point of our agency's short-and-long-term strategic plans, core values, mission statement, and vision statement."[21] Building specific and measureable relationships with parishes became part of planning and annual outcomes measurement for each agency program. These programs now work closely with parishes, and volunteer opportunities for parishioners have been initiated at Charities facilities and housing complexes. Individuals have been recruited as PSM liaisons and placed in every parish. The results are measureable in terms of volunteers who are active, tens of thousands of volunteers hours helping the needy and counseling the vulnerable, and training and workshops for parishioners.[22] The agency summarizes its PSM program this way, "Parish Social Ministry is a resource to assist efforts of parish social concerns committees in the areas of social justice, advocacy, community organizing and outreach to people in need."[23]

- Catholic Charities of the Archdiocese of Denver reorganized its ministries and services in 2004, creating an Office of Mission and Ministry with responsibility for developing a new PSM initiative. After staff attended a regional training in New Mexico sponsored by the national organization, they conducted annual conferences for Denver parishioners in 2004 and 2005. Then they sponsored a regional PSM training for Colorado parishioners in

20. Ibid.

21. Robert McCann, "The Force of Our Parish Partnerships," *Charities USA* 32.1 (2005) 4–6.

22. Ibid.

23. See www.catholiccharitiesspokane.org for agency PSM information.

2006. These efforts have been followed with skill development, intra-and-inter-parish networking, and leadership formation.[24] The Denver agency website indicates that it "works to connect parish communities with issues of justice and charity." It continues, "The organization assists parishes to become active in their expressions of faith."[25]

While PSM has been a major focus of Catholic Charities agencies and Catholic Charities USA for at least two decades, there have been partnership and alliance developments in several other areas of the Catholic world.

OTHER CATHOLIC PARTNERSHIPS AND ALLIANCES

Outside of the context of PSM, in the *2007 Survey* CARA reports that Catholic Charities agencies have partnered with other diocesan offices, Catholic schools, the Knights of Columbus, Mercy Housing, the St. Vincent de Paul Society, and Catholic hospitals and health systems. 101 agencies indicate formal alliances or partnerships with other Catholic Charities and 57 report such formal arrangements with Catholic hospitals or health systems.[26] Because of the size of Catholic healthcare and the scope of these relationships, I want to focus now on partnerships between Catholic Charities and Catholic healthcare. I will discuss underlying rationale for these value-based partnerships or collaboration, some recent and contemporary examples, and then some lessons and challenges that have been identified nationally.

The treatment of the underlying rationale for the collaboration that lies at the heart of the values-based partnerships between Charities and healthcare begins with this insight from the Commission on Catholic Health Care Ministry in their 1988 report of *Catholic Health Care Ministry: A New Vision for a New Century*:

> "Catholic health ministry" is the activity of the whole church—individual members, parish communities, religious congregations, dioceses, and institutions—responding to human suffering with a range of personal and corporate resources. This comprehen-

24. Ernie Geron, "A Good Launching Point for Us," in *Charities USA* 35.1 (2008) 25.

25. See Catholic Charities of the Archdiocese of Denver at www.ccdenver.org for further information.

26. *2007 Survey,* 5, 109.

sive understanding of the ministry was the starting point for the Commission's work and the basis of our vision.[27]

The members of the commission represented the Catholic Health Association (CHA), the U.S. bishops, men and women religious involved in health care, and Catholic medical schools. As the Commission acknowledged in the introduction to the same report, "To the dream of collaboration with and among religious congregations was added the goal of collaboration with and among bishops, parishes, social services, and laity."[28] In 1989, at the recommendation of the commission, the members of the commission, together with Catholic Charities USA, formed the new National Coalition on Catholic Health Care Ministry.[29]

Most people involved in Charities and healthcare could probably name three or four good reasons for collaboration drawn from the contemporary health care and social services environments:

- Catholic Charities and Catholic healthcare face common challenges in the area of Catholic Identity created by pluralism among staff, boards, volunteers, and persons served, by federal and other public funding, and by our common unwillingness to impose religion on our clients or patients as a condition of their being served. What does it then mean to be *Catholic* health care or social services? Leaders in both ministries have been working on helping members better answer this question, including new efforts around mission effectiveness, identity, roots, etc. (Those in Catholic education have faced similar questions, as is reflected in the twenty-year-old common project at Fordham University on Catholic Identity across the three apostolic sectors of education, healthcare, and social services.)

- Both ministries have been greatly challenged, if not threatened, by enormous change within their sectors that can tempt them to be more concerned about survival than about collaboration and the overall health of the communities they serve.

27. Commission on Catholic Health Care Ministry, *Catholic Health Care Ministry: A New Vision for a New Century* (1988), 8.

28. Ibid., 4.

29. See history of commission, coalition, and the New Covenant in Rev. Michael D. Place, STD, "A Hidden Treasure: The National Coalition," in *Health Progress* 81 (2000).

- Both ministries have faced a common challenge in managed care, which health care confronted several years before its incursion into social services ten or twenty years ago. There are not only fiscal challenges here, but challenges to Catholic and professional ethics and especially to the commitment to serve the poor and needy. These people are often least able to pay for care and least likely to be included in a managed care plan, with the exception of the efforts in some states to put the Medicaid program into managed care. Charities and healthcare could work together to share insights and resources, for example around outcomes, outcomes measures, and strategies for moving into the future both financially sound and mission-driven.

- Both ministries trace their roots to the Old Testament responsibilities of the covenant community for the poor, the ministry of Jesus himself, the work of the early church, and the ministries of congregations of religious from the monasteries of the early middle ages to the ship that brought the community of Ursuline sisters to New Orleans in 1727 to begin the first orphanage, home for "women of the street," and health care facility. (The two ministries celebrated that common heritage in Chicago in 2002 when the annual Catholic Health Association Assembly and the Catholic Charities USA Annual Conference were held jointly to celebrate 275 years of ministry in what is now the United States.)

In the early nineties, The National Coalition on Catholic Health Care Ministry: (1) sponsored a 1993 survey on collaborative models entitled *Critical Choices: Catholic Health Care in the Midst of Transformation*; (2) reconfigured itself in 1994 to include the members of the U.S. bishops ad hoc committee on health care; (3) produced a comprehensive manual, *Catholic Health Ministry in Transition: A Handbook for Responsible Leadership*; and (4) sponsored a 1995 national convocation—*New Covenant*—on collaboration. Catholic Charities USA was a co-leader in these various efforts to promote collaboration among the various ministries. The New Covenant then became the moving force in collaboration efforts primarily, but not exclusively, between the ministries of Charities and health care. In various dioceses in subsequent years, New Covenant projects and processes focused on partnering between Catholic Charities and Catholic health care institutions and systems and, sometimes, with others in the Church as well.[30]

In the November 1, 1996 *Catholic Health World*, Jack Curley, president of the Catholic Health Association (CHA), and I. as president of Catholic Charities USA, joined in a common statement of collaboration between and among our ministries. It both reiterated some of the reasons for collaboration above and introduced others. In part it read:

> ...Both Catholic healthcare providers and Catholic Charities have distinguished records of service to people in need.
>
> During recent years, Catholic Charities USA and CHA have called on Catholic Charities agencies and Catholic healthcare providers to vigorously pursue opportunities for collaborations and partnerships. There is reason for that. Both organizations share common values and a common goal—to continue the mission of Jesus in the world. But our shared purposes have not led to as much cooperation and partnering as might be expected.
>
> It may be that we suffer from the old adage that "a little bit of knowledge is a dangerous thing"—and that thinking we know more about each other than we actually do has been an impediment to collaboration. Indeed, some successful collaborators have commented on the need to bridge differing "cultures" in the process of coming together. Part of this process involves replacing preconceptions and misconceptions with facts and understanding.
>
> We are now experiencing dramatic changes both in the social and political landscape of our society and in the American approach to healthcare as well. Underlying this change in part is a growing appreciation among many people that physical health and well-being can no longer be addressed apart from social context.
>
> Jesus brought to the lives of persons and communities a healing presence that recognized the wholeness of persons, as well as the complexity of human illness and brokenness. It is time to recall again the life, work, and teaching of Jesus. This requires attending in an integrated way to both the physical needs of persons and to the social and political realities that affect those needs and the ability to respond appropriately.
>
> So the time is indeed ripe to call on Catholic healthcare providers and Catholic Charities agencies to begin fashioning a uni-

---

30. See, for example, Christopher Root, "New Covenant in Practice: The Diocese of Lansing's New Covenant Initiative," *Charities USA* 29.2 (2002) 23–26.

fied, coordinating approach to meeting the needs of persons and communities.

The time is both ripe and changed. Twenty years ago, as I was ending a five year stint as director of Catholic Community Services of Baton Rouge, the president of the local Catholic hospital and I had never met, unless it was a brief handshake at a diocesan function. Today, those in health care and Charities or other social services are saying that active collaboration is both essential and long overdue on both sides. That assertion in itself can be paradigm shattering, especially when, as the New Covenant coalition, in its phase four, recommended—and some people are making a reality—the collaboration reaches to Catholic schools and parishes as well. That 2000 report was entitled, *Ministering Together: A Shared Vision for Caring and Healing Ministries.*[31]

Ministering Together urged active collaboration within the Church by social services, healthcare, education, and parish ministries. It put forth a new shared vision in these words:

> We commit ourselves to transform our current relationships, structures, and services to create a stronger, unified voice for justice in order to enhance the health and well-being of individuals, families and communities. We will:
>
> *Challenge* our traditional structures, models, and approaches to ministry.
>
> *Advocate* more effectively by speaking as one voice on high-priority social and health policy issues.
>
> *Link* our collective ministries to other community organizations that share our vision.
>
> *Leverage* the gifts and talents of all leaders in ministry.[32]

The New Covenant process also produced a national study of collaboration in 2002, sponsored by Catholic Charities USA and the Catholic Health Association, to assess the work of collaboration in Catholic min-

---

31. *Ministering Together: A Shared Vision for Caring and Healing Ministries* (Silver Spring, MD: National Coalition on Catholic Health Care Ministry, 2000).

32. See New Covenant's 2000 vision statement, contained in "New Covenant's Shared Vision: A Call To Minister Together," *Charities USA*, 30, Special Issue (2003) 3.

istries across the United States. Conducted by Health Systems Research, Inc., the study produced four key findings, as reported in *Charities USA*:

- *Collaboration is occurring across the country.* The researchers identified more than 100 collaborative efforts between ministries, ranging from referral programs to extensive joint service initiatives. . . .

- *Collaboration produces results.* Although relationship-building is often hard work, leaders from both Catholic Charities and health care organizations pointed repeatedly to enhanced services, strengthened relationships within communities, and improved outcomes for the persons and families they serve.

- *The joint efforts are responding to individual and community needs.* In the stories told by local leaders, it is clear that the partnerships entail far more than simply combining organizational capabilities. The efforts respond to human need, often in a way that amplifies the effectiveness of the individual organizations.

- *Lessons for success are available for ministry leaders.* This forthcoming report distills "the best of " key insights from the study for persons looking to start a partnership, optimize their chances for success, and overcome obstacles that are bound to emerge along the way. . . .[33]

After the study and the 1992 joint conference of members of Catholic Charities USA and CHA, the national New Covenant steering committee then morphed into Ministering Together, which later restructured in 2005 and 2006 as a Cleveland-based separate corporation and included a greater variety of Church organizations, especially from the diocesan or local level.

Bishop Dale J. Melczek of Gary, Indiana, chairperson of Ministering Together, describes the organization as follows:

> Ministering Together has helped facilitate significant collaborative efforts in dioceses and Catholic organizations across the country. Our goal is to encourage those ministering in Catholic health care, human services, education, and parishes to assume a more prominent role in this effort.[34]

---

33. Ibid., 2–3.

34. Cf. www.ministeringtogether.org for further details on the organization.

The emphasis on such Catholic collaboration has continued within the Charities network. A new Arnold Andrews Award for Collaborative Excellence—named for the former director of Catholic Charities of Tampa-St. Petersburg and a member of the New Covenant steering committee killed in the 2006 crash of Comair Flight 5191—is now awarded by Catholic Charities USA to recognize and encourage collaborative efforts. In 2008, the award was presented to Catholic Charities of Camden for its Project ONE, which facilitates collaboration of parishes and ministries of the diocese with the long-term disaster recovery programs in New Orleans and Biloxi, Mississippi.[35]

The multi-year experience within Catholic Charities indicates that real collaborations are difficult and can be very fragile. To be effective, in my judgment they require at least five elements:

1. Both institutional and personal linkages, beginning with the respective organizational CEOs and even involving reciprocal board representation. Engagement at all levels of the organizations is even more helpful.

2. Actual commitments of personnel and financial resources to the collaborative;

3. Significant time to develop; parties have to identify short-and-long-term goals and pace themselves in the process of getting to them;

4. A focus on the needs of the community which transcends institutional self-interest; obviously, community assets and needs assessments are a step towards creating and keeping this focus; and

5. Real *parity* in representation on planning, governing, or advisory bodies.

The benefit of attending to the possibilities of collaborative partnerships within the Church community have been shown to be real and long lasting, well worth the time, energy, and resources that must be invested to create success. Charities' partnerships, however, have extended far beyond the Catholic community to embrace both interfaith and other volun-

35. "The Arnold Andrews Award for Collaborative Excellence," *Charities USA* 35.4 (2008) 33.

tary sector allies, in addition to the partnership with government at all levels(discussed below in chapter seven).

INTERFAITH AND COMMUNITY PARTNERSHIPS

Partnerships with religious and other voluntary organizations are a significant part of the work of Catholic Charities, according to the *2007 Survey*. Only about one in five agencies (30 in all) reported having no contracts or alliances with other organizations. In terms of formal alliances or partnerships, 176 agencies reported partnering with other non-profit human services organizations, 50 agencies with other-than-Catholic hospitals or health systems, and 77 agencies with other groups.[36] Agencies also reported that they had performance-based contracts for services as follows: employment and Welfare-to-Work (61 agencies); foster care (67 agencies); residential care (64 agencies); special needs adoptions (52 agencies); and sixteen other services ranging from abstinence-based education and adult day care to trafficking and youth at risk (115 agencies).[37] These could involve public or private organizations, as was the case with 139 agencies who reported participating in public/private partnerships with governmental, non-governmental, for-profit, and non-profit organizations to provide a range of services to their communities.

In discussing interfaith partnerships, Gregory Kepferle, director of Catholic Charities of Santa Clara County and former director in New Mexico, described the range of such partnerships in a single diocese:

> In our community, a Presbyterian congregation sponsors refugees in our refugee resettlement program. A Methodist congregation offers to house our senior day care program. A group of small Christian churches based on the Apostle's Creed gathers to organize outreach to the needy. Members of Christian and Jewish congregations organize to support comprehensive immigration reform and to expand children's health insurance. Our agency recruits a coalition of community and faith-based organizations to develop a coordinated service network.[38]

Kepferle credits two dynamics in Catholic Charities organizations that lay the foundation for interfaith partnerships: the Catholic identity of

---

36. *2007 Survey,* 4–5.

37. Ibid.

38. Gregory Kepferle, "Interfaith Partnerships: Why We Form Them, What Makes Them Work, and What We Gain," *Charities USA* 34.1 (2007) 3–5.

Charities calling for service to all people in need in a pluralistic society and the cultural competency of staff in relating to those of other faith traditions. By "cultural competency" Kepferle refers to the experience and skills of religiously diverse staff who respect clients' "ethnic and cultural identities, including the religious sensibilities that are a key aspect of the cultural identity . . ."[39] Important to this competency is hiring staff and recruiting volunteers who understand and accept the diverse ethnic and religious traditions and staff "who are secure enough in their professional competence as well as in their own spiritual journey and faith tradition that they feel no compulsion to hide their faith or impose it on others."[40]

As with effective partnerships among Catholic organizations discussed above, strong and committed leadership is needed on both sides of the interfaith partnership. Kepferle adds that the following elements are key to sustainable partnering:

- a good relationship among strong committed leaders of the different organizations with security in their own faith traditions and missions without needing to proselytize or be defensive;

- acceptance that religious differences may cause a certain level of discomfort and being willing to work through that;

- common ethical values underlying the partnership;

- open, honest, and frequent communication;

- the maturity to set aside egos for the common good;

- a shared vision;

- a recognition that each member needs the others;

- a commitment of resources beyond a particular grant or funding cycle;

- focus on the needs of the clients and a clarity of each group's roles in accomplishing the mutually agreed upon goal or task at hand; and

- trust in God's grace.[41]

---

39. Ibid., 4.
40. Ibid.
41. Ibid., 5.

Locally, such partnerships may bring together two partners or fifteen. They may focus on disaster response, emergency assistance coordination, advocacy for health care or a living wage, construction of housing, provision of respite care, or care for the environment. At the national level, such partnerships are reflected in the Interfaith Roundtable of Health and Human Services Associations which includes national representatives of American Baptist, Brethren, Jewish, Catholic, United Church of Christ, Episcopal, Quaker, Lutheran, Mennonite, and United Methodist organizations providing housing, aging, caring, health, and human services.[42]

Similar civic alliances and partnerships exist all across the country, often involving Catholic Charities with local foundations, the United Way, hospice, colleges and universities, Head Start programs, YMCA and YWCA, Family Service America, scouts, the Red Cross, the Visiting Nurse Association, the Urban League, Big Brothers Big Sisters, the mental health association, and neighborhood centers. At the national level, the organization of the chief executives of these and other human service networks is known as the "Leadership 18." The abundance of such alliances and associations in American society reflect in part the much quoted observation of French philosopher Alexis de Tocqueville in his 1835 book *Democracy in America*, "Americans of all ages, all stations in life, and all types of disposition are forever forming associations." This is true of Catholic Charities locally and nationally, reflecting the American character, our pluralistic society, and the convening spirit growing from the *Cadre Study* and focused on creating effective alliances for service of those in need and to create a more just and compassionate society.

42. "The Interfaith Roundtable of Health and Human Services Associations," *Charities USA* 34.2 (2007)13–14.

PART THREE

Wonders.

6

Volunteers

The Lifeblood of the Network

*O*NE OF THE MORE *inspiring parts of my visits to Catholic Charities agencies across the country between 1992 and 2001 was meeting volunteers, seeing the work that they did, and hearing the stories about them and their impact on people's lives. A favorite story took place in a Midwest diocese where Catholic Charities had established a home for single, pregnant women in the former convent of an active parish. One Sunday after Mass, a man rang the doorbell of the home and introduced himself to the staff member who answered. He said that he was a parishioner and that for several Sundays at Mass he had experienced a strong sense that God wanted him to volunteer at the home. But, because of his profession, he did not believe that he would be able to help. So he had waited to respond until, this Sunday, the sense of God's call could not be resisted any longer.*

The staff member asked what he did for a living. He said he was a computer programmer. He was shocked by how excited she became. A computer company had donated to Catholic Charities several computers, software, and the necessary accessories to create a computer lab in the home, but none of the staff or residents knew how to make them work. They all still sat in the boxes in which they had been delivered. He was the answer to their prayers! Soon, the computers were networked, the software installed, and the volunteer was teaching residents (and staff) how to learn computer skills, write their resumes, and prepare themselves for computer-related jobs.

❧

According to the *2007 Survey*, the number of volunteers working in Catholic Charities agencies was 230,357, plus another 6,342 volunteer board members.[1] Roughly, it was *a quarter of a million people!* Volunteers made up 76 percent of the total workforce of Catholic Charities, and agencies estimated that they contributed 7,571,708 hours of service. While the number of volunteers fluctuates from year to year influenced by the economy, natural disasters, and other factors, during the first decade of this century it has hovered around a quarter of a million. Ten years ago the total number was 252,984, with 9,638 board members;[2] ten years before that, there were 173,358 volunteers and 7,398 board members.[3] The growth in the 1990s from the 1980s reflects in large part the growth of emergency services (food, clothing, shelter) within the Catholic Charities network and that in turn reflects the economics of poverty and massive cuts in government programs as well. The growth of these emergency services provided the opportunity for, and required the services of, many more volunteers than in previous decades. It also reflected the growing awareness of many Americans that hunger and homelessness had been on the rise in urban, rural, and suburban communities throughout the last part of the twentieth century.

THE WHO, WHAT, AND WHY OF
CATHOLIC CHARITIES VOLUNTEERS

Catholic Charities agencies value their volunteers highly and it is common to honor volunteers at the diocesan agency level and even in particular programs. In the 1990s, Catholic Charities USA began recognizing a National Volunteer of the Year, drawn from nominations made by local member agencies. If we look at the honorees of the past eight years, we can see the diversity of people involved in Catholic Charities, the different kinds of work which they do, and their impact on people's lives. In the process we can highlight a bit of their influence within agencies, how their volunteer work has changed their own lives, and why they became involved.

- *Carol Frenette of St. Paul, Minnesota*—Carol began volunteering in 1987 at the Dorothy Day Center for people who are homeless and

1. *2007 Survey*, 103.
2. *1997 Survey*, 42.
3. *1987 Survey*, 4.

poor. Beginning with peeling carrots, over the next fifteen years she became the full-time coordinator for fifty or more volunteers who provide families and single adults with hot meals, overnight shelter, groceries, furniture, clothing, transportation, health care, hospice, substance abuse treatment, and the comforting presence of those who care. Honored nationally in 2001, Carol worked a full day everyday in the center, which served 500 to 600 persons a day; and by 2001, she had 23,000 hours of service to people in need in the Minneapolis–St. Paul area. As she put it, "I love the people here. For the most part, they're no different than you and me. [Homelessness] can happen to anyone."[4]

- *Kathy and Tom Gess of Baton Rouge, Louisiana*—Tom and Kathy were honored in 2002 for their twenty years of service and leadership in prison ministry. Their activities included: providing screening, counseling, and support services to male ex-offenders at Joseph Homes, a Catholic Charities transitional shelter; visiting inmates at state penitentiaries (Louisiana has the highest per capita inmate population in the U.S.); writing notes and birthday cards to inmates; conducting support groups within prisons; attending parole and probation hearings; tracking legislation and advocating for prison reform; developing a resource book for newly released ex-offenders; and working for restorative justice among offenders, victims, and the community. As Kathy said, "We are only a small part of a much bigger world of volunteers who make what we do possible."[5]

- *Jackie Bushong-Martin of Rhinelander, Wisconsin*—Jackie was honored in 2003 for her work focused on the poor of Haiti and engaging senior citizens of the diocese of Superior in making this happen. Schoolchildren in Haiti must have uniforms to attend school; and, because of the cost of uniforms, poor children often cannot attend and are unable to break free from poverty. Jackie mobilized hundreds of senior volunteers to make 2,000 uniforms and she delivered them to Haiti. She also worked with missionary

4. Anna Chrismer Housman, "Carol Frenette—2001 National Volunteer of the Year," *Charities USA* 28.4 (2001), 19, 32.

5. Anna Chrismer Housman, "Tom and Kathy Gess: Catholic Charities USA's Volunteers of the Year," *Charities USA* 29.2 (2002), 9 and back cover.

agencies to organize a mothers' sewing class in Port au Prince and coordinated efforts to refurbish foot-powered treadle sewing machines for areas with unreliable or no electrical service.[6]

- *Dave Cleveland of Washington, DC*—Honored in 2004, Dave had worked full-time since 1998 as a volunteer attorney for the Immigration Legal Services of Catholic Charities of the Archdiocese of Washington. In this capacity, he represented clients fleeing repressive regimes in places such as Burma, Ivory Coast, Rwanda, Somalia, and Sudan, most of them fleeing religious, ethnic, or political persecution. Dave also worked to increase awareness of Catholic Charities and Immigration Legal Services, recruit other attorneys to do *pro bono* work for immigrants, and conduct educational seminars for immigrants on legal issues. When offered a paid position with Charities, "He thought about it and returned the next day to say that if he could offer his services without costing the Church, he would prefer to continue doing so."[7]

- *Helen Brown of New Orleans*—At 81 years of age, "Miss Helen" was honored in 2005 for a lifetime of volunteer service to Catholic Charities of New Orleans. For several decades, she devoted herself to the girls and young women at St. Elizabeth's orphanage operated by the Daughters of Charity and, later, Catholic Charities. Herself a resident of St. Elizabeth's from the age of eleven after her mother's death, Miss Helen later lived in an apartment across the street to allow her to volunteer mornings, evenings, and weekends while working for the railroad as a clerk-typist. In the last fifteen years before this award, she volunteered in the administrative offices of Catholic Charities for three days a week despite arthritis and open heart surgery in 2001. To other senior citizens she urged volunteering, "You're doing something with your life instead of sitting down looking at the soaps."[8]

6. "Volunteer of the Year Award," *Charities USA* 30.4 (2003); and www.catholiccharitiesusa.org/Netcommunity for further information.

7. "Catholic Charities USA's Volunteer of the Year: Dave Cleveland Helps Asylees Find a Home in the United States," *Charities USA* 31.2 (2004), 20–21, quoting Jeanne Atkinson, program director at Immigration Legal Services.

8. Peter Finney Jr., "Helen Brown: Catholic Charities USA's 2005 Volunteer of the Year," *Charities USA* 32.2 (2005), 28–29. Miss Helen was to receive the award at the Catholic

- *Caldwell M. Prejean of Austin, Texas*—Caldwell had served as vice-president and president on the board of Catholic Charities of Central Texas by strengthening the agency and being a liaison to the African-American community. He was honored in 2006 for multiple initiatives in which the agency was involved. The first was "Seeds of Hope," a community coalition to respond to the needs of children and families of inmates by mentoring, counseling, medical referrals, and helping with family visitations to inmates. In the wake of Hurricanes Katrina and Rita, which devastated his state of origin, Carlton worked with evacuees in the Austin area, helped initiate the Adopt-a-Family program to settle families in apartments, hotels, and homes, and adopted two families himself. He also assisted in the design and development of a new Catholic Charities center.[9]

- *Sam Marascalco, Phil Mooberry, and Nick Mooberry of Tucson, Arizona*—Three generations of dentists in the same family were honored in 2007 for their collective sixty years of providing low-or-no-cost dental care to those without dental insurance. Dr. Sam helped to found the dental clinic at St. Elizabeth's Health Center forty years earlier and continued to volunteer there. His son-in-law, Dr. Phil, joined him in this service twenty years later. His son, Dr. Nick, joined them in this service the year before their collective award. Their service included treating twelve to fifteen patients a month at the health center, caring for more complex patients in their own offices, providing leadership to the annual golf tournament to raise more than $60,000 a year for dental equipment and supplies, soliciting other funding, and recruiting other dentists.[10]

- *Ray Suttles of Wharton, New Jersey*—Ray was honored in 2008 for fifteen years of volunteer service to persons with AIDS at Hope House in Dover, New Jersey, an agency of Catholic Charities of Paterson. Initially volunteering only as a buddy to someone

Charities USA annual conference in Phoenix on September 17, 2005. She did not attend, since she was stranded in her home in a flooded New Orleans in the wake of Hurricane Katrina. The award was presented at a later, more auspicious time.

9. Evelyn L. Kent, "Caldwell Prejean Sows the Seeds of Hope in Central Texas," *Charities USA* 33.2 (2006), 24–25.

10. "Catholic Charities USA's 2007 Volunteers of the Year," *Charities USA* 34.1 (2007), 34–35.

who was facing the last stages of the illness, Ray subsequently had spent about thirty hours each month in support for Hope House. He facilitated a support group for men with HIV/AIDS beginning in 1993, staffed a client advisory board, oversaw the monthly HIV newsletter, helped with fundraisers, assisted the agency with earning its first Council on Accreditation certification, and worked to support HIV-affected families. Most recently, he has helped prepare clients to testify at Congressional hearings on HIV funding. As Ray explained, "The clients bring a face, a name, and a story to the legislation."[11]

As you can see from these outstanding volunteers, the work of the volunteer can be to bring his or her own profession to the service of Catholic Charities—attorney or dentist, for example—or to be more of a generalist, providing whatever caring service is required. Volunteers can serve on the "front lines" of emergency services, in the back office of the administrators, on the board of directors, in parish outreach, or in the essential business of raising money or making the agency and its services better known to the public.

Volunteers also may become involved in legislative advocacy, as we saw with Ray Suttles on HIV/AIDS issues and Kathy and Tom Gess on prison reform. This turn to advocacy often comes only after the volunteer has seen the impact of an issue like HIV or prison conditions in the lives of poor and vulnerable people. The volunteer first works to serve these needy people and then, after seeing more and more people in need for the same reason or reasons, adds advocacy as another means of helping them.

Board members like Caldwell Prejean can be volunteers in many ways. Without even becoming involved in programs as Caldwell did, board members bring multiple skills to an array of tasks that are their responsibility in the non-profit world. They deal with the overall governance of the organization, helping to shape the mission and strategies to achieve it. They may help to develop personnel policies, information systems, employment practices, public relations efforts, and accounting and auditing procedures. In the fundraising area, many organizations expect

11. Maureen Fitzgerald-Penn, "Ray Suttles—A Committed Champion for Men with HIV/AIDS: Catholic Charities USA's 2008 National Volunteer of the Year," *Charities USA* 35.2 (2008), 30–31.

their board members to "give, get, or get off," although—as we saw with many of the national volunteer awardees—fundraising is hardly limited to the members of the board.

Many agencies believe that it is best to work with volunteers in ways parallel to what is expected of staff members. By this they expect potential volunteers to apply to work in the agency, to be interviewed, to be screened (including the expectation of criminal background checks, especially when working with children), and to have a definite job description with expected hours of service that, of course, are negotiated with the volunteer. The *Code of Ethics* provides that, "Volunteers should be held to the same standards, policies, procedures and accountability as are the paid staff of the agency."[12] In the case of the full-time volunteers Carol Frenette of St. Paul and Dave Cleveland of Washington, D.C., they worked such regular hours that many staff did not know that they were volunteers at all! These expectations actually reflect the dependence of the Charities agencies on their volunteers for services essential to their clients and their agency.

Volunteers also may be trained to do the service which they provide to the agency. This may take the form of simple orientation and mentoring to more formal training in the mission, values, and practices of the program and how to deal with the specific problems that impact the lives of those they serve, whether they are elderly, children with disabilities, or refugees. Specific training for volunteers is conducted by 214 agencies or specific programs. The *2007 Survey* also reports that 135 agencies or specific programs have a coordinator or director of volunteers.[13] These coordinators themselves often attend training in the care, supervision, and support of the agency or program volunteers. Catholic Charities USA provides on-line training resources for volunteer managers and other staff who are working with volunteers.[14]

The impact of a quarter of a million volunteers on agencies takes a number of forms. First, they provide essential services to those whom Charities seeks to serve and, without them, many programs simply would not exist. Second, they enable Catholic agencies to serve many more peo-

12. *Code of Ethics*, 4.08(d).

13. *2007 Survey*, 107.

14. See www.catholiccharitiesusa for two training programs: *Everyone Ready*, done in partnership with Energize, Inc.; and its fifty-five minute training series for those working with volunteers.

ple than they could with just their paid staff. Third, they bring otherwise unavailable skills to the agencies needed in direct service, administration, governance, advocacy, and fundraising. Fourth, like Caldwell Prejean in Austin or the three dentists in Tucson, they enable the agency to connect with different parts of the community, whether that is the African-American minority or dental professionals. Fifth, they are an inspiration to staff, board, and those they serve. As his supervisor said of Dave Cleveland, "When we learned he was a volunteer and working the longest hours of everyone in the office, it reminded us all how important the work we do is and how important our clients are."[15]

Why do volunteers do it? Why give so much of themselves to the work of Catholic Charities? If we look back at our national honorees, we can discern a wealth of reasons. For some, like Miss Helen at St. Elizabeth's in New Orleans, they themselves had been helped by the agency or program in the past. For others, like Ray Suttles of Hope House in Dover, it was the news that a good friend had HIV that prompted him to want to do something to help others with the disease. "I just felt such a sense that I had to do something," he said. "I hadn't paid a lot of attention to AIDS. I didn't feel like it was something that would invade my world."[16] The same thing happened to Caldwell Prejean when he saw classmates from high school in New Orleans among the hurricane evacuees in Austin.[17]

Some volunteers take on their responsibilities out of a more general sense that can be phrased several ways. Tom Gess of Baton Rouge cites his and Kathy's common humanity with prisoners, "We try to have the public see prisoners as human beings."[18] Carol Frenette had expressed similar sentiments. Some verbalize this in terms of a return to their community for all the good they have received in life. As the director at St. Elizabeth's said of the three dentists in Tucson, "Volunteering at St. E's is how this family gives back to the community."[19] Others explain it in spiritual terms, as did Ray Suttles when asked why he continued to volunteer after so many years, "We are all children of God, all deserving of His love and

15. Atkinson in "Dave Cleveland," 21.
16. Fitzgerald-Penn, "Ray Suttles," 30.
17. Kent, "Caldwell Prejean," 25.
18. Housman, "Tom and Kathy Gess . . .," back cover.
19. "2007 Volunteers of the Year," 34.

each other's love and support. To give anything less is just not within the teaching that I have learned."[20]

Finally, for some volunteers it is seeing the results in people's lives that keep them coming back day-after-day or week-after-week. Caldwell Prejean put it this way: "It was very, very gratifying to be able to work with individuals, to help see to their medical needs and to help them with access to FEMA, their employers and the resources that they needed to get their feet on the ground."[21]

For Dave Cleveland, the practice of law as a volunteer carried far more meaning than he saw in other cases: "If you win a civil suit, nothing really changes except maybe money exchanges hands. But if you win in immigration court, you established a family."[22] A local Catholic Charities volunteer in Colorado Springs named Frank Mora put it this way, "The best part of my job is that I get to see the results of my work in people's lives."[23]

WOMEN AND MEN RELIGIOUS

Any discussion of volunteers in Catholic Charities in this country must include those who founded and, for more than a century, staffed many of these ministries which are now largely the work of lay men and women, staff and volunteers. Chapter three began with the story of the Ursuline Sisters arriving in New Orleans in 1727 to do whatever was needed by the community and, thus, beginning voluntary social, health, and educational ministries in what is now the United States. The religious—sisters, brothers, and religious order priests committing their entire lives in vowed service to Christ's Church—represent the quintessential volunteer. "Come, follow me," Jesus said; and their affirmative response gave rise to many of the charitable institutions and agencies that comprise the contemporary Catholic Charities network

To look at just one diocese—admittedly a unique one—can give us a glimpse of the breadth and history of what religious did in creating the

20. Fitzgerald-Penn, "Ray Suttles," 31.

21. Kent, "Caldwell Prejean," 25.

22. "D.C. Bar Names Immigration Legal Services Lawyer 'Pro Bono Lawyer of the Year,'" *Impact* 3 (2008) 4.

23. "Diocese of Colorado Springs Awards Frank Mora with 'Spirit of Charity' Award," *Charities USA* 30.1 (2003), 27.

Church's charitable works. That diocese is New York, which celebrated its 200th anniversary in 2008 and included a special celebration honoring two centuries of charitable work done there by religious orders in an area that welcomed millions of poor immigrants over two centuries. Sister Margaret John Kelly, DC, former superior of the Northeast province of the Daughters of Charity was the keynote speaker; and, in her address, she reflected on the congregations who had "quarried, carried and polished the stones which have helped to build the marvelous and massive organization of Catholic Charities extending now over several counties."[24]

In parts of her address, Sister Kelly provided snapshots of the history, congregations, founders, and works that were woven into the fabric of this historical masterpiece of charity:

- In 1817, Mother Elizabeth Ann Seton (now Saint), who had founded the Sisters of Charity of St. Joseph, sent three sisters from Emmitsburg, Maryland, to staff the first charitable institution of the diocese, the Roman Catholic Asylum for Orphans.

- In 1846, the Mercy sisters from Ireland opened their first house of mercy to offer shelter, job training, and hospitality to young women from Ireland.

- In 1848, the De La Salle brothers offered the boys in the Bronx Protectory basic education and job training which the Sisters of Charity also did for girls there.

- In 1854, School Sisters of Notre Dame, working with the German Redemptorists, established an asylum for German orphans to prepare them to live meaningful and independent lives outside the institution.

- In 1855, the Good Shepherd Sisters began working for "wayward women," a tradition that now reaches to rescuing victims of global trafficking.

- In 1881, American Franciscan Sisters of Hastings sheltered homeless street youth at the Mission of the Virgin Immaculate and prepared them for employment.

24. Sister Margaret John Kelly, DC, "Contributions of Men and Women Religious to Catholic Charities: Charity Embracing Justice," *Origins* 37.40 (March 20, 2008), 639–42.

- In 1889, Mother Frances Cabrini (now Saint) and her companions arrived in New York to attend to the needs of Italian immigrants as the newly formed Missionary Sisters of the Sacred Heart.

- In 1890, the Sparkhill Dominicans opened St. Benedict's orphanage for African-American children who were not accepted in any other Catholic orphanage.

- In 1899, Rose Hawthorne Lathrop founded the Dominicans for the Relief of Incurable Cancer to care for those sick and ostracized after this diagnosis.

- In 1912, Katherine Drexel (now Saint) sent to Harlem her sisters of the Blessed Sacrament for Indians and Colored People to serve African-Americans and confront the issue of racism.

- In 1925, the Franciscan Handmaids of Mary, founded in Georgia by the African-American Mother Theodore, began day nursery services for African-Americans.

- In 1928, Angeline Teresa McCrory and a small band of sisters began residential services to the elderly in the Bronx and established the Carmelite Sisters for the Sick and Infirm.

In her review of these accomplishments and others, Kelly described their legacy this way:

> It seems fair to say that the constant motivator and consistent service posture across congregations and across the two centuries has been the conviction that the church must be constantly searching out poor and needy persons to assist them but also to be faithful to our identity and to maintain credibility. Even when logic, limited resources and sometimes opposition urge inaction or great caution, the communities responded in the unique Gospel way.[25]

While New York is unique in many ways, the growth of Catholic charitable institutions from the nineteenth to the twentieth century was truly an astounding tribute to the "volunteers" in religious habit who made it happen. The U.S. bishops summarized the scope of the achievement of religious as follows:

25. Ibid., 640.

By the year 1900, the organized response of the Catholic community in the United States to social needs included more than
800 Catholic charitable institutions. Ten years later, in 1910, 445
Catholic orphanages and institutions were caring for 88,860 dependent children. By 1919, the Sisters of Charity and the Daughters of
Charity operated sixty-two maternity hospitals, infant homes, and
orphanages, and cared for 10,653 infants and children. Sisters of
the Good Shepherd cared for 7,036 delinquent and neglected girls
in fifty-eight institutions. Sisters in more than forty other congregations cared for another 41,000 infants and children. Religious
priests and brothers cared for 4,900 in their protectories, industrial
schools, and orphanages.[26]

While women and men religious are no longer the majority serving in or
even leading many of these charitable works, there remain a number of
religious in leadership in Catholic Charities agencies and institutions and/
or working in the simplest tasks of caring for people in need. They also
have served and continue to serve in leadership positions within Catholic
Charities USA and on various national committees, commissions, and
task forces, despite the significant decline in religious sisters and brothers
in the United States over the past fifty years.

THE DISTINCTIONS AND LIMITS OF
FAITH-INSPIRED VOLUNTEERISM

Since the first President Bush's volunteer emphasis on a "thousand points
of light," we have been engaged in a protracted national debate about the
role of volunteerism. In his son's presidency for the past eight years, this
emphasis was interwoven into his faith-based initiative; and it seems that
it will continue in the presidency of Barack Obama, who is keeping the
faith-based White House office and whose inaugural address highlighted
individual responsibility, one form of which is voluntarism. For skeptics,
too often the emphasis on volunteering and faith-based initiatives in the
past two decades has seemed to accompany and justify efforts to cut the
government's commitment to assisting poor families directly or through
government social service programs. At this point (we will revisit related
issues in the next chapter), our treatment of volunteerism should be fur-
thered by considering what churches and other faith-based organizations

26. *In All Things Charity*, 24, relying as its source on Brown and McKeown, *The Poor
Belong to Us* (see introduction, 2).

(FBO's) can and cannot do in the complex world of social services. I take my lead here from the thoughtful op-ed published in January 2001 in the *Greensboro News and Record* by Professor Bob Wineberg of the University of North Carolina, a specialist in this arena. It was written at the beginning of the presidency of George W. Bush.[27] There are four points to be considered here.

First, congregations and FBO's are extremely active in meeting the social needs of their own congregations and their communities. They care for elderly members of their congregations, work to improve neighborhoods, and promote community well-being in many ways. As Professor Wineberg put it, "They are limited, but essential, partners in a broader community of care."[28] This work is largely done by volunteers drawn from the local congregation, as occurs in many Catholic parishes. Tens of thousands of volunteers work in their Catholic parishes in this way to meet the needs of their members and their local communities.

Second, Catholics, Lutherans, Baptists, Jews, Methodists, and Salvationists (Salvation Army) sponsor vast networks of faith-inspired social service organizations who assist tens of millions of people in need across the country each year. As discussed above, the Catholic Charities USA membership network served over 7.7 million people in 2007. "What is confusing to the public," Professor Wineberg noted, "is that there is not a clear distinction between faith based organizations and service provision coming from congregations." The social service organizations sponsored by churches such as Catholic Charities have professional staff and multiple funding streams, including—*for over a century*—significant government funding. But they also utilize volunteers, space, and funding from congregations, "sometimes making it hard to distinguish between the congregations and their community based organizations." For the Catholic Charities network, as we have discussed, almost a quarter of a million volunteers are part of this second kind of involvement. In addition, as Wineberg noted more generally, many Catholic Charities programs and services are housed within parish facilities, making the distinction even more difficult.

---

27. This treatment of the limits on volunteerism is adapted from my column, "Faith and Works," *The Catholic Commentator* of Baton Rouge, February 7, 2001, 5.

28. Professor Robert J. Wineberg, "The Faith Community Can't Do It All," *Greensboro News and Record*, January 21, 2001.

Third, many congregations have their own social service programs through which paid staff or volunteer members reach out to the wider community to visit the sick, provide after-school care, or serve a hot meal to seniors. Catholic Charities promote these activities through their PSM programs. These encompass direct service activity, as well as parish participation in housing development, diocesan legislative networks, community organizing, and twinning with poorer parishes here or abroad. Professor Wineberg indicated that most local congregations have four such social programs. Other research shows that congregations and their volunteers are far more likely to engage in direct hands-on activities such as providing food or clothing than more intense social services such as mentoring or job training. These latter social services are more likely to be provided by Catholic Charities and similar agencies than by a local parish or church congregation.

Fourth, policy makers must understand that "the religious community's spirit is not housed in a vacuum." On one hand, there is the complex web of volunteer-driven activities fueled by intense faith. "On the other," Professor Wineberg emphasized, "that volunteer spirit works in tandem with, and is often inseparable from the professional service efforts of other faith based, private nonprofit, and even government agencies." One problem in a lot of the debate over faith-based initiatives and volunteerism is that these distinctions are often blurred. Policy makers need to learn about what is really happening in local congregations, about their social service organizations, about what really works, and about what more the congregations believe they can do. They cannot presume that local church congregations have the capacities that are normal to faith-inspired social service organizations such as Catholic Charities with professional capacities made possible by staff and volunteers.

CONCLUSION

Lives are transformed by volunteerism within Catholic Charities, in parishes, and in society at large. The transformation takes place in those served, but also, sometimes in surprising ways, in those who put their time and talents at the service of others. Most come to see the poor and needy and their common humanity in new ways. They also see U.S. society in ways they had never dreamed, both good and bad. They read the Scriptures with more appreciation and deeper meaning. Some become determined advocates when they only set out to serve a hot meal to a hungry family. Others, like the saying of the Jesuit Volunteer Corps Volunteers (many of whom work in Catholic Charities programs), become "ruined for life." They can never accept the status quo again and never go back to "business as usual."

For most volunteers, their engagement in Catholic Charities becomes a matter of the heart. In my first year at Catholic Charities USA, I attended a volunteer appreciation night at a local agency in the Midwest. A "middle" woman—middle age, middle class, middle America—was honored for her decade or so of service to people with HIV/AIDS. She told the story of how she had gotten into the work as a volunteer, how her spiritual director had perceived her desire to do something "more" with her life, and how he had referred her to Catholic Charities where they were "starting a program dealing with a new disease called AIDS." Then, after thanking a number of people by name, mainly those the program served and those who had died, she said what I have heard time-after-time from volunteers, "I have received so much more than I have given."

7

Pluralism

From Jefferson to Obama

IN 1803, LOUISIANA BECAME part of the United States of America when Thomas Jefferson purchased much of the Mississippi River Valley from Napoleon Bonaparte. The Ursuline Sisters in New Orleans were concerned about whether they would be allowed to continue their ministries when New Orleans was no longer part of a Catholic country. So, as Americans are free to do, they wrote to President Jefferson. His handwritten letter in response, dated May 15, 1804, is in the archives of the New Orleans Ursuline community. It reads as follows:

> I have received, holy sisters, the letter you have written me wherein you express anxiety for the property vested in your institution by the former governments of Louisiana. The principles of the constitution and government of the United States are a sure guarantee to you that it will be preserved to you sacred and inviolate, and that your institution will be permitted to govern itself according to its own voluntary rules, without interference from the civil authority. Whatever diversity or shade may appear in the religious opinions of our fellow citizens, the charitable objects of your institution cannot be indifferent to any; and its furtherance of the wholesome purposes of society by training its younger members in the way they should go, cannot fail to ensure it the patronage of the government it is under. Be assured it will meet all the protection which my office can give it. I salute you, holy sisters, with friendship and respect. [Signed Th. Jefferson][1]

---

1. Rev. Michael D. Place, "The Ursulines' Legacy: A History of 'Doing What Needs to Be Done,'" *Charities USA* 29.2 (2002) 16–18.

Thus began the complex and generally positive relationship of Catholic Charities, education, and health care with the government of the United States and, subsequently, various state and local governments. It brought together the constitutional protection of religion ("free exercise"), the voluntary sector of this society, and the desire of government to promote the common good through a variety of means, including religious-inspired services to the population. As we will see, this is another area of extreme complexity.

GOVERNMENT AND RELIGIOUS INITIATIVES

On February 5, 2009, President Barack Obama signed an executive order to create a revamped White House office for religion-based and neighborhood programs. This was to be an expansion of the "initiative started by the Bush administration that provides government support—and financing—to religious and charitable organizations that deliver social services."[2] A news article went on to report on one major unresolved question from the Bush program, namely whether religious groups that receive federal money for social services can hire only those who are members of their denomination. It indicated as well that there are other controversies associated with this program, namely, whether funded churches or groups can proselytize those they serve, whether they can discriminate among those to be served on the basis of religion, and whether religious groups outside the mainstream, such as the Church of Scientology, might participate in government funding for social services. Thus, what may have seemed simple in the time of Thomas Jefferson has become far more complicated in the days of George W. Bush and Barack H. Obama, made more complicated by the availability of public dollars to support such services (although, frankly, no significant new dollars were appropriated for these purposes during the two terms of the Bush administration).

These questions are not new in the world of Catholic Charities, and they are generally discussed under the heading of "pluralism."[3] The debate

2. Jeff Zeleny and Laurie Goodstein, "White House Faith Office to Expand," *New York Times*, January 5, 2009. The White House also announced that there would be a 25-member advisory council to the office and that the president of Catholic Charities USA (Rev. Larry Snyder) would be a member.

3. I have written on these themes a number of times over two decades and am drawing on these writings for parts of this chapter. See, for example, "Pluralism," *Charities USA*

that greeted President Bush's faith-based initiatives and is now beginning for the Obama administration is an important one for the nation; but, for Catholic Charities USA members across the nation, it can be very frustrating. This is because so much history and so much of the social services reality and experience in this country often is unknown or ignored.

For purposes of the current discussion, it is important to note that, in addition to welcoming the Ursuline Sisters to New Orleans, the colony also provided financial support to the work of the sisters because it was seen as serving the whole community. In the letter that Sister Therese of St. Francis Xavier first wrote to President Jefferson on behalf of the Ursulines, she pleaded that their ministries were "for the public good" and that their institution was both "useful" and "necessary." This snatch of history suggests that public-private partnerships are not new in this country and that we might learn much from the many years and experiences of the past.

Since the late 1800s, the partnership that religious social service providers and other organizations have developed with cities, counties, states and the federal government involve regular contracting to care for vulnerable infants, protect children from abusive family situations, operate group homes for severely disabled adults, resettle refugees, provide training for the unemployed, and house elderly residents. Governments are more likely to contract out social services to religious and other agencies that specialize in such services than to provide direct social services themselves. (If you think about it, this is similar to the building of government ships and airplanes, done by major corporations, or medical research that is funded by government at university medical schools.) In addition, in the social arena governments largely retain to themselves the direct functions of income support programs such as Social Security, Unemployment Compensation, Temporary Assistance to Needy Families, and Supplemental Security Income. They also determine eligibility for income programs and benefits such as food stamps, Medicaid and Medicare. On a number of occasions, when social service arrangements between religious providers and governments have been challenged, the

---

14.7 (1987) 23–27; "The Pluralism Diamond," *Social Thought* 14 (1988) 23–36; "Churches and Government" (April 24, 1996), "Churches and Social Services" (May 17, 2000), and "Faith and Fiction" (July 11, 2001) in my regular column in *The Catholic Commentator*, Diocese of Baton Rouge newspaper; and "Public-Religious Partnerships," *America* 184 (2001) 6–10.

U.S. Supreme Court has sanctioned such social service contracts, distinguishing such programs from its much more restrictive rulings on public aid to religious elementary and secondary education.

With this historical pre-note, we can now turn to the current debate over faith-based social initiatives. Since the welfare reform debate during the mid-nineties, our politics have seemed almost silent about the needs of families who are poor and vulnerable. They figured little in the 2000 and 2004 presidential campaign and debates; and, in 2008, concerns about poor families were smothered in the debate over the Iraq war, the general economic downturn, and what candidates would do for middle-America. When President Bush first urged congregations to take a more active role in meeting their communities' social needs, that call had been consistent with the call of the U.S. bishops to Catholic parishes in the two pastoral letters of the 1990s discussed in chapter 5: *Communities of Salt and Light* on the parish's social mission and *Called to Global Solidarity* on parish responsibility for suffering people worldwide. Catholic Charities agencies welcomed the concern of the Administration for mobilizing congregations since much more local action certainly was needed. As indicated earlier, PSM already had been an important emphasis in Catholic Charities for three decades.

As we have seen, Charities agencies also had another, equally important role through which they served as instruments of community service for Catholic dioceses. In this capacity they had cared for cocaine-addicted infants, provided foster homes for abused children, staffed group homes for adult persons with mental disabilities, built housing for the elderly, fed hungry families, sheltered abused wives and children, welcomed refugees and immigrants, and provided job training to welfare recipients. In this Gospel-inspired capacity, they worked in active concert with parishes and with local, state and federal governments who contracted with them for these services to people of all faiths and none. So, what was the big deal about the Bush initiative? What, too, about the plans of the Obama administration in this regard?

This is one of the most frustrating aspects of the faith-based debate, because religiously sponsored social service agencies have had such long-standing partnerships with government. These partnerships are essential to government and to the ability of Catholic Charities to serve more than seven million people in 2007. The mission-inspired tradition of the Ursuline Sisters in New Orleans continues today in more than 50,000 staff and a quarter of a million volunteers whose professional competence and voluntary commitment make Catholic Charities a reality in 1,400 locations nationwide. These partnership commitments usually result from careful government requests for proposals from social service agencies, competition among providers to deliver the most effective services at the least cost, and cautious oversight and appraisal by public officials. Some in the recent faith-based debate have expressed fears about unseemly competition among Churches. These too seem strange to Catholic Charities agencies which often have effective collaborations with Lutheran Services in America, the Salvation Army, Volunteers of America, members of the United Jewish Federation, and other faith-based organizations. Frankly, it is in the areas of social services and advocacy for justice and peace that the most effective forms of ecumenism occur in this country today.

So what advantages might come from this twenty-first-century emphasis at the federal level on the importance of faith-inspired social services? How might such partnerships be improved? When President Bush pledged to simplify bureaucratic requirements and establish a level playing field for religiously inspired and other service providers, Catholic Charities applauded this effort. Government bureaucrats sometimes overreached and, in so doing, threatened the organizational integrity of agencies, as we saw in chapter 2. The poor and vulnerable deserve the best qualified and most effective services. This is why Catholic Charities support efforts to credential licensed professionals, screen out volunteers who may be dangerous to children, and accredit agencies for services. In the view of Catholic Charities leaders, agencies not only can, but should, be both mission-driven and competent. Moreover, to promote more effective partnerships, governments should pay their social service partners in a timely and adequate fashion. When they do not, agencies often have to borrow to meet payroll and pay other expenses, incurring interest charges that are usually not reimbursed by public authorities. Government also should eliminate unfair advantages of for-profit corporations now invading the world of social services with a thirst for margins of profit that may jeopardize the well-being of abused children and the frail elderly.

In the Catholic community, our practice has generally been to establish separate organizations to serve those who are poor and vulnerable. For example, we have Catholic Charities agencies, St. Vincent de Paul societies, and residential care institutions for people with disabilities and abused and neglected children. Incorporating such programs separately from local parishes and dioceses has many advantages, including economies of scale, targeting of fiscal and personnel resources, and the ability to hire professional staff and qualify for accreditation. Entering directly into a government service contract would subject a parish or local congregation to a host of new rules, as well as opening up its budgets to government audits. For most local churches, it is more practical to create or collaborate with a separate non-profit organization to handle administrative headaches. This too might obviate some of the concerns which opponents of faith-based initiatives have about direct assistance to Churches, and the concerns of some churches about becoming "entangled" with government. (These separate corporations are not without challenges, discussed in the next two sections.)

Those in public life also must be made aware of the great need for public-private partnerships for additional housing for low-income families—a goal effectively abandoned by government more than 25 years ago. We could learn much from the highly successful Section 202 housing projects for the elderly and disabled. These government-funded complexes—operated by religiously sponsored and other organizations and sometimes built on church land—are highly successful. Construction was funded by government grants and residents often use a government Section 8 voucher to help pay their rent. In those same facilities, many volunteers may help with recreation, reading, transportation, health care, or a wide variety of other personal supports. One needs only look at the long waiting lists in most communities to recognize the value-add of these partnership arrangements. The second great need for partnerships is for more safe, quality day care for children of working parents. Catholic Charities and other local groups again could help to meet those needs. Despite the significant federal deficits created in the past eight years and the massive accumulated debt, significant federal investments should be made now for both housing and child care, both of which would provide jobs and a much-needed stimulus to the economy. In these and far too many other areas of human need, there are long waiting lines for service and all-too-depleted private resources.

Before a new administration goes too far down the road of some new promotion of so-called faith-based initiatives, however, there are caution signs along this highway that must be noted here. The most telling reports come in the *National Congregations Study* conducted by university researchers in the late nineties and again between 2006 and 2007. What they reveal in part is the distinction at the close of the last chapter in what volunteers do in church congregations in terms of the kinds of services that they render as distinct from church-sponsored social services agencies such as Catholic Charities. That distinction should add more reality to public policy debates on government initiatives in this area. The comprehensive 1998 *National Congregations Study* of 1,236 churches was led by professor Mark Chaves, then of the University of Arizona and now at Duke University. The first significant finding was that large congregations, African-American congregations, and Catholic and theologically liberal or moderate Protestant congregations were most likely to avail themselves of the provisions of "charitable choice," part of the welfare reform legislation that allowed states to contract directly with church congregations to deliver social services.

Those least likely to apply for government funds were congregations described by their leaders as theologically and politically conservative. This first finding contrasted sharply with the national political debate where those who most advocated for charitable choice provisions were political and religious conservatives and those most opposed were political and religious liberals.

The second significant finding was that churches were more likely to engage in activities that address the immediate needs of individuals for food, clothing, and shelter than in projects that require sustained involvement to meet longer term goals. So, the kinds of services most needed by people moving from welfare to work—job training, transportation, child care—were very seldom conducted by churches. This second finding is related to the work of volunteers and was supported by the experience of Catholic Charities nationwide where volunteer numbers had increased substantially precisely as emergency services such as food and shelter programs had increased markedly, as noted in chapter 6. The survey of congregations also indicated that the total number of volunteers provided by individual congregations remained small. They were most likely to be involved in areas such as food and housing, where organizations were able to take advantage of congregations' capacity to mobilize relatively small numbers of volunteers to carry out well-defined tasks.[4]

4. Mark A. Chaves, *National Congregations Study, 1998* (Ann Arbor, MI: Inter-university Consortium for Political and Social Research, 2002) and the study was sponsored by the National Opinion Research Center.

Even more caution now should follow from the findings of the *National Congregations Study—Wave II* as it reports from the second phase of the study, this time of 1,506 congregations. The key finding of this 2006–2007 study, after six or seven years of the Bush faith-based initiative, is this:

> And even after the Bush administration's faith-based initiative, *there is no increase* since 1998 in congregations' involvement in social services, receipt of public funds for their social services work, or collaboration with government.[5]

A number of other changes in church congregations nationwide were reported in the survey, but no change was reported in this key area on which so much public policy debate and time had been expended in the nineties and earlier in this decade.

If that is the case, how have we arrived at this 2009 heralding of the faith-based initiative which in fact has produced little effect? To understand we have to return to the welfare reform debate of the mid-nineties and persistent and even strident messages of the proponents of charitable choice and other provisions of that legislation. First, they argued that private religious providers are better than public providers, so government programs for the poor should be reduced. In making this argument, proponents continued trying to separate church and government in ways that were not true to history nor to the present realities of social services. For example, one U.S. senator observed to me, "The church social services have millions of volunteers, but few people ever volunteer at the welfare or social security office." To this I responded there was a broad middle ground, where agencies like Catholic Charities or Lutheran Social Ministries use government dollars for programs in which there are thousands of volunteers as well. This middle ground was an uncomfortable truth for those trying to demonize government and glorify Church programs.

Later, when Catholic Charities USA and other major religious social services providers opposed the logic of dividing church and government in this way—and the resulting draconian cuts in government social services and family support programs—the same people then argued that

---

5. Mark Chaves and Shawna Anderson, "Continuity and Change in American Congregations: Introducing the Second Wave of National Congregations Study," *Sociology of Religion* 699 (2008) 415–40 at 420 (emphasis added).

government money corrupts the private religious provider who is restricted in terms of proselytism and thus denies to the poor the essentially
religious component of needed personal change that could only come in a
church-based program. Therefore, it was argued, government should cut
back on supporting welfare and social services programs for the needy (in
effect including the work of religiously-sponsored social services) and let
the churches pick up the slack with tax-exempt contributions, an army of
volunteers, and muscular spiritual reform for welfare dependent families.
The White House faith-based office was an outgrowth of this thinking
that, with a lot of fanfare and some small financial investments, local congregations would transform their communities and the poor. From the
national study above, it does not appear that such has occurred or was
possible.

To conclude this section, it should be clear at this point that the debate over government funding and encouragement of "faith-based initiatives" needs to make at least one major distinction that seems to have
eluded those who see the world only in terms of the church-government
"either/or":

- First, there are Church-sponsored social services agencies—
  Catholic Charities, Lutheran Social Services, Jewish charities,
  etc.—that have a longstanding relationship to government that
  has given rise to the current partnerships that generally have
  these key indicators: service to people in need without regard
  to their religion; refusal to proselytize the poor in serving them;
  religious and ethical values to which the agency is committed
  and which guide its identity, purposes, and means; hiring of staff
  and recruitment of board members who respect and are committed to the agency's mission and identity, even if they do not
  belong to the sponsoring church; the possible retention of certain positions within the organization for co-religionists, such as
  the chief executive officer, the mission officer, and, in Catholic
  Charities, the director of PSM; fiscal and service accountability
  of the agency to the funding partners; and some formal affiliation
  with the sponsoring church. These characteristics seem to have
  weathered decades of testing in various forms and to validate
  these partnerships from both sides (church and state), allowing
  both government funding and tax exemptions. These relation-

ships are not, however, without problems, as discussed earlier and in the next section.

- Second, there is the basically new proposal of the past decade or so to fund churches or congregations directly by government to deliver social services. This proposal and, to whatever extent implemented in the past ten years or so, has continued to raise a number of religious and legal questions: whether hiring of all staff can be restricted to co-religionists; whether proselytizing is allowed and, in the context of the welfare reform debate, necessary to "cure" the poor; whether certain religions will be "tainted" by government money or government relations; whether to allow government to regulate the practices of churches such as service quality, finance, and hiring; and whether social services could be restricted only to those of the same religion. These arrangements continue to be highly debated, are questionable at best within the constitutional framework that has evolved over the past century, and, as we have seen from the *National Congregations Study*, have had little impact.

One might well conclude, then, that the initiative that received major impetus from the proponents of the "welfare reform" of the 1990s—proposed as the cure for poverty and dependence—and was implemented in part in the Bush administration's White House Office was not only badly conceived; but it was not needed, doubtfully legal, and has not taken root in American social services or in American churches.

THE PLURALISM OF CATHOLIC CHARITIES

In the wake of the confusing history and dubious state of the faith-based initiative of the past decade or two, it would be good to look more carefully at the complex and nuanced position of Catholic Charities on pluralism—as articulated and practiced in various ways across the country. In the discussion above in chapter 3 of the *2007 Survey* by CARA, the areas of government contracts for services and the amounts of funding involved were briefly described. The actual survey data is broken down into subcategories, as, for example, twenty-five separate categories of funding from health and human services programs ranging from Medicaid and Medicare to Child Day Care, Mental Health Services, and

Hurricane Katrina Relief Programs. In chapter 5, we saw the reports on the number of performance-based contracts and alliances with public and private organizations. Suffice it to say, there are literally thousands of separate agreements between Catholic Charities agencies and some branch and level of government to provide services to people in need in this country, and they involve hundreds of millions of dollars of program services. This has prompted a long history within the Catholic Charities family of focusing on the meaning of pluralism in social services in this country and, specifically, within Charities agencies. How do agencies view and maintain their Catholic identity within these realities? The answer supplements the discussion of Catholic identity in chapter 2 with this chapter's treatment of pluralism.

The most participative and formal statement on this pluralism came from the development of the 1987 policy statement of Catholic Charities USA entitled "Catholic Charities and Pluralism." The statement was developed in draft by a task force of members, discussed in regional meetings around the country, and then, after debate and amendments, approved by the membership congress at their meeting in San Antonio—the same meeting that Pope John Paul II addressed (see chapter 1). That statement reads as follows:

> *Pluralism in this paper means that state or conditions of affairs in our country in which a variety of religious traditions live and work under a constitutional, democratic government which recognizes persons' rights to religious freedom and freedom of conscience.*
>
> 1. *Catholic Charities agencies and institutions are voluntary associations* which incorporate a religious identity and, as such, are concrete dynamic expressions of the human and constitutionally protected rights of freedom of religion and association.
>
> 2. *When viewed theologically,* Catholic Charities agencies and institutions can be considered to both transcend and enhance the interest of the state to the extent that they are grounded in and embody religious meaning and values.
>
> 3. *Catholic Charities agencies and institutions have a prophetic, critical* role to play in drawing from their value system to participate in education and public debate about social issues.
>
> 4. *Catholic Charities agencies and institutions enhance genuine pluralism* by enabling choice, promoting action in society, and by

joining with other religious bodies and social agencies in ongoing dialogue that fosters individual freedom and liberty, and to discern, call attention to, and oppose the causes of oppression.

5. *As advocates for and contributors to the common good,* Catholic Charities agencies, as well as other voluntary social agencies which make similar contributions, deserve not only acceptance but support which should not be conditioned on requirements that weaken agency identity and integrity.

6. *The state, as the political entity formally responsible for the common good,* may appropriately require accountability of Catholic Charities and other voluntary agencies for standards of service and expenditures of public monies.[6]

As you can see, the statement combines positions on constitutionality within the framework of the United States (freedom of religion and association, pluralism, and free speech) with those drawn from Catholic social teaching and theology (the common good, justice, advocacy, and subsidiarity).

In my opinion, there are five key assertions in the policy statement: (1) Catholic Charities agencies are an expression of First Amendment rights of freedom of religion and association; (2) in theological terms, Catholic Charities agencies are essentially more valuable ("transcends" is the final language[7]) in a way than the political entities that fund and regulate them since Charities express and embody religious beliefs and values; (3) in keeping with the principle of subsidiarity and U.S. pluralism, Catholic Charities agencies and services enrich the world of social welfare by providing variety and freedom of choice in society; (4) since Catholic Charities embody constitutional rights, enrich social welfare, and contribute to the common good, government should not only support their work, but also try not to undermine their identity and integrity by *intrusive* funding or regulatory requirements; and (5) Catholic Charities acknowledge that they must be held accountable for money received from government and the services that they contract to deliver to people in need.[8]

6. "Catholic Charities and Pluralism," 1987 Policy Statement of Catholic Charities USA, *Charities USA* 14.9 (1987) 27 (emphasis in original).

7. The earlier draft debated in regional meetings read: of a "higher order."

8. Adapted from "Pluralism Diamond," 24.

At the time of the development of the policy statement, I was asked to make a presentation on the topic at a meeting of Catholic Charities representatives from the mid-South region. From that initial presentation in 1987 and discussions at the Catholic Charities USA annual Leadership Institute between 1992 and 2001, I tried to capture the reality of pluralism within Catholic Charities with the tensions that arise from the combination of democratic and religious values in our pluralism, the diversity of staff and persons served, the tensions in American political life, the variety of funding sources, the regulatory and ethical requirements, and the demands of different constituencies. I first used the image of a "diamond;"[9] and, because of both its durability and beauty, it still captures the array of forces, factors, and opportunities of these agencies. Light shining through a diamond also reflects and is refracted in many ways.

In trying to conceptualize key areas of stress associated with pluralism, the diamond identified certain institutional and other relationships—stakeholders, we might say—for a Charities agency that both create its pluralism and can create problems as well. The three points on left side of the diamond represent funding constituencies, the primary three being the Church (dioceses and the Catholic faithful), the civic community (United Way, foundations, corporations, and private donors), and government at various levels. The right side of the diamond mirrors the left and represents major influences on the shape of services provided by agencies: "who, what, how, when, where, and why." The three points of influence are:

- the Catholic Church with its values, principles, norms, and compassion drawn from Scripture, theology, Catholic social teaching, and Catholic Christian spirituality that inspired the very creation of these agencies and that sustains them today;

- the legal and regulatory framework and specific requirements imposed by government in enabling legislation, regulations, and contractual provisions that attach to specific funding as well as its general constitutional and legal framework; and

- the ethics and skills of the professions (social workers, therapists, attorneys, accountants, fundraisers, public relations specialists, etc.) represented in the staffs and services, that often are stan-

---

9. Ibid., 32.

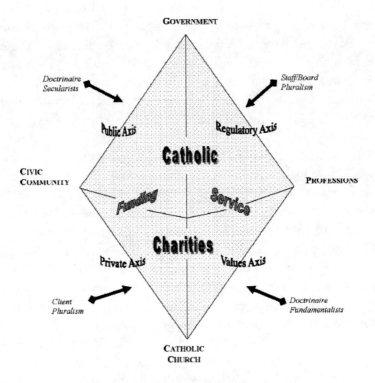

THE PLURALISM DIAMOND

dards expected and monitored by the civic community, funding sources of all kinds, individual donors, and accrediting bodies.

The Catholic Charities agency is at the center of these forces and is influenced by each of them in different ways. It is the pressure of these diverse forces, like the earth's pressure on carbon, that creates the hardened and beautiful diamond that is Catholic Charities in this country. The challenge is—no small feat of strength, balance, or even grace—to keep them all in proper proportion so the diamond is not split or crushed.

Outside the diamond I have identified four key sources of tension in maintaining this balance. They exist because of the multiple constituencies and funding sources of Charities—Church, government, civic community, including the poor, and the professions. First, in the upper left are what the 1987 pluralism task force called *doctrinaire secularists*. These are the folks pushing on the "public axis" (government and civil society) who, in pursuit of extreme forms of Church-state separation, urge cutting off government funding to sectarian agencies, tying one hand—the advocacy arm—of tax-exempt groups, trying to eliminate competition with business by non-profits, or imposing controversial values or practices that conflict with the religious values of the agencies (for example, insisting on abortion referrals, adoptions by gay couples, reports of undocumented clients to civil authorities, or mandatory staff health insurance coverage for contraception).

In the lower right corner, pressing on the "values axis" where Catholic Charities blend elements drawn from the Catholic Church and the professions of staff, are those I call the *doctrinaire fundamentalists*, here both Catholics and Protestants who have a very narrow view of religion and its role in public life. From this outside pressure point, state licensing and professional ethics are challenged in the name of religious freedom and religious values, such as objections to requiring licensing of counselors or handicapped accessibility of buildings. Some Catholics insist on only their own narrow interpretation of what Catholics and Catholic Charities should do about war or abortion in the public sector, that all adopted babies should have Catholic parents, or that collaboration with "suspect" religious or secular groups should be avoided.

In the lower left-hand corner is the pressure on the "private axis" than comes from *client pluralism*. Catholic Charities and Church leadership actively promote the service of all in need in the community and this openness usually is required by government and civic funders as well. Here the problems come when a client wants an abortion referral or contraception information, insists on only seeing a Catholic counselor, demands as a Catholic to be moved to the top of the adoption waiting list ahead of non-Catholics, or expects free service regardless of the sliding scale designed to give some recognition to the priority concern for the poor in Catholic social thought.

The fourth stress-point can be *staff and board pluralism*, coming in from the upper right along the "regulatory axis." Moved by nondiscrimination requirements of government and civic funders, the need for professional staff to meet often-highly-specialized service requirements, the recognition of the richness that an ecumenical staff brings to service delivery, and the decline in the number of priests and religious in Charities agencies, staffs have become immensely varied in terms of religious affiliation (or none).[10] In addition, prompted by funding sources, by practical ecumenism, and by the need to involve the wider community and persons of varying skills and backgrounds in policymaking and fundraising, many agencies have expanded board membership beyond the Catholic community. This is true with corporate boards and, where the corporate board members remain the bishop and a few others, it is the case of advisory boards that often exercise genuine policy leadership.

This staff and board pluralism can strain the ability to agree on agency goals and priorities or ethical norms for professional and other services, to project a consistent image in the midst of the civic community's pluralism, and even to coalesce within the agency around a coherent mission and identity. This can make Charities vulnerable to critics in the civic community and even those within the Catholic community who do not understand the complexity of Catholic mission and identity. Ultimately it could threaten the moral and financial support for the future of the agency.

As you can see, while each constituency and each funding source brings its own strengths and support to Catholic Charities, individually or in combination they can present challenges to the identity and survivability of the agency. What does an agency need to do, then, to maintain its balance and sustain the beauty and strength of the diamond? A number of concrete steps[11] are necessary:

1. Catholic Charities must identify the agency and its mission as both Catholic and as an expression of the social mission of the Roman Catholic Church, an embodiment of the servant model of Church, explicitly authorized by the local diocesan bishop, and actively linked to Catholic parishes and the larger Catholic community. Clarity about mission and identity gives the agency a strong foundation to address other issues.

2. Agencies should adopt and adapt as appropriate the *Catholic Charities USA Code of Ethics* and educate all board members,

10. In my experience as a local director at Catholic Community Services in Baton Rouge, our other-than-Catholic staff were among the most loyal to the agency and its mission, often sharing deep values and religious commitments in their work for the agency and those it served.

11. These are adapted from "The Pluralism Diamond," 34–36. See also, Msgr. Charles J. Fahey, "The 'Catholic' in Catholic Charities," *Who Do You Say We Are*, 19–23 on "essential elements."

staff, and volunteers on its substance, relevance, and everyday requirements.

3. Charities must respect the pluralism of all clients based in their natural rights, dignity, and freedom. They must serve all clients, without regard to their religious affiliation, but within the limited means so often available to the agency and the priorities arising out of its mission and identity.

4. Agencies must deliver quality services and, where appropriate, seek the licensing and accreditation that assure that quality to clients, collaborators, and the entire community.

5. Charities should hire staff and develop boards that perceive and are committed to the mission of the agency and to act in accord with the Church's basic values and principles as applicable to the agency. This "hiring for mission" and "recruiting for mission" must respect the religious diversity of staff and board within the limitations of these values and principles.

6. Agencies should enhance the identity of staff and boards by purposeful exploration of agency identity and mission, by improving their knowledge and skills, and by values clarification. They should promote a spirituality of professional service by providing opportunities to staff and board to explore their mission, to raise consciousness as to the service of others by the people of God, and to unite work with prayer. Again, these practices must be offered in ways respectful of staff religious diversity. (Chapter 9 will continue this discussion of spirituality.)

7. Management must work with the agency board and staff to engage them regularly in processes that insure organizational integrity, renewal, and development regarding mission, strategic planning, quality improvement, regulatory compliance, fiscal and program audits, practices to insure transparency, and staff and volunteer development.[12]

8. Charities should maintain an active political responsibility, in collaboration with the diocese, including advocacy on social issues, pluralism, and human life and dignity.

---

12. *Code of Ethics*, section 3.02.

9. Agencies should maintain the well-earned place of Catholic Charities in the public sector, delivering quality family and social services, and resisting every effort to dilute their identities for the sake of securing or maintaining public or other funding.

10. Charities should continue and enhance collaboration with government, civic partners, and even those whose views are antithetical to those of the agency on one or another social or family issue. They should respect the shared values of other religious groups by ecumenical convening and collaboration in action within the scope of their common values.

11. Boards and management must provide fiscal accountability to governmental and other funders and regulatory and contract compliance with requirements that do not unduly intrude upon their protected freedoms and their underlying mission, values, and purposes.

These expectations and requirements are not new in the world of Catholic Charities, but they are the lessons of decades of experience and found in the practices of those agencies that are able to hold together their various stakeholders in ways that forward the mission of Charities and serve many people within their communities.

WHY PARTNER WITH GOVERNMENT?

Although Catholic Charities and other religiously-sponsored non-profits have worked out their partnership arrangements with government over much of the past century, we can see from the preceding section that it is not without a lot of care and effort on the part of agency boards, management, and staff and not without occasional misunderstanding or conflict. Why not simply eliminate the governmental partners and simplify the work of being a Catholic Charities agency?

In June of 1997, I was with the Volunteers of America (VOA) for their national meeting. Like Catholic Charities, VOA local agencies have a high percentage of government contracts with funding supporting a variety of their programs. As a religious organization that spun off from the Salvation Army in the early part of the twentieth century, VOA makes no apology for their partnerships with government. As Catholic Charities has done, they affirm the positive values of their public-private partnership and did so in these words in various materials that I received in connection with this meeting:

> Many Volunteers of America services receive some local, state and federal government support. Enhancing this long-standing partnership with the citizen, we also engage the American spirit of giving through foundations, corporations, churches and individual donors, and the work of thousands of dedicated volunteers. The result is an efficient and accountable organization. More than 85% of combined Volunteers of America revenues go directly to program services.

VOA's description of a "long-standing partnership with the citizen" was very striking. Decisions about government programs for the poor and vulnerable are ways in which elected officials choose to meet the needs of citizens with the taxes paid by citizens and in programs often adopted at the request of citizens. Rather than a negative, VOA in effect begins with this positive consideration.

In the "ten ways that Catholic Charities are Catholic" in chapter 2, the one point in my experience that is most surprising, even to Catholics, is number nine: *Catholic Charities support an active public-private partnership with government at all levels.* It could also be the most controversial. In my years at Catholic Charities USA, I found that this reality was unknown to most people, a practical mystery to liberals, and a sometimes scandal to conservatives. The partnership positioned Catholic Charities in a middle place between those who would have social services delivered solely by government or entirely secular organizations and those who eschew any relationship with government and any role of government in the delivery of needed social services or care of the poor. As we have seen in this and earlier chapters, this partnership between Catholic Charities and government is hardly new in this country and at least 1500 years old in other parts of the world.

This brings us to the central discussion of this section, why Catholic Charities do and *should* enter into such partnerships with local, state, and Federal governments. Even this discussion, however, must be seen in light of the responsibility of all the community to care for those in need in their midst. In their 1999 statement *In All Things Charity: A Pastoral Challenge for the New Millennium,* the U.S. Catholic bishops posed the question, "Who can and should respond to the call for charity and justice?" In their answer, they specifically mention every baptized person, families, parishes, religious congregations, lay associations, dioceses, and the public, private, and voluntary sectors of society. Meeting the needs of the poor and vulnerable is everybody's business and everyone's contribution is needed today in a country where tens of millions of people still live in poverty.

Government, however, has a moral responsibility for justice in society in Catholic Social Teaching. Pope Benedict emphasized this in his first encyclical (see the discussion in chapter 1). The U.S. bishops explained this responsibility earlier in their 1999 pastoral letter on charity:

> Our Catholic tradition teaches that the moral function of government is to protect human rights and secure basic justice for all members of the commonwealth. Society as a whole and in all its subsidiary parts is responsible for building up the common good and for responding to the needs of the poor and vulnerable. But government is responsible for guaranteeing that the minimum conditions for social activity, including both human rights and justice, are met.[13]

The bishops go on to describe particular government policies that are included within its moral responsibility, including the provision of certain services to insure basic human needs.

> How society responds to the needs of the poor through its public policies serves as the litmus test for whether it conforms to the demands of justice and charity. The Church has long supported minimum wage and fair labor standards as essential for the protection of workers. For those who cannot find fair wages or cannot work due to age, disability, parental responsibilities, or another cause, the economic safety net must be ensured by government insurance and income support systems. "The programs that make up this system should serve the needs of the poor in a manner that respects their dignity and provides adequate support."[14]

This provision of social welfare programs received attention from the Second Vatican Council, which the bishops also cite in their pastoral letter.

> Catholic social teaching assigns a positive role for government in social welfare. Thus the Fathers of the Second Vatican Council

---

13. *In All Things Charity,* 38.
14. Ibid., quoting *Economic Justice for All,* 210.

declared that "the growing complexity of modern situations makes it necessary for public authority to intervene more frequently in social, cultural and economic matters in order to achieve conditions more favorable to the free and effective pursuit by citizens and groups of the advancement of people's total well-being." As a result of the Great Depression, which lasted from 1929 to 1941, it became evident to people of the United States that only the government could develop resources to ensure regular income support for aged, disabled, or otherwise needy families. It has accomplished this by establishing such vehicles as Social Security; retirement, disability, and survivors' programs; unemployment compensation; workers' compensation; food stamps; and dependent children programs. No private charity has the resources, for example, to provide steady monthly support to families without adequate income. These beliefs and principles, however, have come under attack during the latter part of the twentieth century as a negative attitude developed with regard to the responsibility of government to develop the policies and programs that make it possible for all people to fulfill their basic human needs.[15]

The bishops' discussion balances a variety of roles: all in society have a responsibility for those in need; government has a special responsibility to assure human rights and basic justice; and, in fulfilling its role, modern government has to assure the provision of basic income and social service to those who cannot work or have special needs.

Does government have to be the provider of all social services to people in need? Not at all. As we already have seen, in the U.S. a partnership has evolved in which government decides to fund a service needed by the elderly, abused children, the homeless, or people with disabilities; and it contracts with a non-profit organization to provide those services. As the bishops described this, "For at least a century, religious and community-based nonprofit organizations have been providing social services under contracts with governments at all levels. This system of joint responsibility has served children and families, communities, and society very well."[16] Two concrete examples may help to explain the complementarity of government and social service agencies. Nowhere is this more evident than in the child welfare system, where government exercises its legal powers to remove abused children from their homes and supports them financially.

15. Ibid., 38–39, citing *Gaudium et Spes*, 75.
16. Ibid., 42.

Then government entrusts many of these abused children to the care of private agencies in a variety of group homes, foster care placements, and institutions. And, while religious agencies have public funds and do not use them to proselytize, they do in fact attend to the full person: physical, emotional, intellectual, and spiritual. Similarly, when refugees come to the U.S. fleeing war and persecution, our government admits them to the country and provides basic funds for core resettlement services and even time-limited welfare support to the refugee family. Yet it is church volunteers recruited by religious social services providers who are the sponsoring families, offering friendship and teaching the refugee family about U.S. customs, and volunteers and staff who provide intense social and personal support in the critical first months of resettlement.

With this framework in mind, why would Catholic Charities choose to be one of those nonprofit agencies who agree to participate with government in meeting social service needs of the poor and vulnerable? Why not leave this to other groups? There are a number of compelling reasons:

First, these partnerships strengthen Charities' gospel-based mission of diakonia (service). Put very simply, the mission of Catholic Charities begins in service to people in need, and these partnerships make it possible for agencies to carry out that mission more effectively and widely. As Pope Benedict emphasized, this *diakonia* lies at the heart of the identity of the Church; and, without it, the Church is not true to its inner nature and its mission in the world. Whether the means are surplus government grain in the fifth century, good will donations in the "poor box" in the parish, or contemporary partnerships with a city or state, service to the needy is an intrinsic part of this Church. It is who we are and who we are called to be.

Second, these partnerships greatly expand the ability of Catholic Charities to bring quality care and compassionate service to people in need. Partnerships with public authorities multiply church and community resources many times over, allowing agencies to bring their expertise, commitment to quality, and Gospel-based compassion to millions more people and in a greater variety of programs and services than would be available otherwise. They help as well to strengthen agency infrastructure which in turn facilitates broader services to communities. The ability to use public funds, however, is often dependent on the religious and other human and financial resources of the agencies. These resources initially create the organizations, staff and fund their core competencies, establish their capacity to partner with governments, and often provide a financial "match" of some sort required by the public partner.

Third, these partnerships support the public sector's responsibility to serve the common good and protect the most vulnerable in society. As we have seen in chapter one, the common good represents "the sum total of social conditions which allow people, either as groups or as individuals, to reach their fulfillment more fully and more easily."[17] While the common good is everyone's responsibility, these partnerships allow Charities specifically to assist public bodies in their special responsibilities for its promotion and for the care of the poor and vulnerable.

Fourth, these partnerships promote the Catholic principle of subsidiarity by having the actual delivery of services, even those which government must fund, performed by religious and other non-profit community-based organizations. As the U.S. bishops had indicated in their pastoral on charity, there are some things best done by government, such as the determination of eligibility for benefits and direct assistance payments. But, in the area of social services to the poor and vulnerable and in service to American pluralism, government's responsibilities can and should be served in a variety of ways and by a number of providers who bring a wealth of trained staff, volunteers, private funds, and dedicated commitment to their part of this partnership. The bishops put it this way: "This pluralism has been an essential characteristic of twentieth-century social service delivery in the United States. Pluralism in public programs is strengthened and made more genuine when individuals can choose to receive social services through a variety of providers, including religiously affiliated social services organizations."[18] The availability of a plethora of organizations to partner with government is a richness developed in U.S. communities across the country, and it allows government to bring services to people in need through local and familiar outlets. The Salvation Army, Lutheran Services, Jewish Federation, Volunteers of America, YMCA, Catholic Charities, senior and community centers, and hundreds of other organizations are a richness not found in comparable number and scope in other countries. In so partnering, government and its partners insure pluralism, consumer choice, and community responsiveness

17. *Compendium*, 164, quoting *Gaudium et Spes*, 26.
18. *In All Things Charity*, 39.

in the delivery of greatly needed services to our most vulnerable citizens whether funded from city hall, the state capitol, or Washington.

Fifth, these partnerships bring the Catholic Church into sectors of society where it may not normally be present, enhancing its reputation for good among the general population and enabling it to reach populations it might not otherwise touch. Being able to provide housing to the elderly, re-settlement services to refugees, or care for persons with disabilities allows the Catholic Church through the instrumentality of Catholic Charities to be present to people with whom it may only have occasional contact at Sunday Mass or, in the case of other-than-Catholics, none at all. It is an enormous source of credibility for the Gospel and for the Catholic community, creating immense good will in many communities.

Sixth, these partnerships enable the Church to exercise faith-based influence on a major sector of civil society—as we can do in education and health care—whose roots are actually in the Church. Because the Catholic Church sponsors the largest voluntary social services, education, and health care networks of institutions in the United States, we are able to bring our Gospel-based values and experience to these critically important fields of human endeavor so central to the common good of any society. These three sets of professions and institutions, however secular they may seem, all had their roots in the ministries of the Catholic Church. In the world of social services and social welfare, the very size and scope of the Catholic Charities network gives it the opportunity to bring its values, ethics, and passions into debates over the shape of social services and the professions associated with it. Combined with the social work schools in Catholic universities, this network has an enormous opportunity for influencing social work practice and social institutions. This is especially important as a growing number of for-profit corporations are moving into the field of human services and the strictures of budget cuts and managed care threaten the quality of care in the interest of the bottom-line.

Seventh, these partnerships give Catholic Charities both familiarity with the workings of publicly funded services and a set of practical relation-ships with policy makers from which to advocate for more effective social policies and programs. The word here is "credibility." Providing assistance to seven million people in a year is an incredible experience to bring to the national debate about the common good and how to care for the poor and vulnerable. Even more particularly, by actually operating programs and providing services that elected officials have decided are needed by the public, Catholic Charities can work with these same officials to try to insure that programs are as effective as possible in meeting those needs. This advocacy, as noted in chapter four, may take the form of legislative testimony, regulatory advocacy, working on government commissions, participating in research, or informal communications with elected or appointed officials. It is also in dialogue with public officials and by working with them that Catholic Charities and others in the voluntary sector are able to bring innovative programs, initially funded by other sources, to the attention of policy makers as models for future legislative or administrative initiatives.

Eighth, these partnerships are effective "good news"—immensely good people in faith-based organizations reaching out to the least of these. This partnering with cities, states, and the national government is effective charity, an immense treasure of the Church, and something of which all Catholics—liberal and conservative, Republican and Democrat and Independent—can be proud. Enormous human, financial, and spiritual resources are brought together in the service of those most in need in U.S. society. In addition, the hands-on work of Catholic Charities, done together with an array of public and private partners, puts flesh on the bones of the Church's teaching about the just and caring society. As Pope John Paul II put it, "Today more than ever, the Church is aware that her social message will gain credibility more immediately from the *witness of actions* than as a result of its internal logic and consistency."[19]

CONCLUSION

Pluralism, as we have seen, is both an opportunity for Catholic Charities and a challenge. "Getting it right" has taken almost a century; but it remains a constant task at which the leaders and staff of agencies must work carefully. The opportunities of weaving together so many stakeholders and so rich a variety of resources should not be taken lightly, nor should they be easily dismissed by outside commentators unfamiliar with the realities and complexities of contemporary social welfare in this country.

19. Pope John Paul II, *Centesimus Annus* (1991), 57.

8

Quality and Innovation

Doing Good as Well as Possible

*W*HEN I VISITED CATHOLIC *Charities of San Diego in the late nine-ties, Sister RayMonda DuVall, the director, showed me their Food Resource Center (FRC) and proudly explained how their agency had turned direct food assistance into a more empowering program for those they served. The clients of the program are mostly single mothers who in the past had been given a basket or box of food prepared by staff or volunteers after appropriate screening of family needs and resources. Such a food distribution program exists in many Catholic Charities agencies and other community groups. She had challenged her staff to consider ways that food services could be transformed into a more empowering program of the agency.*

After some coaxing from Sister DuVall, instead of simply distributing food, the staff set up a small grocery-like center where the food was arranged on shelves similar to those we might find in food stores and supermarkets. After screening, clients were allowed a certain amount of "credit" to shop for food for their families and determined how many times a year they would do so. The empowering began in people making choices for themselves and their families about the food they would prepare and eat, instead of being handed a bag or a box of food someone else had selected. The process continued with staff working with clients about food choices and then, through group processes, recognizing their own resources and their ability to leverage other resources, develop peer support, and gain the skills needed to access those resources.

As the staff reported two years ago about the Food Resource Center, "Over the years, we have received numerous letters from FRC members, describing the sense of dignity and self-respect that they felt by this simple act of 'shopping' for food."[1] *The empowerment approach of the agency is also critically important to its highly rated Welfare-to-Work Program, its refugee resettlement program, and the Rachel's Women's Services for homeless women. The Rachel's Women's Center also sponsors the Tomorrow Project, a shop and production facility that functions as a job readiness program for homeless women who "assemble and sell our unique, chef-created soups, and rubs." The goal of the Project is to "learn life skills and evolve into confident, productive individuals with a future."*[2]

It is difficult to measure or generalize about the innovative character and quality of so many diverse services offered by hundreds of locally directed Catholic Charities agencies across the country. Instead, it may be more helpful to discuss an array of indicators of how many who care for the poor and vulnerable in Charities are constantly searching for better ways to do what they do, much as the staff and leadership in San Diego have done. The indicators described in this chapter are: outcomes-focus, research, accreditation, innovation, and, yes, awards. If a person unfamiliar with Catholic Charities wanted an overview that captures many of these indicators, they might watch video replays of two 1999 installments in season six of the award-winning PBS series *The Visionaries* with host Sam Waterston. There, in two hours, are captured a micro-business program of Catholic Charities of Omaha, housing and neighborhood revitalization by Charities in Brooklyn, a greenhouse project employing persons with disabilities of Catholic Charities Bureau in Superior, Wisconsin, a Catholic Charities program for the elderly in Honolulu, a child day-care center in Denver, and a Charities job-training program in Minneapolis. Together they visually capture agency inventiveness, concern, and effectiveness, shown in the lives of the people whom they serve.

OUTCOMES AND RESEARCH

In the last twenty years public and private funders have placed an increasing emphasis in human services on outcomes and outcomes-measures. In many cases, these are replacing the older "units of service" (e.g. number

1. "Empowerment: Finding the Chicken in the Soup," *Charities USA* 33.3 (2006) 10–11.

2. See Tomorrow Project at www.tomorrowproject.org for details and contact information.

of meals served, number of hours of counseling, number of clients, etc.) or at least supplementing them. The *2007 Survey* asked the respondents to report in three ways on outcome evaluation of programs. Reports were made by both diocesan Charities agencies and by some programs within diocesan agencies, so the totals in some cases exceed the 171 diocesan agencies reporting. The first question was about data sources used for outcome evaluation. This can be one of the most difficult challenges of the current emphasis on outcomes from funders, since progress in many cases may be more difficult to measure or, indeed, even subjective. Agencies were asked about four specific data sources and the following numbers were reported for those using each source (an agency may use more than one of these)[3]:

Client Records	250
Client Satisfaction Systems	233
Client Tracking Systems	209
Pre/Post Test	174
Other	82
None	4

CARA indicated that a majority of the reporting agencies in fact did use client records, satisfaction systems, tracking, *and* pre-and-post testing.

The survey then asked about a variety of methods commonly employed in outcome evaluation, and the number of agencies using each follows[4]:

Comparison of Benchmarks	199
Formal Program Evaluation	179
Goal Area or Peer Review Teams	155
Retrospective Analysis of Data	152
Longitudinal Studies	37
Other	48
Not conducting analysis	15

3. *2007 Survey*, 6.
4. Ibid.

As you can see, Catholic Charities agencies are least likely to use longitudinal studies as a method of outcome evaluation.

Agencies were also asked to indicate their preferred methods for reporting program outcomes. As CARA noted, "Agencies tend to prefer either a contract/funding report or internal management reports, although nearly as many display program outcomes in an annual report." Respondents did indicate at least a dozen other formats for reporting program outcomes either internally or to the public or grantors.

In 2007, over thirty agencies reported being involved in research regarding their services and/or the people being served. Research concerned a wide range of topics including: the effects of exercise on cognition among seniors; family homelessness; hurricane evacuees; prison inmate literacy; the effect of mental health disorders on program participation; Head Start families; healthy marriage relationships; domestic violence; refugee resettlement; homeless women; addiction services; health practices of families with children with disabilities; aging in adults with mental retardation; early reading programs; open adoption; mentoring children of prisoners; and children with asthma.

Most reported research is being conducted with universities, including Union College, Loyola University of Chicago, University of Dayton, University of Buffalo, Johns Hopkins University, Michigan State University, UCLA, Norwalk Community College, Tuffs University, University of Delaware, Temple University, Stanford University, and St. Louis University. Research was also reported with the National Center on Family Homelessness, the National Resource Center for Family Centered Practice, the Atlantic Social Research Corporation; the Urban Institute; and the Constella Group. Public research was reported in conjunction with the states of New York, Ohio, and Hawaii and the City of New York, as well as federal research dealing with substance abuse and mental health, mentoring kids of prisoners, and the Marriage for Keeps program. While participation in research does not in itself prove the quality of Charities' program methods and services, it does seem to indicate a desire to understand what truly helps and a willingness to make improvements where indicated.

ACCREDITATION

In 1977, the Child Welfare League of America and Family Service America (now the Alliance for Children and Families) began the now international Council on Accreditation (COA) to improve human services. Catholic Charities USA was one of the early supporters and is today one of the fourteen Sponsoring Organizations, along with the two founders and Lutheran Services in America, the Volunteers of America, the Association of Jewish Family and Children's Services, and others. The nineteen-member Board of Trustees includes representatives of three Catholic organizations, two from the U.S. and one from Canada.[5] COA describes its mission in this way, "The Council on Accreditation (COA) partners with human service organizations worldwide to improve service delivery outcomes by developing, applying, and promoting accreditation standards."[6] In terms of the scope of their work, "In 2007, COA accredited or was in the process of accrediting more than 1,800 private and public organizations that serve more than 7 million individuals and families in the United States, Canada, Bermuda, Puerto Rico, England and the Philippines."[7] COA's reports to Catholic Charities USA indicate that approximately seventy-five diocesan Charities agencies and an additional thirty other member organizations are included among those who have been accredited,[8] a process that must be repeated every third or fourth year, depending on the length of each period for which an agency is accredited. Several other agencies are accredited through other accrediting entities.

COA accredits private organizations, such as Catholic Charities, as well as public organizations, such as those operated by a state or county. There are separate standards for each, both of which are in their eighth edition and are extremely comprehensive. For example, the standards for private organizations cover administration, management, services, ethics, human resources, risk prevention, finances, audits, training, supervision, client rights, and, currently, forty-six different types of social and human

---

5. The three members are Sister Ann Patrick Conrad (chairperson) from the National Catholic School of Social Services at Catholic University, Sister Linda Yankoski of Holy Family Institute in Pittsburgh, and Christopher Leung, CEO of Catholic Social Services of Edmonton, Canada.

6. See, COA website at www.coanet.org for further information.

7. Ibid.

8. Email message of February 17, 2009 from Jane Stenson of Catholic Charities USA, liaison to COA.

services. The initial stages in the process involve initial applications, fees, study of a seventy-eight-page Policies and Procedures Manual, adapting agency practice to COA standards and COA guidelines, appointment of a full-time COA coordinator within the agency, staff training, and a comprehensive self-study which may last a year or more. A site visit is then conducted for a minimum of a day-and-a-half by a team consisting of a team leader and one or more peer reviewers, all of whom are volunteers from outside the agency and have received at least fifty hours of training for their responsibilities. There are four sets of final ratings of the agency and, depending on these, corrections must take place in agency practices and procedures to qualify for accreditation, if at all. Each year until the reaccreditation, the agency must prepare a Maintenance of Accreditation Report for COA.[9]

While accreditation may be necessary to qualify for certain types of licensing or insurance payments for services, COA suggests that the benefits are more wide-reaching, including improved service delivery, improved internal processes and procedures, improved employee morale, and recognition from governments, foundations and grant makers. A typical testimonial from an agency was sent out on December 17, 2008 from Gordon Wadge and Jim Kelly, Co-Presidents of Catholic Charities of the Archdiocese of New Orleans:

> We are delighted to inform you that Catholic Charities has been accredited by the Council on Accreditation. As you know, we have been working diligently toward this goal since December of 2005, when, in a post-Katrina world, we re-committed ourselves to excellence in everything we do. Since accreditation by COA covers the *entire* organization, this is an acknowledgement that the work we have done is based on best practice standards performed by a skilled staff providing the highest quality service at all levels of the organization.
>
> This achievement reflects three years of work on the part of a full-time staff person as well as countless staff hours and the support of the Board and Mission Committee. We become one of only twelve agencies in Louisiana to achieve COA accreditation. This recognition is similar to accreditation granted to hospitals and universities.

---

9. More on COA accreditation can be found at www.coanet.org and, in addition, at www.coastandards.org for standards and guidelines.

The journey is not over. Accreditation is a living, breathing process. As we move forward on this path, the processes implemented along the way, such as Performance and Quality Improvement (PQI), Corporate Compliance, Risk Management and our Strategic Plan, will challenge us to continue to provide the most innovative, highest quality care for those we serve.

We thank you, the members of the Catholic Charities Board, for providing the leadership and impetus that allowed us to achieve this distinguished recognition.[10]

As a member of the Board and Mission Committee, and knowing the devastation experienced in Catholic Charities facilities and services in New Orleans from Hurricane Katrina, I can personally attest to the value placed upon accreditation by local Catholic Charities leadership and the tremendous investment of time, personnel, and other resources to make this a reality.

As a means of promoting quality, Catholic Charities USA continues to encourage accreditation among its members in its publications and at various meetings during the year. A number of Charities leaders and managers have taken the training to become team leaders and peer reviewers, trying to bring quality to both public and private organizations in human services in this country. Accreditation is one more way to try to improve the quality of their services to clients and to strengthen the overall organizations in their service, advocacy, and convening responsibilities.

INNOVATION AND AWARDS

In the *2007 Survey*, CARA asked agencies to report on new or innovative services or programs developed or implemented during that year. Eighty-five agencies reported new or innovative programs, many of which indicated more than one or even many new initiatives. The list and brief descriptions cover twenty pages of the survey report.[11] From studying that report and the national organization's magazine, my subjective selection of six initiatives described in the following paragraphs can suggest the scope and purposes of innovation within the Catholic Charities USA network.

---

10. Letter of Gordon Wadge, Co-President & CEO, and Jim Kelly, Co-President & CEO, to the Catholic Charities Board, Archdiocese of New Orleans, December 17, 2008.

11. *2007 Survey,* 46–66.

In terms of asset-building and empowerment, Catholic Charities of Santa Clara County operates an Individual Development Account (IDA) program that matches savings for low-income individuals and families, combining education on financial matters with a two-to-one savings to develop a "nest egg" for the future. Taught in three languages—English, Spanish, and Vietnamese—fifteen hours of money management classes cover such topics as personal bank accounts, budgeting, and regular savings. As a result, 440 savers reached their goals, amassing enough savings for home purchases, education, small business start-ups, or retirement. In the first seven years, the participants with matching funds had saved $2,646,497.[12]

As a complement to its foster care programs, Catholic Charities, Archdiocese of New York, inaugurated a novel city-funded, NYC Works Initiative, a collaborative program in which they partnered with the AFL-CIO and the Consortium for Worker Education to move "aged-out" foster children ages 17–21 into the work force. Charities begins the effort with eight weeks of training in job skills and financial literacy. The Consortium then provides further training in various high-pay, high demand union trade positions, including construction and culinary services. Afterwards, the AFL-CIO hires these youth as soon as they are ready for the work force. All through the process, Charities follows these youth with necessary social supports and networking as a foundation for success.[13]

To address the cycle of poverty and people in financial crises, Catholic Charities of Evansville, IN combines faith, life skills education, and financial literacy in fourteen sessions of its Neighbor to Neighbor program. The goals include learning the skills needed in order to become financially stable and self-sufficient. Participants are urged to use their faith and faith-sharing as a source of personal strength and motivation to stay with the program, move beyond previous negative behaviors, and produce productive, healthy lives. Participants also develop personal and family budgets, learn social skills, and practice responsible accountability, leading to a personalized action plan with goals and definite action steps

---

12. "Individual Development Accounts: Matched Savings Program Aids Families in Building Assets," *Charities USA* 33.3 (2006) 15.

13. "NYC Works Initiative: Innovative Program Keeps Aged-Out Foster Children from Poverty," ibid., 17–18.

to achieve them. They leave the program strong, confident, and hopeful about their futures.[14]

To complement its mental health and outpatient chemical dependency services, Catholic Charities of Buffalo opened a Creative Edge Arts Studio to engage people recovering from mental illness and/or addictions, funded by the local John R. Oishei Foundation. In the six month first phase, Creative Edge introduces participants to a variety of art expressions—visual and written arts, music, and drama—to promote a stronger sense of self, social and problem-solving skills, and purposeful life choices. A second three-month phase further develops their experience in one or two art modes by linking participants to a community-based art program, developing their own portfolios, and learning to mentor others in the program.[15]

After some years of being the largest provider of transitional housing and shelter for the homeless in Minnesota, Catholic Charities of St. Paul and Minneapolis opened a pay-for-stay shelter offering real beds, with pillows and sheets, a locker, and access to counseling for $3 a night. By paying for his stay, the homeless man earns much needed self-respect and dignity and agrees to abide by stricter rules concerning behavior, substance abuse, and respect for others. He also makes an investment in his future, since half of the money he pays is returned to him when he secures a more stable housing situation. The facility fills its 126 beds each night. In its first fifteen months, the program assisted 130 men to move into stable housing.[16]

To expand the scope of its employment programs, in 1990 St. Patrick Center of Catholic Charities of the Archdiocese of St. Louis opened McMurphy's Grill in downtown St. Louis to provide the first-in-the-nation full-service restaurant for training homeless/mentally ill clients. Their mission is to enable men and women in the program to develop good work habits, acquire food service skills, and discover successful careers in the restaurant business. Three to six months of training in "back" kitchen duties and "front" service functions, combined with job coach-

14. "Neighbor to Neighbor: Faith Combined with Life Skills Education and Financial Literacy," ibid., 14–15.

15. "Catholic Charities in Buffalo Opens Therapeutic Arts Studio Program," *Charities USA* 30.3 (2003) 27.

16. "A Roof, a Bed, and a Little Dignity: Pay-for-Stay Homeless Shelter Offers More Than a Night's Stay," *Charities USA* 30.4 (2003) 25.

ing and job placement, helped 43 of 65 clients find employment in 2007. Optional training and certification are also provided, taught by St. Louis Community College instructors, to enhance employability.[17]

While these are only six examples (more will be discussed as award-winners, below), one benefit of the existence of the national network of Catholic Charities is that innovative programs often become the subject of workshops at annual conferences and at meetings of the diocesan directors of Charities or those of specialty groups. Others are described in various publications. Then those programs that seem effective and replicable often are duplicated or adapted by other agencies within the network. Thus innovation can spread throughout the nation rather easily. Awards for innovation and creativity do the same.

Americans seem to love awards and see them as a way to thank people and organizations for a job well done and to encourage others to do the same. This is true in the world of human and social services, including the management of voluntary organizations. Considering awards in this chapter can give a further flavor of the areas of innovation and excellence that concern Catholic Charities agencies in this country. The following sample of a half-dozen national, state, and local awards presented to Charities agencies and leaders over the past six years highlight quality outcomes, individual commitment, service to the vulnerable, collaborative leadership, innovative excellence, and even workplace flexibility:

- 2003—Catholic Charities of Wilmington received the United Way of Delaware's Community Impact Award for 2003. Along with other agencies, Charities was recognized for its exemplary leadership among social service agencies geared to creating a quality Outcomes Management System that promotes caring, quality programs. In the same year the agency was also honored for its services to people with disabilities and its program to connect volunteers to assist low-income taxpayers in filing returns under the Earned Income Tax Credit program.[18]

- 2004—Mario Villanueva, director of the Diocese of Yakima Housing Services was honored with the Skip Jason Community

17. Kelly Peach, "McMurphy's Grill: It's not just a restaurant … it's a mission!" *Charities USA* 35.2 (2008) 17.

18. "Catholic Charities in Wilmington Wins Community Award," *Charities USA* 30.3 (2003) 28.

Service Award presented by the national Housing Assistance Council in 2004. As founder of the housing services agency, Villanueva's organization had developed and managed seven housing projects to provide farm workers and their families with affordable housing and the educational and social support they need to be successful and contributing members of their communities.[19]

- 2005—In 2005, Governor Sonny Perdue honored the domestic violence program of Catholic Social Services of Atlanta as a model program in the State of Georgia. The honor included a $93,850 grant to improve the functioning of the criminal justice system with an emphasis on serving the needs of adult female victims of violent crime. Agency services to refugee, immigrant, and undocumented women who are victims of domestic violence include crisis intervention, counseling, training, and outreach services. In the Governor's words, "Catholic Social Services is providing an effective and compassionate community response to assist the victims of domestic violence."[20]

- 2006—In June 2006, Sister Maureen Joyce, director of Catholic Charities in Albany, NY, was honored by Jewish Family Services (JFS) at its annual banquet, the first non-Jewish recipient of the award. Sister Joyce had worked closely with JFS in creating an innovative program to help seniors deal with health and aging issues while remaining in their homes and communities as long as possible. Serving over 800 seniors, the program makes available case management, healthcare assistance and monitoring, senior volunteer opportunities, shopping assistance, and friendly visiting.[21]

- 2007—Begun in 1989, the DIGNITY program of Catholic Charities of Phoenix was honored in 2007 as one of the three national

---

19. "Yakima Housing Director Receives National Award," *Charities USA* 32.1 (2005) 31. By 2009, now as Catholic Charities Housing Services, Villanueva's program and staff have developed nine projects and begun to build "New Life Homes" for first-time homebuyers in the diocese. See agency website at www.ccyakima.org for details.

20. "Georgia Governor Honors Atlanta Agency with Grant," *Charities USA* 32.2 (2005) 35.

21. "Albany CEO Maureen Joyce Honored by Jewish Family Services," *Charities USA* 33.3 (2006) 40.

recipients of the prestigious Peter F. Drucker Award for Nonprofit Innovation from the Drucker Institute at Claremont Graduate University in California. The DIGNITY program offers a comprehensive array of rehabilitation and diversion services—support groups, counseling, case management, 24-hour hotline, jail diversion, and housing—that help women break away from the destructive life of prostitution with the goal of rebuilding their lives. Eighty-two percent of the women who complete the program continue to live free of prostitution, alcohol, and drugs.[22]

- 2008—In 2008, the Alfred P. Sloan Award for Business Excellence in Workplace Flexibility was presented to Catholic Charities of the Diocese of Winona by the United States Chamber of Commerce. Sloan Award honorees are employers offering workplace flexibility programs, policies, and practices that exceed the standard of excellence established by the National Study of Employers conducted by the Families and Work Institute. Charities worked to eliminate inefficiencies, utilize new technologies, develop better communications among employees, and provide family and workplace flexibility for staff, while still remaining effective on the job. The evaluation process includes employee verification of award-winning workplace practices.[23]

In addition to these awards from outside evaluators, since 2005 Catholic Charities USA, in partnership with the Annie E. Casey Foundation, annually has recognized its members' outstanding programs in family strengthening with awards of $25,000. The focus is on giving children what they want and need—strong, capable, and economically successful families. In 2008, the national organization honored four programs with the Family Strengthening Awards:

1. The Homebase Program of Catholic Charities Brooklyn and Queens works closely with families who are on the brink of entering the shelter system so this emergency step either can be

---

22. "Phoenix's Prostitution Diversion Program Wins Drucker Innovation Award," *Charities USA* 35.1 (2008) 46.

23. "Catholic Charities Diocese of Winona Wins National Award," *Charities USA* 35.3 (2008) 43.

shortened or eliminated altogether; the program has assisted over 1,700 families since its founding.[24]

2. The Kinship Care Resource Network of Catholic Family Center of Rochester, NY, collaborates with four other agencies to support the needs of families in which a child is being raised by a relative other than the biological parent, such as a grandparent or sibling. In 2007, Kinship Care helped 331 caregivers and 483 children, a 42% increase over the previous year.[25]

3. The Our Daily Bread Employment Center of Catholic Charities of Baltimore is a comprehensive resource center which helps clients overcome their barriers to employment, thus enabling them to better support themselves and their children. Over 80% of their clients live below the poverty line. In a single day, Our Daily Bread provides a hot daily meal to over 600 people, as well as employment counseling, recovery support, and education.[26]

4. St. Margaret's Shelter of Catholic Charities of Spokane, provides emergency and transitional shelter to homeless women and mothers with high-risk newborns and works to improve family self-sufficiency and economic condition with case management, tutoring, parenting classes, and life skills and job training. Dedicated in 2000, St. Margaret's has provided shelter and services to over a thousand women and children.[27]

In addition to these four awardees, Catholic Charities USA also honored five family strengthening finalists in 2008.[28] These awards and honors for finalists are one way to continue to promote quality care for families that is so important to strengthening the social fabric of this country.

---

24. The Homebase Program is found at www.ccbq.org/homebase.htm for details. A description of each awardee is also found on the website www.catholiccharitiesusa.org of the national organization.

25. The Kinship Care program is found at www.cfcrochester.org/pg/kinship-care for details.

26. Our Daily Bread is found at www.catholiccharities-md.org/emergency/odbec. html for details.

27. See St. Margaret's on the agency website at www.catholiccharitiesspokane.org for details.

28. "Family Strengthening Awards Finalists," *Charities USA* 35.3 (2008) 28–29.

PROTECTING THE VOLUNTARY SECTOR

Not all innovation is good for quality of programs and services or good for the poor and vulnerable in the voluntary sector. While everything from operating prisons to protecting State Department employees in war-torn Iraq is being contracted out to for-profit corporations, Catholic Charities has taken a lead in opposing or at least limiting widespread incursions of for-profit corporations into the area of caring for the poor and vulnerable in our society without strong protections for those to be served.

No one denies that the for-profit sector has an important role to play in the reduction of poverty in this country and the provision of financial support for U.S. families. As the U.S. bishops made clear in their pastoral letter *Economic Justice for All*, "*The first line of attack against poverty must be to build and sustain a healthy economy that provides employment opportunities at just wages for all adults who are able to work.*"[29] This is even more important in the context of the economic crisis worldwide in which we now find ourselves. Corporations, businesses, and unions all can play a strong role in providing a decent livelihood for families which lifts them out of poverty or keeps them from falling into it. Jobs with decent wages and benefits also reduce welfare dependency and eliminate the need for charity except in times of emergency.

In addition, as the bishops noted in *In All Things Charity*, business and labor can support and complement the work of voluntary sector organizations such as Catholic Charities by providing volunteers, financial support, and expertise; and they can support advocacy for better community and public responsiveness. They can do even more, however, as the bishops indicated: "As charities grapple with more complex issues and with the need for productive employment, business and labor organizations can supply additional resources—technical assistance, business skills, and capital—to support more creative responses, such as domestic and international micro-enterprise loan programs, cooperative development, and construction and rehabilitation of housing."[30] We have seen some of this collaboration in earlier discussions of economic development and housing and in some of the above examples of innovation.

What seems new in the last two decades is a move to expand what has been called "privatization" in social and human services to include

29. *Economic Justice for All*, 196 (emphasis in original).
30. *In All Things Charity*, 37.

for-profit businesses. This is driven often by considerations of "devolution" (highly touted by the proponents of so-called welfare reform during the nineties), managed care, and cost-effectiveness. Privatization might take the form of contracts, the use of vouchers, joint ventures, and managing the managed-care dollars. Privatization in the past has provided strong benefits for the public good, historically by non-profit or voluntary organizations, more recently by non-profits and for-profits or collaborations between them. The fear is that privatization will be submerged in a tidal wave of "profitization" in human services.

In early 2000, the CEO's of eighteen of the nation's most well-known charities or voluntary organizations, including Catholic Charities USA, warned about the unconditional incursion of for-profit organizations into the social service arena. The statement was entitled *The Profitization of Social Services*. In part, it reads:

> At a minimum, we must ensure that profitization at the expense of people in need does not occur. Profitization is a form of privatization that puts profit ahead of individuals and communities in need. It substitutes profit maximization for essential care, limits access to critically needed services, delivers substandard services to consumers, and/or sets inadequate reimbursement for providers.
>
> Our society must not abandon its long history of public responsibility and accountability. While the market may play a role in the efficient delivery of social services, we must ensure that it does not undermine the provision of services that meet fundamental human needs.[31]

The non-profit sector leaders cautioned about the trend of profitization and proposed fourteen principles to govern the changes implied in the growing movement of for-profits into the sector. The principles were developed under the headings of "contracting for quality," "protecting the rights of consumers," and "accountability for public funds." (The introductory statement and the principles are included as Appendix B.) The implementation of these principles is a responsibility of governments, as payors and as responsible for the care of their vulnerable citizens, and also

---

31. Statement of eighteen nonprofit CEOs, *The Profitization of Social Services: Where do we set limits on a market-driven social service system?* (February 2002), was reprinted in *The NonProfitTimes*, February 2000. The Principles were also approved by the Board of Trustees of Catholic Charities USA and also printed in *Charities USA* 27.1 (2000) 11, 30–32. See Appendix B of this volume.

of non-profits and for-profits, as contractors with government and service providers to the poor and needy.

The issues highlighted and the principles proposed in the 2000 statement on profitization reflect genuine concerns for the quality and integrity of the services which are delivered in the human and social services sector of society. As such, they are part of the continuing service and advocacy responsibility of Catholic Charities agencies both locally and nationally and they complement Charities' own efforts to improve the quality of their services in local communities.

9

Spirituality

Seeing the Divine in Their Midst

BILL JONES OF CATHOLIC Charities of Covington, Kentucky, began working for the agency in 1981. When I later met him, he had become the associate director and, in 2005, became the diocesan director of the agency. In
the series of reflections for Lent developed by Catholic Charities USA from
their members and for their members, Bill's reflection tied his experience in
the U.S. Army to that of the people served by his agency in order to highlight
the service to which Charities workers are called. In his words:

> As a young man, I served as a 2nd Lieutenant in the U.S. Army.
> Part of our training in the summer of 1973 at Fr. Bragg was a unit
> called IRT (Interrogation Resistance Training) involving several
> days of classroom preparation followed by two days of "simulated"
> experience as a prisoner of war. During those two days we did not
> sleep and had little to eat or drink. Those days were among the most
> difficult I have ever endured. During debriefing, we were informed
> that the training was designed to let us experience what it is like to
> lose our freedom—to become slaves.
>
> My mind has often gone back to that experience of helpless-
> ness, dependence and rage as I encounter those who ask for help
> at Catholic Charities here in Covington. They have been deprived;
> their bodies and minds tortured: sometimes through poor choices;
> sometimes through the abuse, neglect and exploitation of others; but
> most often, because of the deprecations of poverty, discrimination or
> mental and physical conditions over which they have little control.
> They have lost their freedom—they have become slaves. How ironic
> it is that in doing so they have become God's chosen ones!
>
> In today's Gospel Jesus defines a mission of service whose highest
> expression becomes the sacrifice of our own "freedom" on behalf of

those who are enslaved: ". . . the great ones make their authority felt. But it shall not be so among you. Rather . . . whoever wishes to be first among you shall be your slave. Just so, the Son of Man did not come to be served but to serve and to give his life as a ransom for many."

Each of us experience in our own lives, and in the lives of those with whom we journey, a sense of captivity and the need for ransom. The Lord teaches his disciples that when we turn away from what our culture defines as power and success and become servants for the sake of others, we share in the Kingdom that offers riches beyond imagination.

In his reflections Bill named spiritual themes that I have found to be among the hallmarks of the workers within Catholic Charities—common humanity with those who come for assistance, an emphasis on service, God's special love for the least among us, a recognition of our common need for salvation, and the incredible ways this work enriches those involved.

In the introduction to *Salted with Fire: Spirituality for the Faithjustice Journey*, I described "spirituality" in these terms:

> Spirituality is essentially about seeing God's presence and activity in the midst of human reality. In a way, we look through or past the apparent object and event and see its inner self, trying to discern the movements of God's grace and the opposing forces of evil, their interplay, and our own roles in the conflict . . . It insists on seeing reality in its social or structural manifestations which reveal the three-dimensional depth of all our relationships, including our relationship to God.[1]

In keeping with this multi-dimensional insistence, in this chapter I will treat the spirituality of Catholic Charities under three headings: institutional spirituality, workplace spirituality, and personal spirituality. The first form of spirituality is structured especially into the inner life of the agency as an institution. The second reflects efforts of the past twenty years or so to focus more explicitly on spirituality in the Catholic Charities workplace among staff and volunteers, usually in group discussion, reflection, and retreats. The third reflects the kind of spiritual characteristics

---

1. Fred Kammer, SJ, *Salted with Fire: Spirituality for the Faithjustice Journey* (1995; reprint, Eugene, OR: Wipf and Stock, 2008), 8.

that are often found among those who staff and volunteer in the agencies, what we might call their key spiritual virtues.

INSTITUTIONAL SPIRITUALITY

While theologians in recent decades have written of "sinful social structures"—what Pope John Paul II called "structures of sin"[2]—some also have written of graced social structures. These are those institutions and systems that promote life, encourage fidelity, dignify human beings, strengthen communities, and reinforce loving behaviors in the external world.[3] We might think of the triple activities of service, advocacy, and convening in the Charities mission as being expressions of its external character as a graced social structure. But Charities agencies, like all institutions, also have an internal face reflected first in their organizational structures, decision-making modes, personnel policies, and by the staff and volunteers themselves.[4] Whether the internal face is largely graced or not will affect the spirituality of the institution and can affect the relationships among, and spirituality of, all of those who are employed or engaged as volunteers, including board members. It is this internal aspect of the institutions upon which this chapter's first part is focused.

When we look at the *Code of Ethics* of Catholic Charities USA, there are a significant number of principles, values, and ethical standards that address themselves to the relations between and among the staff, board, and volunteers. To the degree that they reflect the better practices of the diverse network, they give us a sense of their internal framework. (They also tend to be elements included in the accreditation process for agencies.) Naturally, many provisions are addressed to the standards and care with which clients are to be treated. But many others are set out to determine the inner life and spirit of the agencies and influence the people working or volunteering there. Some examples follow:

1. Under the principle of Human Dignity, "Catholic Charities affirm that each person served and *engaged with our work* will be held in great esteem and with great respect."[5]

2. Pope John Paul II, *Sollicitudo Rei Socialis*, 36.

3. In *Doing Faithjustice*, 206–7, I introduced the concept of "mixed social structures" as a more realistic description of most systems and institutions.

4. See discussion in *Salted with Fire*, 56–60.

5. *Code of Ethics*, 8 (emphasis supplied).

2. Under the principle of Solidarity with the Poor, "Catholic Charities affirm that our staff and boards should engage those served to have representative voice in decisions impacting policies and programs. Accordingly, we affirm the need to create structures and processes for obtaining *appropriate input from stakeholders*."[6]

3. Under the fundamental value of Truth, "Catholic Charities affirm that transparency and accountability will always be pursued in our communication and work."[7]

4. Under the fundamental value of Freedom, "Catholic Charities affirm that we will always assist our clients, *staff and volunteers* to live in socially responsible freedom, to exercise their authentic autonomy in light of objective truth and to actualize their inherent potential as beings created in the image and likeness of God."[8]

5. Under the fundamental value of Justice, "Catholic Charities affirm that we will work to expand and maintain diversity and excellence in our *membership, board, leadership positions, and staff*."[9]

6. Under the ethical standard on Fiduciary Duty, the board is expected to provide an accessible and safe communication process for staff to make known any unfair discriminatory practice, sexual harassment, or "other conduct inconsistent with the identity and/or values of the corporation or of the employees . . ."[10]

7. Under the ethical standard on CEO/Management Team Responsibilities, "The CEO/Management Team are expected to ensure that their own personal and professional behavior are consistent with the norms of the Catholic Charities USA Code of Ethics; in doing so, *they shall model ethical behavior and decision-making for those whom they are appointed to lead*."[11]

---

6. Ibid., 9 (emphasis supplied).

7. Ibid., 10.

8. Ibid. (emphasis supplied).

9. Ibid., 11 (emphasis supplied).

10. Ibid., section 2.03(e).

11. Ibid., section 3.01(d).

8. Under the same standard, "The CEO/Management Team are expected to lead with integrity."[12]

9. Staff, in turn, under the ethical standard of Colleague Relationships, are expected to: respect the rights and views of their colleagues; treat them with respect, fairness, and courtesy; respect confidences shared by colleagues; not to engage in negative criticisms of a colleague with clients or with other professionals with whom they work; and, in the case of colleagues impaired by personal problems, psychological distress, or substance abuse, to consult first with the colleague and then seek informal or even formal resolution of the matter.[13]

While some or even many similar provisions might be found in the personnel manuals of for-profit corporations or other voluntary organizations, the terms indicated above and the full scope of the *Code of Ethics* help to shape the inner face and spirituality of the Charities organization—encouraging and embodying relationships as sisters and brothers to one another and as children of a loving and caring God.

The inner spirit also is shaped by salary and benefit programs that reflect the fullness of modern Catholic Social Teaching which would mean, for example, paying a family wage, providing worker's compensation and unemployment compensation, subsidizing retirement benefits, funding a substantial part of medical and related benefits, and providing family-friendly workplace policies. These become a matter of workplace justice and can be a major challenge to managers when the payers—government, foundations, and others—may be trying to limit their budget outlays for contracted services. From my own experience, I know that many a director has been caught between the justice owed to staff and the funding constraints being imposed by funders. Fair and just pay and benefits honors the sanctity and human dignity of the staff which they in turn are then encouraged to honor in how they treat one another and those they serve.

For thirty years now, authors and social scientists have focused on a critically important negative experience for those in the helping professions that can turn the worker from a caring professional into more of a

---

12. Ibid., section 3.01(g).
13. Ibid., section 4.06.

bureaucratic functionary or simply bring a promising career in human or social services to a halt. That experience has been called "burnout."[14] Earlier analyses of this phenomenon focused on the psychological and spiritual characteristics of the person affected and the remedies proposed for the condition. Later writing, however, began to uncover the organizational and environment factors that contributed to or even were primary causes of the problem. Key organizational causes involve the absence of shared decision-making in the workplace, conflicting and changing role expectations, role and organizational conflicts, and the absence of staff development opportunities. These problems often are more acute in newer organizations, those that are underfunded, those without experienced middle-managers, or those that are so focused on mission that they neglect the well-being of those working in the agency.[15] Thus the *Code of Ethics* wisely lays out requirements for management, staff, and volunteers which include written job descriptions, evaluation processes that include reciprocal dialogue, opportunities for training and professional growth, and contracts for services that allow for just salaries for staff.[16]

It seems safe to say, then, that the spirituality of a Catholic Charities agency as an institution is molded by its external mission in service of the Gospel and the poor and vulnerable *and* its internal character as an ethical organization whose policies and practices reverence those who are involved as board, staff, and volunteers. In this coherence of external mission *and* internal character, the spirituality of individuals is enhanced in significant ways that also are in keeping with the mission and their own sanctity and dignity. Recent decades have taught that nurturing that spirituality also requires explicit attention to spirituality within the workplace.

WORKPLACE SPIRITUALITY

When the Catholic Identity Project task force began its work in the mid-nineties in conjunction with the Vision 2000 process of Catholic Charities USA, one of its first activities was to solicit ideas and materials from local

14. My attention initially was focused on burnout among Jesuits in social ministry and among legal services attorneys among whom I worked in the seventies and eighties. Burnout is the focus of the first chapter of *Salted with Fire*, entitled, "From Compassion Fatigue to Burnout."

15. Ibid., 31ff.

16. See *Code of Ethics*, Ethical Standards, sections 4 and 6.

agencies. Ninety-five agencies responded; twenty-two of them sent materials used locally in planning and/or orienting staffs, boards, and volunteers regarding mission and identity of the agencies.[17] Perhaps surprisingly, many agencies were focusing on the spirituality of their workers as part of these efforts. Their experiences with reflection groups, shared prayer, and time for staff spiritual nurturance were created in ways respectful of the religious diversity of staff and volunteers and yet focused on the mission, identity, and spirituality of the work. Some of these materials were included in the 1997 Catholic Charities USA publication, *Who Do You Say We Are?—Perspectives on Catholic Identity in Catholic Charities*.

Two years later, during Lent of 1999, the national organization piloted a weekly workplace spirituality resource for groups of local staff and volunteers to use in exploring mission and values in their work. Catholic Charities USA followed this effort with a monthly resource in September and October, 1999, and then a weekly resource again during Advent, 1999.[18] Over the following decade, under the leadership first of Br. Joseph Berg, CSC and then Sister Therese Wetta, ASC, the provision of workplace spirituality materials continued. Notable among these efforts was the 2001 publication of a five-session *Study Guide* for *In All Things Charity*, which invited local staff and volunteers to reflect together in a Scriptural context on the themes enunciated in the US bishops' 1999 pastoral letter.[19] Today, led by Robert Colbert, Director of Mission Integration/Catholic Identity, the national organization provides several sets of workplace spirituality materials for the use of member agency staff and volunteers.

During Lent and Advent for each of the past three years, Catholic Charities USA members have provided daily reflections on the Scripture readings for the liturgy of the day. Members also are supplied with group reflection resources on topics relevant to their mission together, which include readings, questions for reflection and discussion, and individual and group prayers for use during these sessions. These resources are introduced on-line as follow: "This series is meant to be practical. Each reflection is designed to be used by Catholic Charities agency staff to further their understanding of mission and to learn how to interpret the mission

17. *Who Do You Say We Are,* 2.

18. Fred Kammer, SJ, "Workplace Spirituality," in *President's Report to the Board of Trustees* (September 1999) 2.

19. Rev. Stan De Boe, OSST, *Study Guide for In All Things Charity* (Alexandria, VA: Catholic Charities USA, 2001).

of the agency into their individual work." The first set of reflections for group use focus on the mission of their agency under various headings, including spirituality and the religiously diverse workforce common to most agencies:

- Our work is a Sacred Mission
- Leadership Skills are Integral to Our Mission
- Mission and Spirituality
- Mission and Catholic Social Teaching
- Mission Expressed as Hospitality
- Mission and the Religiously Diverse Workforce
- Mission-Based Hiring
- Mission as Expressed Through Core Values[20]

Other reflection materials provided address the organization's Campaign to Reduce Poverty in America, in addition to the Lenten and Advent reflections indicated above.

Besides these reflection resources, spirituality in the workplace is promoted by providing a series of prayer resources for use at the local agency. The introduction to these prayers on their website reads in part as follows: "Prayer and reflection are part of the fabric of our work at Catholic Charities. Through prayer we draw support and inspiration from God. The Church Fathers at Vatican II describe prayer and liturgy as 'at the foundation of the Catholic social mission.' The prayers below represent a compilation of prayers submitted by agencies across the Catholic Charities network. It is only a beginning; we view it as a 'work-in-progress.'"[21] Members are then invited to submit additional prayers for inclusion in this on-line resource for other members. Topics included for prayers are also indicated on-line:

Days and Seasons

- Advent
- New Year

20. Found at www.catholiccharitiesusa.org under Our Catholic Tradition heading.
21. See www.catholiccharitiesusa.org under the Prayer Resources heading.

- Lent
- Thanksgiving
- National/International Observances

Prayers for Different Occasions

- Birthdays
- Death of a staff member's loved one

Prayers for Special Occasions

- Dedication and Blessing

Meeting Prayers

Twenty-four separate prayer themes for meetings are indicated, including: Beatitudes; Care for the Homeless; For an End to Racism; God of Strength, God of Mercy; Hear Us and Challenge Us; Justice for Immigrants; Prayer to Be Worthy of Serving the Poor; and That None Should Be Lost.

Other Religious Traditions

- Buddhist
- Hindu
- Jewish
- Muslim
- Native American[22]

In addition, local agencies have developed their own prayer and reflection materials for use by their own staff, board, and volunteers. Examples would be *Inspirations: A Collection of Reflections, Prayers, and Thoughts for the Journey,* created by Catholic Community Services of Western Washington in 2004 and *Let Us Pray: Short Prayers and Meditations for Use in Group Settings,* produced by the Secretariat for Catholic Human Services of the Philadelphia Archdiocese in 2003. Similar materials have been prepared by Catholic Relief Services in 2004 for its even more diverse staff and

22. Ibid.

volunteers who carry on the charitable work of the Church across the world (*Prayers without Borders: Celebrating Global Wisdom*).

In local agencies the responsibility to encourage such workplace spirituality discussions and prayer, while respecting the religious diversity of staff and volunteers, is shared by directors, managers, and, more recently, by persons holding positions with specific care for the mission and Catholic identity of the agency and/or the spiritual care of the staff and volunteers. For example, in Philadelphia the position is Director, Mission Integration; in Hawaii it is Director, Catholic Identity and Mission; Dallas has a Missions/Social Concerns Coordinator; Peoria employs a Mission Director; and Charities of Kansas City—St. Joseph includes a Director, Mission Integration and Community Services. In other agencies, the PSM director may have a special care for this area of the inner life of the agency. Still others, such as Catholic Charities of the Archdiocese of Washington, D.C., have a Spirituality Committee composed of staff to promote this kind of reflection and prayer and to develop resources for use within the agency and, in Washington, to plan an annual Spirituality in the Workplace Retreat.[23]

Workplace spirituality efforts reflect a growing awareness among member agencies of the importance of attending to the interior life of staff and volunteers that recognizes that, for many of those involved of many faiths, working at Catholic Charities is a crucial expression of deeply held religious values. It also nurtures the ability of staff to sustain the difficulties of this work, to be more supportive of those whom they serve each day, and to become more deeply committed themselves to the mission and values of the agency.

SPIRITUALITY AND VIRTUES

In recent years, moral theology has focused in new ways on the role of virtues in the moral life. It asks the self-understanding question, "Who are we?" This question focuses interest not on particular moral acts *per se* so much as on who the actor is as person and what kind of person they ought to become. The virtues become a way of assessing who the person is and also setting goals for oneself in terms of acquiring or

---

23. Joan Fowler Brown, "Making Meaningful Connections between Faith and Work: Washington, D.C., Agency Staff Retreat Focuses on Spirituality, Relationships, and Prayer," *Charities USA* 31.2 (2004) 7.

developing certain key virtues. Parallel developments have occurred in the field of spirituality, turning the focus from ascetical practices to relationships to God and others and attitudes of heart. Spirituality looks at these relationships, how we experience God daily and hourly, and how that experience shapes our living and working each day. It looks at holiness in ordinary life, at discipleship lived "outside" the sanctuary, and at the virtues that shape our ways of acting towards others in light of our relationship with God.

In this part, I want to turn to the ways Catholic Charities people act in relationship to God and others. I do this by reflecting their own ways of describing what they do and ought to do in terms of six key virtues that seem to me to be central to their way of proceeding: *accompaniment, hospitality, service, solidarity, hope,* and *sacred love.* In this part I am drawing in large part on the Advent and Lenten reflections of Catholic Charities members from their Reflections offerings,[24] as well as my thirty years of being with the people who make Catholic Charities a reality in communities across the nation.

Accompaniment

Accompaniment takes many forms among the staff and volunteers of Catholic Charities: the foster parents who care for infants being placed for adoption during the period between initial surrender of the child by the birthmother and formal adoption; a counselor who spends hours one-on-one with the person working to become free of addictions; the sponsoring family teamed with a refugee family as they adjust to a new country, new language, and new culture; a social worker partnered with a single pregnant woman as she goes through nine months of discernment about her future and that of her child; and "friendly visitors" who spend hours with men or women in nursing homes or in prisons. Accompaniment involves patient listening and a caring presence, being companion to the other. The word *companion* has at its roots the meaning of one who breaks bread with another, and this companionship is a foundation for much of the work within Catholic Charities agencies.

---

24. These Reflections, drawn from www.catholiccharities.usa, are from Lent for 2008 and 2009 and Advent for 2008. In further footnotes, for the sake of simplicity, only the person's name, position, and date of the Scripture reflection are given.

Another very simple term for this caring presence would be that of the "neighbor," as Father Ragan Schriver of Tennessee indicates:

> Each day I see staff and volunteers spending time working and speaking *with* the poor, understanding the issues they face and engaging them in building a better community. When we engage with others we build up what the greatest commandment calls for: love of neighbor . . . it may be important to share food and shelter with others but it is most essential to live with a deep and pervasive attitude of neighborliness toward the vulnerable and marginalized on our society . . . We at Catholic Charities all over the country are so involved in the lives of the clients we serve each day, we are truly living out fundamental neighborliness with those we serve.[25]

Accompaniment begins with presence and listening, but it leads to understanding and *compassion*, a word whose roots mean to "suffer with." George Garchar of Youngstown explains: "Especially in today's tough economic times, people can easily fall into the trap of bitterness and condemnation—the politicians are only looking out for themselves, the illegal immigrants are taking our jobs, the greedy bankers sold us down the river—instead of focusing on positive actions that might be taken. Even in our work with Catholic Charities, we can be tempted to judge our clients, assigning blame where, instead, a measure of understanding is needed."[26] This understanding and compassion is not easy work, because the lives of those Charities serves are not easy lives.

Sister Mary Lou Stubbs, DC, of Arkansas explains: "We are asked to walk into the difficulties of people's lives and not only provide them help, but also create hope in their lives. This is often a thankless job, and many days we do not know how to start or what success will look like."[27] In her description, Sister Stubbs is naming two distinct characteristics of this accompaniment—its difficulty and the great unknowns involved. Moralist James Keenan, SJ, describes this involvement in terms of the trademark Catholic virtue of "mercy," which he defines as "the willingness

---

25. Rev. Ragan Schriver, Executive Director, Catholic Charities of Eastern Tennessee, March 12, 2009.

26. George Garchar, Associate Director of Social Action, Diocese of Youngstown, March 9, 2009.

27. Sister Mary Lou Stubbs, DC, Diocesan Director, Catholic Charities of Arkansas, December 8, 2008.

to enter into the chaos of another so as to respond to the other . . ."[28] Many of those served by Catholic Charities come from abusive home environments, life on the streets, a world of addictions, chronic unemployment, and the grinding world of persistent poverty—what Keenan would call "the chaos of the margins."[29] Listening to and sharing in their experience of difficulty and chaos is a first step towards recovery or freedom or self-empowerment or simple dignity.

How one can be willing to make this difficult journey begins for many in Charities with a spiritual acknowledgement of their common humanity with those they accompany. They share common humanity and a common sinfulness. The traditional Catholic morality within which I grew up reminded us in moments of judging others less fortunate, "There but for the grace of God go I." Bill Jones of Covington expressed that in his comments at the opening of this chapter about our common slavery and the need for freedom which we all share. We even know that we have a common tendency to ignore the poverty and suffering around us. Greg Kepferle of Santa Clara County explains:

> Since becoming an executive director with responsibilities for fund raising and managing the budget, I have learned to pray "give us this day our daily bread" with a certain pragmatic earnestness. And the prophetic calls for repentance, forgiveness, and sacrifice challenge me. It is easier for me to say, "Woe are you—other people" who neglect the poor while living the high life, who pass laws that cut services to the widows and orphans, and needy. It is harder for me to look at myself and acknowledge when I have turned my back on those in need right in front of me, whether it be a colleague, a staff person, a client, or a stranger.[30]

Encouraged by this acknowledgement of our common humanity and our common proclivity to sin, even against the poor and vulnerable, Charities workers enter into their accompaniment of those they serve.

28. James Keenan, SJ, "Virtues, Chastity, and Sexual Ethics," Lecture Paper for the Catholic Common Ground Initiative, at www.nplc.org/commonground/papers/kennan-paper.htm. Keenan has written extensively on this topic for two decades or more.

29. Ibid.

30. Greg Kepferle, Chief Executive Officer, Catholic Charities of Santa Clara County, March 4, 2009.

Hospitality

Hospitality in Catholic Charities personnel shows itself most vividly when people provide a home for single women with unplanned pregnancies, when others operate a shelter for families who are homeless, when workers staff group homes for abused children, when volunteers provide hot meals and shelter to disaster evacuees, when staff supervise a halfway house for ex-offenders, or when agencies create and staff apartments for persons who are old or disabled. The components of hospitality variously are a safe place, words of welcome, hot and healthy food, respect for individual dignity, and, sometimes, "all the comforts of home." Hospitality begins, often enough, with simple words of welcome. Mary Ellen Blackwell of Trenton explains:

> From the moment we answer the phone or greet a person at the door or the desk, our ministry of hospitality begins. Even if we are not able to provide the needed service or do not have the funds available to assist them with rent or utilities, we can be cordial and courteous. When there are messages on the office answering machine, we need to remember as the psalmist remembers, "When I cried out, you answered," and build in time each day to call back those who have left requests for information, referrals, and assistance.[31]

This virtue of hospitality often directs itself towards those who are rejected or despised in society, as Rosio Gonzalez of Idaho puts it: "Every day we encounter people who have been turned away by society. We embrace immigrants who are not welcomed. We open our hearts to people who are homeless and purposefully forgotten. We visit prisoners and emotionally hold their families as they struggle to reconnect with humanity."[32] Embracing immigrants, opening hearts to the homeless, and visiting prisoners or their families reflect the justice of the Jewish Scriptures which was central to the faith of Israel and directed toward widows, orphans, strangers, and the poor. They also reflect a Scriptural emphasis on hospitality.

Such graced hospitality was extended by Abraham and Sarah in Genesis 18, when their hospitality to three strangers on the road is re-

---

31. Mary Ellen Blackwell, Director, PSM, Catholic Charities of Trenton, February 14, 2008.

32. Rosio Gonzalez, Executive Director, Catholic Charities of Idaho, February 28, 2008.

warded by the God who was present in these strangers. That same sense of God's presence also shapes the virtue of hospitality among Charities today. The Good Samaritan in Luke 10, one of Pope Benedict's "three great parables of Jesus," is about hospitality; and it is critical to understanding who is my "neighbor" today. As Benedict explains, the earlier more narrow definition of neighbor within Israel is now "abolished." He continues: "Anyone who needs me, and whom I can help, is my neighbor. The concept of 'neighbor' is now universalized, yet it remains concrete. Despite being extended to all mankind, it is not reduced to a generic, abstract and undemanding expression of love, but calls for my own practical commitment here and now."[33] The Good Samaritan is important to our understanding of hospitality in another important way. It enriches hospitality with the concept of healing. Just as the Samaritan poured wine and oil into the wounds of the stranger by the road and carried him to an inn to care for him, so the practice of hospitality in Catholic Charities is often about healing the wounds of abuse, neglect, homelessness, and various forms of psychological and spiritual sickness.

Service

Service of others in need takes many forms within the world of Catholic Charities: mental health counseling, job training, English as a Second Language tutoring, respite care, legal representation, transportation to doctors, dental care, and even the simple provision of food. It is the daily business and ministry of most staff. The more varied the needs in the community, the more comprehensive the services are likely to be. The model for this virtue, however, is very simple and menial: Jesus washes the feet of his disciples (John 13). That image provides an understanding that service begins in simple care for others, often involves divesting ourselves of external power, includes suffering for others, and connects the one serving to the Eucharist.

What most Charities staff do each day are simple tasks of service that make life more bearable for others. Anthony Mullen of Rockville Centre provides us with an example:

> As I stood outside the medical examiner's office the refrain "from death into life" kept running through my mind. Ronnie, a Catholic Charities' driver for our Meals on Wheels program, died in a car

33. *Deus Caritas Est*, 15.

accident earlier that day as he finished his meals route . . . Ronnie, like countless Catholic Charities employees lived a life of service, bringing much needed food to vulnerable seniors. Ronnie's was not a "morsel" of betrayal but a meal of sustenance, and a witness to hope, love and dignity. He used the delivery of the meal as a way to make contact, share a joke, and let those whom we are called to serve know that they are not alone.[34]

The serving is often just as simple as that provided by Ronnie to senior citizens. As such, over time it can be what one staffer calls, "beautiful drudgery,"[35] working face to face with poverty, homelessness, hunger, fear, and sadness on a daily basis. Service, however, also can involve great difficulty and pain. Heather Reynolds of Fort Worth acknowledges, "I know how very busy and stressful these times are for us. We are being asked to do more with less and are seeing so much pain with the families we serve."[36]

In addition, service of others—just as washing the disciples' feet—brings the Charities worker into the mystery of the selflessness, suffering, and transformation that lies at the heart of the mystery of the Eucharist. According to Briston Fernandes of North Dakota:

> In a deliberate attempt at "trans signification," John inserts the washing of the feet at the very place of the institution of the Eucharist in the synoptic gospels. The "Gospel of Signs" conveys to us the profound and sacramental connection between the Eucharist and a life of service. First by example, then by word, Jesus teaches us that to be his followers we must live the Eucharist through a life of selflessness, simplicity and humble service. Jesus turns our world upside down and our lives inside out.
>
> Whether we are direct service staff, managers or directors, we are called to "remove our outer garments" of power, position and authority, gird ourselves with the humility of a servant and care for the most lowly and vulnerable amongst us. When we divest ourselves of the exterior trappings of power, we will be given the power of the Spirit that Jesus promised us not only to provide help

34. Anthony Mullen, Chief Community Services Officer, Catholic Charities of Rockville Center, April 7, 2009.

35. Nancy Hickman, Coordinator of Pregnancy Adoption Services in Camden, quoting a colleague, April 2, 2009.

36. Heather Reynolds, President/CEO, Catholic Charities of Fort Worth, March 17, 2009.

and create hope, but also to transform lives by our gentleness and integrity as followers of Jesus.[37]

Simple service, then, is the most basic of virtues and yet it contains within itself caring for another person and the seeds of transformation of the one serving, a point to which we will return at the end of this chapter.

Solidarity

As a virtue among Catholic Charities workers, solidarity can be seen in individual advocacy with a state agency for a person with disabilities, negotiating with the power company for a poor family threatened with a utility cut-off, door-to-door neighborhood visiting on behalf of safe schools, writing a letter to Congress about housing, or legislative testimony to improve drug treatment programs. In a way, this is a new "virtue." While used by Pope John XXIII in *Pacem in Terris* in 1963, the term solidarity found its way into our Catholic virtue lexicon most explicitly in the writing of Pope John Paul II, where he explicitly says, "Solidarity is undoubtedly a Christian virtue."[38] In his encyclical *Sollicitudo Rei Socialis*, the Pope explains in one of his most quoted texts:

> It is above all a question of interdependence, sensed as a system determining relationships in the contemporary world in its economic, cultural, political and religious elements, and accepted as a moral category. When interdependence becomes recognized in this way, the correlative response as a moral and social attitude, as a "virtue," is solidarity. This then is not a feeling of vague compassion or shallow distress at the misfortunes of so many people, both near and far. On the contrary, it is a firm and persevering determination to commit oneself to the common good, that is to say, to the good of all and of each individual because we are all really responsible for all.[39]

This solidarity among Catholic Charities personnel begins in their seeing the connections between individual client suffering and social realities, calls them to add advocacy to their commitment to service, requires work

---

37. Briston J. Fernandes, Executive Director, Catholic Charities of North Dakota, Holy Thursday, April 9, 2009.

38. *Sollicitudo Rei Socialis*, 40.

39. Ibid., 38.

towards reconciliation in society, and demands a faithful commitment to the prophetic task.

Tina Andrade of Hawaii expresses her insights connecting the experiences of clients to the structures of society in this way: "In our ministries we see that sometimes our brothers and sisters are "banished" from their own land. They are denied basic dignity and rights to safety and shelter. Some may lack these basic necessities as a result of their personal choices; yet today's economic situation reveals that many experience impoverished situations because of societal structures and the choices we collectively make."[40] Social workers and community volunteers do not immediately make this move to advocacy, nor is it an easy transition for many to make. That reluctance has a long Scriptural history, comments Susan Stevenot Sullivan of Atlanta: "The call to solidarity with people on the margins, those who are poor and voiceless, is not one that prophetic messengers initially welcome. The usual reaction in scripture is to object—that we are not suitable or are not ready. Those called are reminded that what must be done, though difficult, will be accomplished with God's authority and assistance and timing."[41] The incorporation of the commitment to solidarity into the initial call to service of the poor and vulnerable then has certain repercussions.

One is the need for staff and volunteers, recalling the hesitancy of many of the prophets to speak God's word publicly, to beg for the grace of fidelity to the fullness of solidarity. Karen Johnston of Green Bay believes that this quality is needed now more than ever:

> We see each day in our work at Catholic Charities opportunities to look to the Lord for strength. In the faces of compassion we offer to those who are at our door, in our struggle to speak truth to power, and in our advocacy for those we serve we stand strong and faithful to the covenant the Lord has given us through his life and witness. . . . We are called to be faithful to God's promise and keep his word. There has never been a time when the world has needed more prophetic witness than the one we may offer.[42]

40. Tina Andrade, Catholic Identity and Mission Director, Catholic Charities of Hawaii, March 7, 2008.

41. Susan Stevenot Sullivan, Director, Parish and Social Justice Ministries, Catholic Charities of Atlanta, March 7, 2008.

42. Karen Johnston, Director, Catholic Charities of Green Bay, March 13, 2008.

Another repercussion from this awareness of the lack of solidarity in so much of our society and across the world is a renewed focus on bringing people together across society's divisions. This call to reconciliation has been made by Elizabeth Lilly of Santa Clara County: "In my work with Parish Social Ministry I meet many new brothers and sisters. Each cares deeply about reconciling our lives, building solidarity, and working to overcome and remove barriers to full participation in community. I look for opportunities to introduce brother to brother, sister to sister, across barriers and divisions of race, language, immigration status, and need. With the focus on the Campaign to Reduce Poverty, I work to raise awareness of the need for reconciliation as a society."[43] Solidarity then fits into the overall picture of virtues within the Catholic Charities network, acknowledging that the challenges are real, can be difficult, and require the grace of fidelity to stay focused and committed to what can be very unpopular. The call then is to be people of hope, part of a community of hope empowered by God's Spirit to remain at this task.

Hope

Hope as a virtue is crucial to the people of Catholic Charities. It may take shape in working with adoptive parents and birthparents to create a future for an infant, building assets through a matched savings program for the distant goal of buying a first home, providing rigorous job skills training to a long unemployed worker, nurturing determination in an addict to remain sober one day at a time, or encouraging a community group to combat drugs in their neighborhood. Such hope is essential to the faithfulness of the charity worker to these often difficult tasks, but it is also critical that it be communicated to those with whom Charities works.

To many clients, hope is essential to the willingness and persistence needed to confront what are often immense challenges. Edward Lis of Philadelphia thinks this is central to the mission of God in which Catholic Charities participates: "Isaiah's God speaks such uplifting words to those who find themselves so burdened: "*I will help you . . . I will grasp your hand . . . I will answer you . . . I will not forsake you.*" God's mission, and thus ours, is to encourage bruised and broken people to believe and hope again. Our compassionate care invites them to risk the audacity of

---

43. Elizabeth Lilly, Director, Community and Parish Partnerships, Catholic Charities of Santa Clara County, February 15, 2008.

hope in the face of immense challenges because 'if God cares and you care, then I must be worth caring about.'"[44] This "audacity of hope" is even more needed in the hard economic times which have hit this country and especially affected those who are poor. To Celeste Matheson of Peoria this means that Charities have important opportunities as bearers of hope to those they serve:

> Today more than ever it seems people are losing hope. We know all too well that during these tumultuous economic times, it is our clients—those facing home foreclosure, or who wonder where their next meal will come from, or how they will clothe their children—who may feel particularly hopeless ... Could it be that at Catholic Charities, we have the awesome opportunity to help those less fortunate begin to believe once again? The things we do each and every day to help those less fortunate could be just what they need to begin to believe in a better tomorrow. It is up to us to send that message of hope, or in the words of John's Gospel, for us to be the visible, wondrous sign of God's love.[45]

The call to embody hope can be challenging to Catholic Charities staff and volunteers when they face increasing demands from clients created by these hard times and when they themselves and their families also may be affected adversely. Efforts at advocacy and community organizing are made more difficult in tighter economic times as well.

Heather Reynolds of Fort Worth counsels that these hard times make it all the more important for staff and volunteers to stay rooted in God who can create and sustain hope: "However, our first call is to God by spending time with Him in fellowship, prayer, and study. When we seek His heart, all else falls into place ... And when we focus on being men and women after God's heart, all who we meet and serve will sense it. This is when we truly become a beacon of hope in our communities."[46] In terms of hope, Jay Brown of Washington, DC, urges Charities members to take the longer view and to rely on the promises of God for the strength to make charity and justice a reality:

44. Edward Lis, Director of Catholic Mission Integration, Catholic Human Services of Philadelphia, December 11, 2008.

45. Celeste Matheson, Director of Communications, Catholic Charities of Peoria, March 23, 2009.

46. Heather Reynolds, President/CEO, Catholic Charities of Fort Worth, March 17, 2009.

Our work is focused on the future; our work is focused on the promise of what is coming for the individuals with whom we serve, and the communities in which we work; but the promise isn't reality—yet.

God promises that there are days to come when there will be an end to suffering. Our task is to hold onto our faith in that promise and continue to work towards the realization of that promise. ...Let God's promises strengthen us as we carry out works of charity and justice. Let our work move the world toward fulfillment of what God has promised—in days to come.[47]

Hope is a much unappreciated virtue, but critical to those who work in adverse circumstances and sometimes against what seem to be overwhelming odds.

In 1986, Czech Poet-President Václav Havel described hope in words that for me capture the distinctiveness of this virtue and its ability to help Charities workers to continue at their difficult work even in hard times:

Either we have hope within us or we don't; it is a dimension of the soul, and it's not essentially dependent on some particular observation of the world or estimate of the situation. Hope is not prognostication. It is an orientation of the spirit, an orientation of the heart ...

Hope, in this deep and powerful sense, is not the same as joy that things are going well, or willingness to invest in enterprises that are obviously headed for early success, but rather, an ability to work for something because it is good, not just because it stands a chance to succeed.

Hope is definitely not the same thing as optimism. It is not the conviction that something will turn out well, but the certainty that something makes sense, regardless of how it turns out ... It is this hope, above all, which gives us the strength to live and continually try new things, even in conditions that seem as hopeless as ours do, here and now.[48]

What Havel describes as "hopeless conditions" in the final lines quoted here is his homeland under communism. Amazingly, three years later,

---

47. Jay Brown, Spirituality Committee Member, Catholic Charities of Washington, D.C., December 1, 2008.

48. Václav Havel, *Disturbing the Peace: A Conversation with Karel Huizdala* (New York: Vintage, 1991), chap. 5.

communism collapsed in most of Europe. What so many people had hoped and prayed for during so many years suddenly became a reality.

Many Charities workers, then, embody this virtue of hope and, by bringing it to their workplace, help to give those they serve new hope for the future. Joan Fowler Brown of Washington, D.C., contends that this gift can be given even in hard times and despite limited resources:

> It would seem, though, that scarier than living through a disaster or scarier than getting up every day wondering if my family will have a place to live, would be doing it without any hope for the future. And, while our agencies may not be able to provide a program to address a specific need or we may not have the funds to do all that we want to do, we can open a door to hope. We can all learn to hope, and as we become hope-full we also become fear-less.
> Then see what amazing things we can all do with Him.[49]

Hope, then, is indeed a virtue important in the world of Catholic Charities, one with which many staff and volunteers are endowed and which they in turn share with those they serve.

Sacred Love

The sacred love that is found all across the world of Charities shows itself in staff outreach to the rejected of society, great concern extended to even resentful people, forgiveness for those whom others have despaired of, protection of those who are self-destructive, and persistent joy in the face of repeated failure and defeat. In its most powerful form, this love extends itself to the despised and the guilty. Tricia Wallin of Kansas City-St. Joseph believes this most reflects who God is and is only made possible by God:

> In my work with the agency, I encounter many who society would detest. Parents who choose to physically abuse their children to relieve their own stress, children who crave love and affection so much they will violate others to meet their own needs, and parents who find comfort for their afflictions in substances which cloud their judgment and alter their mood ... [God] wants all to be loved and respected, no matter what the offense. He can enlighten our eyes as His servants to demonstrate His love and compassion for

---

49. Joan Fowler Brown, Chairperson, Spirituality Committee, Catholic Charities of Washington, D.C., March 24, 2009.

humankind. It is only truly through Him that we can carry His message of love to others.[50]

This universality of God's love for humanity in the work of Catholic Charities staff and volunteers not only reaches those despised by society, but even those who despise themselves.

Such work is seldom easy. Yet, the experience of being loved first by God lays the foundation for the ability to love others, even those who appear most unlovable. This is the same love that we humans have experienced from God, even when we rejected and crucified Christ. Father Dick Bresnahan of Peoria sees this as the roots of difficult loving:

> As we look at the cross today, God says to us, "No matter what you do to me, no matter how terrible it might be, I still love you." Nothing, but nothing, can destroy God's love, not even the cross. In fact in and through Christ on the cross God speaks that love in a very powerful way under the worst of circumstances.
>
> We see and deal with so much suffering in our world and in our work that we are tempted to take a 'fight or flight' attitude. But in the cross God teaches us not to run, not to reject but to stay committed, to stay present and to work hard to love as best we can, even when circumstances encourage us to turn away. In the cross, God says to us as nothing else does or can "I love you." In our lives and in our work, the cross calls us to love even in the most difficult moments.[51]

This empowering love of God—despite human rejection—sustains the ability of Charities staff and volunteers to reach out in love to even the most difficult people, even to those who reject their offer of loving care.

Not only does God's love make it possible for staff and volunteers to love those they serve, but their love in turn communicates to others God's presence, God's power, and God's compassion. Lori Fox of Charlotte believes that this is an honor for the Charities worker and a source of powerful hope:

> But for many, the comfort of God seems so distant and intangible. ... We ask, how do we know God is here? What is our proof? Jesus said that through his works, all can see that the Father is in him

---

50. Tricia Wallin, Foster Care Program Manager, CC of Kansas City-St. Joseph, March 2, 2009.

51. Rev. Dick Bresnahan, retired pastor and member of the Board of Catholic Charities of Peoria, Good Friday, April 10, 2009.

and he is in the Father. With every one of his works, he shows us that God's mighty power, tender compassion, and healing transformation are being poured upon us.

Jesus also said that what he has done, we can do too, because God is within us as well. We at Catholic Charities have the honor of carrying out so much of God's good work. With every bag of healthy food, every hand that wipes away a tear, every penny that keeps a family from being evicted from their home, we share the God that is within us with those who so badly need to see and believe. Our works, just as Jesus' works, give proof that God is here . . .

By merely doing our jobs, we show our brothers and sisters that their cries have reached God's ears. Through us he rescues his people from the power of the wicked and hope is restored to empty hearts. Rocks are dropped from slack fists and the souls of the empty are filled with the certainty that Emmanuel, God is with us.[52]

Louis Cocchiarella of Toledo echoes these sentiments by emphasizing the expectations that clients have about Charities staff and volunteers and how they will be treated by "God's people": "In a recent survey one of our clients wrote, 'I like Catholic Charities because God's people are there.' When people come to Catholic Charities for help they expect that they will find God's people working there and will be treated accordingly. As long as we see ourselves and the people we serve as God's people, we can be assured that we will continue to be refreshed and sustained by God's love and grace and that we will receive the strength we need to continue to do God's work in the world."[53] This experience of the love of God confirms the insight of St. Ignatius of Loyola and many saints that love shows itself in deeds, not in words. As Pope Benedict put it in *Deus Caritas Est*, when writing of the charitable activity of the Christian, "He knows that God is love (cf. 1 Jn 4:8) and that God's presence is felt at the very time when the only thing we do is to love."[54]

Loving in the power of God affects the staff member or volunteer as well. Emily McCue of Kansas City, MO, believes that it should be a great source of joy. In her words, "Each of us should have a heart of joy, no

52. Lori Fox, LCSW, Director of Counseling Services, Catholic Social Services of Charlotte, April 3, 2009.

53. Louis Cocchiarella, Executive Director, Catholic Charities of Toledo, March 20, 2009.

54. *Deus Caritas Est*, no. 31(c).

matter what our task or who sees us doing it, because we are spreading the light of God's grace and love to those who need to see it in action in order to believe that they are loved.[55] To Becky Reiners of Baton Rouge, such loving service is a privilege which transforms staff and volunteers even as they serve: "What a privilege is ours, that God allows us to share in the work of redeeming the world; what an honor, that God uses our living hands to heal, our voices to comfort, our arms to strengthen and uphold the 'little ones' at the margins of our society. And as we reach out our hands each day to the hungry, the homeless, the despairing, we ourselves are transformed, becoming in truth what we claim to be: the healing, comforting, living Body of Christ."[56]

Finally, Sister Joan Jurski, OSF, of Raleigh believes that God's love and God's activity in working with those who are poor and vulnerable call the Charities worker to quiet moments to appreciate that she stands on holy ground:

> Holy people, holy places! Wherever I will stand today may I think of that place as holy because God's things are happening there. It may be my office cluttered with paper and overdue reports, a homeless shelter, a family center, a counseling room and a myriad of other places. I will take a moment to be still and know that where I am God is and this is holy ground.
>
> "Amen I say to you whatever you did to the least of these brothers and sisters you did to me."[57]

For Sister Jurski and others, it is clear that the sacred love of God is embodied in their work with the poor and vulnerable, empowers their daily work, and enriches their own lives in miraculous ways.

To hear the women and men of Catholic Charities themselves speak of spirituality is to appreciate how their virtues touch their lives and their work. We also hear from them how these same virtues call them to greater accompaniment, hospitality, service, solidarity, hope, and sacred love. These virtues and others weave the fabric of their spirituality, a holiness that they learn from one another and from those they serve and a holy

55. Emily McCue, Accounts Payable, Catholic Charities of Kansas City, MO, March 13, 2009.

56. Becky Reiners, Coordinator, PSM, Catholic Charities of Baton Rouge, February 8, 2008.

57. Sister Joan Jurski, OSF, Office of Peace and Justice, Catholic Charities of Raleigh, February 11, 2008.

graciousness that they share daily with so many others in marvelous ways. These virtues also bring a fitting close to this effort to understand and celebrate the faith, the works, and the wonders of Catholic Charities today.

An Historical Outline

Important Dates in the History of Catholic Charities
and Catholic Charities USA[1]

1727   Ursuline Sisters arrive from France to open an orphanage, school for street girls, and health facility in New Orleans, LA. This is the first organized Catholic Charities apostolate in present day USA.

1775   Missionaries and religious orders in colonial times followed the earliest settlers in order to care for the orphaned and widowed, to heal the sick, and to teach the young.

1800   By the early 1800s, some twenty religious orders had established schools, orphanages, hospitals, homes for widows, the aged and infirm, and missions in almost every state.

1845   The founding of the St. Vincent de Paul Society in the United States occurs in St. Louis. A national organization was founded by 1864 and held ten national meetings by 1910.

1850   By the mid-nineteenth century, lay Catholics, particularly the Society of St. Vincent de Paul, joined in charitable efforts at the parish level to help the needy, dependent children, prisoners, the aged, the sick, and persons with disabilities.

1895   The *St. Vincent de Paul Quarterly* begins publication to promote developments in the field of social work, continuing until 1916.

1900   By the turn of the century, more than 800 institutions under Catholic auspices provided care to children, the aged, and the ill.

1910   On the campus of Catholic University of America, at the invitation of Bishops Thomas Shahan, CUA's President, the National Conference of Catholic Charities (NCCC) was founded to promote the foundation of

1. This thumbnail history is adapted and updated from that developed by me for our leadership institutes and then published in conjunction with launching the celebration of the 90th anniversary of Catholic Charities USA in 1999.

diocesan Catholic Charities bureaus, to encourage professional social work practices, "to bring about a sense of solidarity" among those in charitable ministries, and "to be the attorney for the poor."

1910   Msgr. William J. Kerby of Catholic University was selected the first Executive Secretary of NCCC, an office that he held until 1920. NCCC met every other year until 1920, when it began meeting annually.

1916   Fourteen diocesan directors—all priests—present at the NCCC annual meeting proposed formation of the Diocesan Directors Committee within the National Conference, drawing priests more formally into leadership.

1917   With the support of the Superior Council of the Society of St. Vincent de Paul, NCCC begins monthly publication of the *Catholic Charities Review*, replacing the *St. Vincent de Paul Quarterly*. It was edited by Msgr. John A. Ryan.

1920   Msgr. John O'Grady assumes the office of Executive Secretary of NCCC, which he will hold until 1961.

1920   The Conference of Religious was formed within NCCC to provide religious with opportunities for peer support and to promote specialized training and leadership development.

1922   Thirty-five Central Bureaus of Catholic Charities had been formed in cities or dioceses.

1922   NCCC publishes the first *Directory of Catholic Charities*.

1923   NCCC publishes *A Program for Catholic Child-Caring Homes*, a work of the Conference on Religious to stimulate improvement of standards in existing homes.

1929   The depression and its aftermath prompted more intense activity by NCCC and diocesan bureaus to promote social legislation based upon Catholic social principles. Msgr. O'Grady became a major national voice on social reform.

1934   The National Catholic School of Social Service is founded at Catholic University of America at the urging of NCCC with Msgr. O'Grady as its first dean.

1934   An NCCC bulletin to diocesan directors is initiated to update them on legislative and other national developments.

1935   The Social Security Act passes Congress for the first time, with strong support from NCCC for insurance benefits based upon rights as opposed to a needs test for benefits.

1937   Sixty-eight diocesan bureaus had been organized in thirty-five states.

1939   The Continuing Committee of Diocesan Directors becomes the Standing Committee.

1940 NCCC sponsors an institute for Catholic prison chaplains at Washington, D.C.

1943 An NCCC bulletin to directors of child-care institutions is initiated to keep them abreast of national developments.

1946 Msgr. O'Grady testifies before the Senate Committee on Education and Labor on behalf of universal health coverage.

1947 A Standing Committee of Religious was established within NCCC, which was parallel to the Standing Committee of Priest Directors. Its focus included institutional issues.

1947 A new NCCC Information Bulletin is initiated for all members who subscribed, covering a wide range of social issues.

1949 A new constitution and bylaws for NCCC was approved by the Executive Committee and membership. It established a Program Committee for planning of the annual meeting, inaugurating the use of more panels and workshops in place of speeches and papers.

1949 The National Housing Act is passed with strong support from NCCC and Msgr. O'Grady, culminating twenty years of O'Grady's leadership of the Catholic community and the nation on housing needs.

1950 The NCCC annual meeting is moved from Miami to Washington DC due to racial segregation in the planned facility.

1951 The first meeting of the International Conference of Catholic Charities (later *Caritas Internationalis*) is held in Rome. Msgr. O'Grady was one of the founding committee.

1960 President Eisenhower and Cardinal Spellman join NCCC in New York for its 50th Anniversary.

1960 The Association of Ladies of Charity of the United States is founded in conjunction with the 50th Anniversary of NCCC.

1960 NCCC takes a leadership role in the White House Conference on Children and Youth.

1961 Msgr. Raymond J. Gallagher becomes Executive Secretary of NCCC, serving until 1965, when he was named a bishop.

1965 Msgr. Lawrence Corcoran is named Executive Secretary of NCCC, serving in that capacity until 1982.

1969 At the NCCC annual meeting in Houston, Msgr. Joe Alves of Brooklyn moves for a professional study of the conference, beginning the development of the "Cadre Report."

1972 At the annual meeting in Miami, NCCC membership approved the *Cadre Report Toward a Renewed Catholic Charities Movement* with its triple goals of quality service to people in need, humanizing and transforming society, and calling the larger church and society to join in this struggle.

1973 NCCC begins its parish outreach program, later evolving into the current Parish Social Ministry program.

1974 The first membership Congress is held at the annual meeting. In the Cadre spirit, it was designed to be a member forum to discuss mutual concerns elicited from regional meetings and to develop policy statements. More prominent statements were: housing (1985), feminization of poverty (1986), pluralism (1987), and a just food system (1989).

1978 Msgr. Joseph Semancik's study of Catholic Charities leadership reveals the demographics and backgrounds of diocesan directors and describes their overall responsibilities.

1982 Father Thomas J. Harvey succeeds Msgr. Corcoran as Executive Secretary, later President/CEO, of NCCC/Catholic Charities USA until 1992.

1983 NCCC helps to found the federal Emergency Food and Shelter Program, providing approximately $130 million each year to local voluntary organizations across the U.S.

1983 NCCC adopts the Code of Ethics to promote quality service, Catholic values, and ethical standards. Reprinted in 1987, 1989, and 1997 with only minor changes until 2007.

1985 NCCC celebrates its 75th Anniversary in San Francisco, with greetings from Pope John Paul II and President Reagan.

1986 NCCC becomes Catholic Charities USA.

1987 Pope John Paul II addresses the annual meeting of Catholic Charities USA in San Antonio.

1990 An agreement is entered into with the National Conference of Catholic Bishops for Catholic Charities USA to coordinate domestic disaster response on behalf of the conference.

1991 Catholic Charities USA is "discovered" by the *Non-Profit Times* as the nation's largest voluntary social service network.

1992 Father Fred Kammer, SJ, succeeds Father Harvey as President/CEO of Catholic Charities USA.

1993 The Board of Trustees of Catholic Charities USA launches Catholic Charities USA: Vision 2000 to refocus the work of Catholic Charities locally and nationally in the tradition of the "Cadre Study" of 1972.

1994 Catholic Charities USA publishes its position paper Transforming the Welfare System to bring its experience to bear on the nation's debate about welfare reform.

1995   On January 9th, Catholic Charities USA launches *Advofax,* its weekly legislative update for members.

1995   The Racial Equality Project, one of the "early initiatives" of Vision 2000, was created.

1996   The Board of Trustees approves the Vision 2000 Task Force final report, concluding three years of intense dialogue within the membership and with others in Church and society.

1997   The Catholic Charities USA membership approves new bylaws that incorporate the Vision 2000 report's recommendations. The Board of Trustees was reconfigured to represent diocesan directors more directly and member sections were created.

1999   *In All Things Charity: A Pastoral Challenge for the New Millennium* was approved by the National Conference of Catholic Bishops. Bishop Joseph Sullivan, member of the "Cadre" and episcopal liaison to Catholic Charities USA, chaired the writing committee.

1999   Bishop William Skylstad is appointed new episcopal liaison to Catholic Charities USA, succeeding Bishop Sullivan. Catholic Charities USA celebrates its 90th anniversary on the steps of McMahon Hall at Catholic University of America, its founding site in 1910.

2001   Father J. Bryan Hehir succeeds Father Fred Kammer, SJ, as President/CEO of Catholic Charities USA. The "9/11" World Trade Center bombing occurs his first week in office.

2002   Catholic Charities USA and the Catholic Health Association hold their joint celebration in Chicago of the 275th anniversary of the 1727 arrival of the Ursuline Sisters in America and the beginnings of Catholic health care and charitable ministries in this country.

2003   Father Hehir returns to the Archdiocese of Boston at the end of 2003 to assist with the recovery from the clergy child sexual abuse scandal and its aftermath.

2004   Mr. Thomas A. DeStefano becomes President/CEO for the year following Father Hehir.

2005   Father Larry Snyder becomes President/CEO of Catholic Charities USA.

2005   Pope Benedict XVI publishes his first encyclical, *Deus Caritas Est,* on charity.

2006   Catholic Charities USA publishes *Poverty in America: A Threat to the Common Good.*

2007   The Campaign to Reduce Poverty in America is launched in January. Its goal is to cut the domestic poverty rate in half by the year 2020.

2007   The substantially revised *Code of Ethics* is completed and published.

2008   *Poverty and Racism: Overlapping Threats to the Common Good* is published.

2009   Catholic Charities USA begins its 2009–2010 centennial celebration at its September annual meeting in Portland, Oregon.

The Profitization of Social Services

Where Do We Set Limits on a Market-driven
Social Service System?[1]

FEBRUARY 2000

BACKGROUND

SOCIAL SERVICES ARE NEEDED to help America's people in need—from caring for the elderly to child day care, from providing for the homeless to helping people enter or re-enter the work force, from working to turn around the life of a troubled teen to helping abused, neglected, or abandoned children find safety and stability in loving families. Community-based, non-profit organizations have been providing these services and many more for over 200 years. For many of these years, these non-profit agencies have provided services under contracts with public agencies. This is often referred to as privatized service delivery. Public funds are used to support the work of community-based, non-profit agencies that are highly valued and trusted by the communities they serve.

This system of joint responsibility has served children and families, communities, and society well. However, in a climate of devolution, the responsibility for ensuring and managing the resources to support social services is being shifted first from the federal government to the states, and then from the states to localities and the private sector in the name of greater efficiency, cost-effectiveness, and local control. Providers are ex-

1. *Charities USA* 27.1 (2000) 11, 30–32.

pected to deliver quality services and also to share potential rewards and financial risks in managing the money. All over the country, non-profit agencies are stepping up to the plate and assuming major financial risks in order to fulfill their missions and commitments to their communities.

In this government clamor for a more efficient and cost-effective way of serving people in need, for-profit entities see business opportunities. Many for-profits are entering the social services market because of the potential financial rewards in managing the dollars. Public purchasers are attracted by the capital and technology that for-profit agencies bring to the table. Traditional non-profit agencies also are finding new ways to collaborate with proprietary agencies: creating joint ventures or subcontracting with one another. Some of these new alliances will introduce needed innovation into under-funded systems. However, before unconditionally embracing the entrance of the for-profit organization into the social service arena, society, and particularly government, has an obligation to confront some real conflicts of interest and install safeguards to protect the nation's most vulnerable citizens.

At a minimum, we must ensure that profitization at the expense of people in need does not occur. Profitization is a form of privatization that puts profit ahead of individuals and communities in need. It substitutes profit maximization for essential care, limits access to critically needed services, delivers substandard services to consumers, and/or sets inadequate reimbursement rates for providers.

Our society must not abandon its long history of public responsibility and accountability. While the market may play a role in the efficient delivery of social services, we must ensure that it does not undermine the provision of services that meet fundamental human needs.

What is Privatization? Privatization is a broad term that refers to the transfer of *public* assets and services to the private sector. There are several common forms of privatization, including *contracts* (hiring a private company to provide public services, such as foster care placement or fire-fighting), the use of *vouchers* (for example, providing families with public funds to use for private child care), and *volunteerism* (recruiting volunteers or charities to provide services formerly provided by government). Privatization has proven to provide strong benefits to the public good, historically by non-profits, and more recently by non-profits and for-profits, as well as through appropriate collaboration between the two.

ISSUES SURROUNDING PRIVATIZATION
AND PROFITIZATION

The presumed benefit of allowing competition in the marketplace is that it will lower costs and increase quality. In most marketplaces, this may occur. However, as for-profit organizations enter the social service marketplace, there are inherent conflicts of interest that should be recognized by policy-makers and public purchasers.

The Profit Motive

A for-profit company is accountable to its shareholders to maximize profits. That is its primary mission. Can it also deliver quality services? Certainly. However, in the for-profit world, profit margins are the bottom line. After contractual obligations are met, a proprietary agency's surplus revenue is distributed to investors.

As newcomers to the social service community, a for-profit's roots are shallow. There are no community commitments to hold a proprietary agency in place when the profits are nonexistent or less than expected. For-profit organizations may opt out of a service or market as clients who can be served through fewer or less intensive services move out of the client pool. This practice leaves other providers to stretch scarce resources to cover the needs of clients requiring more costly and intensive services.

Non-profit organizations, on the other hand, are accountable to voluntary boards of directors and to the communities and clients they serve. This is not a small distinction.

A non-profit agency's surplus revenue is reinvested into more services for the community to either augment existing services or fill unmet needs. Non-profit agencies don't abandon people in need when resources disappear or are unexpectedly cut. They dig deeper, work harder, and strive to raise more charitable dollars to supplement limited public funds. They are mission-driven, and their mission is to improve the lives of the people who count on them, in good times and bad.

The profit motive changes the climate in which decisions are made, goals are determined, and progress is monitored. Government must balance cost issues with other considerations of the public good, including protecting vulnerable populations and achieving priority goals such as promoting long-term self-sufficiency. Concern arises when the profit motive inherently changes this ideological balance that has sustained the delivery of social services since the founding of our nation.

Public purchasers should carefully weigh the differences in proprietary and non-profit organizations. It is ultimately the responsibility of the public purchaser to ensure, through contracts and monitoring, that the profit motive does not undermine the quality, availability, or appropriateness of the services delivered. It is the public purchaser's responsibility to ensure that profit limits and reinvestment strategies are in place to capture excess dollars and invest them back into services. It is the public purchaser who must weigh factors other than the lowest bid when selecting a partner. It also must examine the contractor's experience in delivering the services and its commitment to the community.

Accountability for Public Funds

A government-funded program must be directly accountable to the public and the individuals the program serves. When a social service program is contracted to a for-profit company, there may be no assurances that the company's actions will be in the best interests of the consumers, because the company's main responsibility is to the shareholders.

In order to ensure that all contractors act in the best interests of the community served, consumers must have access to decision-makers. Consumers must be essentially involved in the implementation and evaluation of the program or service. Contractors must be held accountable for meeting the needs of consumers and interested stakeholders—not simply their shareholders.

Public purchasers can ensure accountability for public funds by providing financial incentives and penalties that are linked to performance in all contracts they sign. Specific quality standards should be established, and contracts should be closely monitored to ensure contractual compliance with all obligations. Appropriate grievance and appeals procedures should be established. Periodic contract evaluations and outcome reports should be made available to the public.

THE NEED FOR PRINCIPLES

Some non-profits have extensive experience in the provision of social services and thus have enhanced public services and the public good. Some for-profits are drawing from their experiences in the private market and entering into the management and business side of social service provision; others are attempting to deliver actual social services without prior experience. It is from these diverse experiences that key issues have arisen and the need for widely accepted principles has become clear.

Statement of Principles on the Privatization of Social Services[2]

Ensuring quality services, protections for individuals and families in need, and accountability in the use of pubic funds.

CONTRACTING FOR QUALITY:

1. Contracts and subcontracts must be sufficiently funded.
2. Professional standards must be met.
3. Outcome measures must be established and monitored.
4. Contracts must establish profit limits and reinvestment formulas.

PROTECTING THE RIGHTS OF CONSUMERS:

1. Contracts must include grievance and appeals mechanisms to protect consumers.
2. Public purchasers must establish an ombudsman program for human service contracts.
3. Contracts must ensure that all consumers are treated with respect and dignity.
4. Contracts must ensure diverse provider panels and program staff.
5. Contracts must, wherever possible, allow consumer choice and monitor customer satisfaction.
6. Contracts must establish and enforce standards for the responsible management of consumer information.

---

2. These Principles are included here without the published explanations for each or the notes included in the original statement.

ACCOUNTABILITY FOR PUBLIC FUNDS:

1. Stakeholder involvement must be central to planning, implementing, or evaluating contracted social services.

2. High-quality community safety net providers must be preserved.

3. Reimbursement rates and schedules must be fair and equitable.

4. Public purchasers must create a level playing field.

These principles have been developed and approved by the following executives of major national non-profit health and human services organizations:

Commissioner John Busby
National Commander
The Salvation Army

Reverend Fred Kammer, SJ
President
Catholic Charities USA

Kirsten Nyrop
Executive Director
United Cerebral Palsy Associations

David S. Liederman
Former Executive Director
Child Welfare League of America, Inc.

Marsha J. Evans
National Executive Director
Girl Scouts of the USA

Carolyn S. Markey
President & CEO
Visiting Nurse Associations of America

Michael Faenza
President & CEO
National Mental Health Association, Inc.

Dr. Prema Mathai-Davis
Chief Executive Officer
YWCA of the USA

Peter Goldberg
President & CEO
Alliance for Children and Families

David R. Mercer
National Executive Director
YMCA of the USA

Fred Grandy
President & CEO
Goodwill Industries International

Joanne E. Negstad
President & CEO
Lutheran Services in America

Wilfred A. Isaacs
Executive Director
United Neighborhood Centers of America

Hugh Price
President
National Urban League, Inc.

Jere B. Ratcliffe
Chief Scout Executive
Boy Scouts of America

Isabel Stewart
National Executive Director
Girls Incorporated

Stewart Smith
National Executive Director
Camp Fire Boys and Girls

Judy Vredenburgh
President & CEO
Big Brothers Big Sisters of America

Index

advocacy, x, 2, 5, 6, 9, 10, 14, 23, 29, 30, 34,
    39, 42, 44, 45, 46, 68–84, 85, 88, 89,
    91, 92, 102, 110, 112, 124, 131, 134,
    136, 144, 151, 158, 160, 163, 177,
    178, 180
Aid to Families with Dependent Children
    (AFDC), 4
Alinsky, Saul, 78
Alves, Msgr. Joe, 189
anawim, 9, 10, 32
Anderson, Shawna, 127
Andrade, Tina, 178
Andrews, Arnold, 99
Andry, Connie, 6
Aroz, Raoul, 6
Atkinson, Jeanne, 108, 112

Barretto, Laurie, 76
Benedict XVI, Pope, 18–22, 23, 25, 33, 35,
    36, 37, 39, 40, 65, 87, 139, 141, 175,
    184, 191
Berg, Brother Joseph, CSC, 167
Blackwell, Mary Ellen, 174
Bresnahan, Rev. Dick, 183
Brown, Dorothy M., x, 116
Brown, Helen, 108
Brown, Jay, 180–81
Brown, Joan Fowler, 170, 182
Buck, Dr. Anna Campbell, 32, 56
Bush, President George H. W., 116
Bush, President George W., 117, 121, 123,
    124, 127, 129
Bushong-Martin, Jackie, 107
Byron, Rev. William, S.J., 27

Called to Global Solidarity, 38, 88, 123
Cadre and Cadre Report, 3, 4–5, 10, 11, 17,
    23, 30, 43, 44, 46, 81, 85, 86, 102, 189,
    190, 191
Caritas Internationalis, ix, 4, 23, 189

Carr, Jennifer, 76
Casey Foundation, Annie E., 156
Catholic Campaign for Human
    Development (CCHD), 11, 17, 18,
    38, 68, 79, 87, 90, 92
Catechism of the Catholic Church, 25, 26
Catholic Charities (Catholic Social Services,
    Catholic Community Services), of
    Albany, 155
    Atlanta, x, 155, 178
    Baltimore, 90, 157
    Baton Rouge, ix, xi, 2, 31, 55, 68, 91, 107,
        112, 135, 185
    Brooklyn and Queens, 85, 146, 156
    Buffalo, 153
    Camden, 99, 176
    Central Texas, 109
    Charlotte, 183–84
    Chemung County, NY, 82
    Chicago, 76
    Covington, KY, 161, 173
    Dallas, 170
    Denver, 82, 92–93, 146
    Detroit, 55
    Edmonton, Canada, 149
    Evansville, 152
    Ft. Worth, 83, 176, 180
    Galveston-Houston, 76, 90
    Green Bay, 178
    Hawaii, 170, 178
    Kansas City-St. Joseph, 170, 182–83,
        184–85
    Minneapolis-St. Paul, 107, 146, 153
    Monroe County, MI, 55
    New Orleans, ix, xi, 99, 108–9, 112,
        150–51
    New York, 114, 152
    Omaha, 82, 146
    Paterson, 109
    Philadelphia, 169, 170, 179–80

Catholic Charities (cont.),
    Phoenix, 155
    Peoria, 170, 180, 183
    Raleigh, 185
    Rochester, NY, 83, 157
    Rockville Centre, NY, 91, 175–76
    San Diego, 145–46
    Santa Clara County, 100, 152, 173, 179
    Santa Fe, 75, 100, 152, 173, 179
    Santa Rosa, 76
    St. Louis, 43, 83, 153–54
    Spokane, 49, 92, 157
    Superior, 107, 146
    Tampa-St. Petersburg, 99
    Toledo, 184
    Trenton, 76, 174
    Tucson, 109, 112
    Washington, DC, ix, 16, 108, 111, 170,
        180–81, 182
    Western Washington, 169
    Wilmington, 154
    Winona, 156
    Yakima, 154–55
    Youngstown, 55, 172
Catholic Charities USA, ix, xi, 2, 5–18,
    22–29, 31, 32, 34, 37, 43, 44, 45, 47,
    48, 53, 55, 56, 66, 68, 70, 74, 75, 80,
    85, 86, 89, 90, 93, 94, 95, 96, 97, 98,
    99, 106, 111, 116, 117, 119, 121, 122,
    127, 130, 131, 132, 135, 138, 149, 151,
    156, 157, 159, 161, 163, 164, 166, 167,
    187–92, 198
Catholic Health Association (CHA), 85, 94,
    95–97, 191
Catholic identity, 31–50, 55, 56, 86, 94, 100,
    130, 166, 167, 170, 178
Catholic Relief Services (CRS), 18, 38, 68,
    88, 90, 169
Center for Applied Research in the
    Apostolate (CARA), 32, 56–67, 73,
    75, 93, 129, 147, 148, 151
Centesimus Annus, 19, 27, 144
Chaves, Mark, 126–27
Church in the Modern World (*Gaudium et
    Spes*), 26, 27, 28, 33, 140, 142
Cleveland, Dave, 108, 111, 112, 113
Cocchiarella, Louis, 184

Code of Ethics, 22–23, 29, 30, 34, 43, 48, 49,
    81, 111, 135, 136, 163, 164, 165, 166,
    190, 191
Colbert, Robert, 167
Collum, Polly Duncan, 86
common good, ix, 13, 28, 29, 39, 86, 101, 121,
    131, 139, 142, 143, 177, 191, 192
Communities of Salt and Light, 38, 87, 88,
    91, 123
*Compendium of the Social Doctrine of the
    Church*, 23, 24, 28, 40, 142
convening, x, 2, 4, 5, 10, 23, 30, 85–102, 137,
    151, 163
Conway, Bishop Edwin, 17
Conrad, Sister Ann Patrick, 149
Corbin, Brian, 6, 55–56
Corcoran, Msgr. Lawrence, 189, 190
Council on Accreditation (COA), 110,
    149–51
counseling, 8, 36, 37, 55, 59, 61, 62, 65, 82,
    92, 107, 109, 147, 153, 155, 156, 157,
    175, 185
Curley, Jack, 96

Daly, Sharon, 11, 68–69
Daughters of Charity, 108, 114, 116
De Boe, Rev. Stan, OSST, 167
DeStefano, Thomas A., 6, 191
Deus Caritas Est, 18–22, 27, 35, 36, 37, 39,
    175, 184, 191
Di Marzio, Bishop Nicholas, 17
DiPietro, Sr. Melanie, SC, 56
diversity—racial, ethnic, and cultural, 12, 79
diversity—religious, 136, 167, 170
Dolan, Francis, 76
Dulles, Rev. Avery, SJ, 43
DuVall, Sister Raymonda, 145–46

Economic Justice for All, 24, 42, 72, 139, 158
empowerment, 7, 10–11, 29, 42, 44, 46, 77,
    78–81, 89, 146, 152
Eppinga, Joannie, 49

faith-based initiative, 116, 127, 129
Family Strengthening Awards, 156–57
Fernandes, Briston, 6, 176–77
Finney, Peter, Jr., 108
Fitzgerald-Penn, Maureen, 110, 112, 113

Index

Flynn, Dr. Patrice, 10
Fox, Lori, 183–84
Frenette, Carol, 106–7, 111, 112

Gallagher, Bishop Raymond, 189
Galvin, Jane, 82
Garchar, George, 172
Gaudium et Spes, see Church in the Modern
    World
Gautier, Dr. Mary, 32, 56
Geron, Ernie, 93
Gess, Tom and Kathy, 107, 110, 112
Gilmartin, Msgr. John, 6, 13
Gonzalez, Rosio, 174
Goodstein, Laurie, 121

Haggerty, Michael, 6
Harvey, Rev. Thomas, 190
Havel, Vaclav, 181
healing, 37, 97, 175, 184, 185
Hehir, Rev. J. Bryan, 14, 45, 191
Heidkamp, Mary L., 89
Heins, Peggy Prevoznik, 89
Hickman, Nancy, 176
Hogan, Rev. Timothy, 6
housing, 4, 12, 36, 41, 55, 56, 58, 59, 61, 63,
    64, 65, 69, 74, 75, 76, 79, 82, 83, 92,
    93, 102, 118, 123, 125, 126, 143, 146,
    153, 154, 155, 156, 158, 177, 189, 190
Housman, Anna Chrismer, 107, 112
Hubbard, Bishop Howard, 17
human dignity, 28, 29, 34, 35, 73, 80, 163, 165

Ignatius of Loyola, 33, 184
immigrants, 16, 32, 34, 69, 71, 76, 108, 114,
    115, 123, 169, 172, 174
immigration, 55, 61, 63, 74, 75, 76, 100, 108,
    113, 179
In All Things Charity, 17–18, 24, 38, 41, 85,
    88, 116, 138–40, 142, 158, 167, 191
innovation, 10, 47, 145–60, 194

Jefferson, President Thomas, 120–22
Jezreel, Jack, 90
Jesuit Volunteer Corps, 119
John Paul II, Pope, 5–6, 12, 19, 25, 34, 35, 36,
    37, 42, 43, 130, 144, 163, 177, 190
Johnson, Patrick, Jr., 6

Johnston, Karen, 178
Jones, William, 161–62, 173
Joyce, Sister Maureen, 155
Jurski, Sister Joan, OSF, 185
JustFaith, 90

Keenan, Rev. James, SJ, 172–73
Kelly, Jim, 150–51
Kelly, Sister Margaret John, DC, 114–15
Kent, Evelyn, 109, 112, 113
Kepferle, Gregory, 75, 100–101, 173
Kerby, Msgr. William J., 80, 188
King, Lauren, 83
Kinship Care Resource Network, 157

Ladies of Charity, 4, 17, 189
Lally, John M., 43
legal services, 55, 59, 108, 113, 166
Leung, Christopher, 149
liberation, 15
Lilly, Elizabeth, 179
Lis, Edward, 179–80
Lund, James R., 89
Lutheran Services in America (LSA), 124,
    142, 149, 198

managed care, 15, 16, 95, 143, 159
Marascalco, Sam, 109
Massaro, Rev. Thomas, SJ, 27
Matheson, Celeste, 180
Matsusaka, Eugene, 6
Mauck, James, 6
McCann, Robert, 92
McCue, Emily, 184–85
McGowan, Kathleen, 6
McGuigan, Dr. Corrine, 92
McGuire, Dr. Terry, 48
McKeown, Elizabeth, 10, 116
Melczek, Bishop Dale, 98
Merici, Saint Angela, 53
migrants, 34, 63, 74
migration, 16, 18, 88
Ministering Together, 97–98
mission, x, 1–30, 32, 38, 40, 42, 43, 44, 45, 47,
    48, 49, 53, 56, 61, 66, 70, 77, 86, 87,
    91, 92, 94, 110, 111, 123, 124, 128,
    135, 136, 137, 141, 149, 150, 153, 154,

161, 163, 166, 167, 168, 170, 178, 179, 180, 195
Mockler, Rick, 41
Mooberry, Nick, 109
Mooberry, Phil, 109
Moore, Sister Barbara, CSJ, 6
Mora, Frank, 113
Mullen, Anthony P., 91, 175–76

National Coalition on Catholic Health Care Ministry, 94–96
National Conference of Catholic Charities (NCCC), 2–4, 5, 89, 187, 188, 190
National Congregations Study, 125–29
New Covenant, 94–99

Obama, President Barack, 78, 116, 120, 121, 122, 123
O'Grady, Msgr. John, 3, 4, 80, 188, 189
option for the poor, 2, 27
Orzechowski, Edward J., 6, 16
Our Daily Bread Employment Center, 157

parish social ministry (PSM), 14, 22, 38, 45, 74, 85, 86–93, 179, 190
Peach, Kathryn Mahon, xi
Peach, Kelly, 154
Perdue, Governor Sonny, 155
Place, Rev. Michael D., 94, 120
pluralism, 10, 49, 70, 94, 120–44, 190
Poverty and Racism, 13, 192
Prejean, Caldwell, 109, 110, 112, 113
privatization, 17, 158–59, 193–99
profitization, 159–60, 193–99

quality, 3, 4, 7, 10, 12, 23, 47, 69, 125, 129, 136, 137, 141, 143, 145–60, 178, 189, 190, 194, 195, 196, 197, 198

Racial Equality Project, 12, 191
racism, 11–13, 79, 115, 162, 192
Ramirez, Bishop Ricardo, CSB, 17
refugees, 16, 32, 34, 65, 71, 74, 75, 100, 111, 122, 123, 141, 143
Reiners, Becky, 185
religious, women and men, 18, 33, 94, 113–16
Reynolds, Heather, 176, 180

Ricard, Bishop John, SSJ, 17
Root, Christopher, 96
Ryan, Msgr. John A., 188
Ryle, Msgr. Edward J., 81

Saint Margaret's Shelter, 157
Saint Vincent de Paul Society, 3, 4, 17, 38, 93, 124, 187, 188
Salamon, Lester, 8–9, 15
Salvation Army, 55, 62, 117, 124, 137, 142, 198
Schlichte, Kristan, 6
Schriver, Rev. Ragan, 172
Semancik, Msgr. Joseph, 190
Shahan, Bishop Thomas, 2, 187
Shields, Dr. Joseph J., 74
sinful social structures, 11, 12, 163
Skylstad, Bishop William, 92, 191
Snyder, Rev. Larry, 121, 191
social justice, 3, 5, 10, 23, 25, 26, 34, 38, 40, 42, 77, 92
social services, 4, 17, 23, 33, 40, 41, 45, 53–67, 66, 69, 85, 89, 94, 95, 97, 117, 118, 121, 122, 124, 126, 127, 128, 129, 130, 137, 138, 140, 141, 142, 143, 149, 154, 159, 160, 166, 184, 193–99
social workers, 61, 91, 132, 178
solidarity, 3, 9, 21, 22, 27, 29, 38, 46, 71, 88, 123, 164, 171, 177, 178, 179, 185, 188
Sollicitudo Rei Socialis, 163, 177
spirituality, x, 14, 47, 48, 132, 136, 161–86
Stenson, Jane, 149
Strange, Rosemary Winder, 74, 89
Stubbs, Sister Mary Lou, DC, 172
subsidiarity, 28–29, 40, 55, 131, 142
Sullivan, Bishop Joseph, 6, 17, 85–86, 191
Sullivan, Susan Stevenot, 178
Supplemental Security Income (SSI), 4, 57, 122
Suttles, Ray, 109–10, 112, 113

Temporary Assistance to Needy Families (TANF), 4, 57, 64, 122
Terrazas, Barbara, 6
Thibault, Lisa, 76
Timm, Betsy, 76
Tocqueville, Alexis de, 102

Index

Ulrich, Tom, 89
unions, 17, 39, 78, 81, 158
United Way, 35, 39, 64, 102, 132, 154
Ursuline Sisters, 34, 35, 53–54, 66, 95, 113, 120–22, 123, 187, 191

Vatican Council II, 4, 26, 27, 28, 33, 38, 139
Verdieck, Dr. Mary Jeanne, 74
Villanueva, Mario, 154
Vision 2000, 6–16, 18, 30, 43, 46, 47, 80, 81, 88, 166, 190, 191
virtues, 163, 170–86
Vitillo, Rev. Robert, 17
volunteers, ix, x, 1, 2, 6, 7, 9, 11, 13, 16, 17, 18, 22, 23, 32, 34, 35, 39, 40, 41, 43, 45, 46, 49, 60, 61, 62, 63, 65, 66, 67, 74, 75, 77, 78, 83–84, 92, 94, 101, 105–19, 124, 125, 126, 127, 128, 136, 141, 142, 145, 150, 154, 158, 162, 163, 164, 166, 167, 169, 170, 171, 172, 174, 178, 180, 182, 183, 184, 185, 194
Volunteers of America, 124, 137, 138

Wadge, Gordon, 150–51
Wallin, Tricia, 182–83
Webber, Alan M., 82
Wetta, Sister Therese, ASC., 167
Who Do You Say We Are? 14, 48, 56, 135, 167
Wineberg, Robert J., 117–18

Yankoski, Sister Linda, 149
Young, John, 6

Zeleny, Jeff, 121